Kamikaze Biker

Ikuya Sato

Kamikaze Biker

Parody and Anomy in
Affluent Japan

With a Foreword by Gerald D. Suttles

The University of Chicago Press   *Chicago and London*

IKUYA SATO is associate professor of cultural anthropology on the Faculty for the Humanities and Social Sciences at Ibaraki University, Japan.

The University of Chicago Press, Chicago 60637
The University of Chicago Press, Ltd., London
© 1991 by The University of Chicago
All rights reserved. Published 1991
Printed in the United States of America
00 99 98 97 96 95 94 93 92 91   5 4 3 2 1

Library of Congress Cataloging-in-Publication Data

Satō, Ikuya, 1955–
    Kamikaze biker : parody and anomy in affluent Japan / Ikuya Sato;
with a foreword by Gerald D. Suttles.
        p.   cm.
    Includes bibliographical references and index.
    ISBN 0-226-73525-7
    1. Motorcycle gangs—Japan.   2. Juvenile delinquency—Japan.
3. Subculture.   I. Title.
HV6491.J3S29   1991
364.1'06'0952—dc20   90-48610

The paper used in this publication meets the minimum requirements
of the American National Standard for Information Sciences—
Permanence of Paper for Printed Library Materials, ANSI Z39.48-1984.

To my late brother, Koya Sato

Contents

Illustrations

Foreword

We are everywhere hunting the bluebird of romance, and we are hunting it with automobiles and flying machines. The new devices of locomotion have permitted millions of people to realize, in actual life, flights of which they had only dreamed previously.
—Robert E. Park, "Community Organization and the Romantic Temper" (1925), p. 117.

Something of a nomad himself, Robert Park was fascinated by locomotion. Elsewhere he virtually took it as the defining feature of phylogenetic differentiation. "If the planets have minds, as some people assume they do, they must be of that brooding, vegetative sort characteristic of those mystics who, quite forgetful of the active world, are absorbed in the contemplation of their own inner processes. But the characteristic of the animal, and of the higher types of animal—everything above the oyster, in fact—is that they are made for locomotion and for action" ("The Mind of the Hobo" [1923], p. 157). Park was not entirely inclined to see in this progression a satisfying example of progress. Locomotion might become an end in itself if the "casualness of labor" (ibid. p. 160) permitted our disengagement from family and community. Thus, he especially admired the Japanese who, he thought, "seek God in their own village" (ibid.).

As the United States and Japan converge in their affluence, they continue to find in each other a reflection in which their commercial cultures are elaborated and enlarged. They are not ordinary reflections, of course, but more like those found in fun houses where unforeseen caricatures allow us to edge past the previous boundaries of intelligibility and moral acceptance. Narcissus was transfixed and made sessile by a single, overly satisfying image. The Japanese and the Americans are confronted by numerous less satisfying images that

All citations are from the Heritage of Sociology edition of *The City* (Chicago: University of Chicago Press, 1967). The original articles were published in 1923 and 1925.

keep them on the move. What makes this fun house fun, then, is not its capacity to flatter or fully satisfy but the endless possibilities for parody. As we locomote past these cunningly designed mirrors, we discover in them unrealized reflections of self, the mockery of our companions, moment-to-moment novelty, and a little world of action and self-engrossment.

It has taken a Japanese sociologist to follow up where Park left off. Sato differs from Park, however, in that he is a bit less nomadic. This is an extraordinarily thorough study which stalks its "fiendish" *bosozoku* through the streets of Kyoto from the time they are "carefree" *Yankii* ("Yankees") to the time they are "ordinary" *ippanjin.* From there we begin to discover how the frontiers of these youth cultures edge outward to create new consumer markets that gradually draw other youth into their orbit just enough to propel *bosozoku* and *yankii* experimentation a bit further. But each expansion of the moral frontier also arouses a mixture of pity and suppression. And, unlike the United States, Japan still has sufficient room in its prisons and sufficient dread of its police for them to be effective. The party over, *bosozoku* withdraw momentarily to their hangouts like *tamuru,* stagnant pools of water.

This, of course, is not the end of the *bosozoku.* What makes it all hang together, for them, is that it can be truly fun to go roaring down the main street of Kyoto in unison, toying with the police, swapping drivers in mid-course, alarming pedestrians, drawing the willing or unwilling attention of girls. With their exhausts roaring, their cars and bikes modified to convey the "feel" of the road, the requirements of concentration are sometimes such that action and self are one, and a kind of psychological flow occurs like that discovered by Csikszentmihalyi among mountain climbers, marathon runners, and basketball players. Improbable brothers under the skin, I suppose, but locomotion is where the action is.

Of course, the *boso* run can be dangerous too. Some may go to the *kankan* (juvenile "home"). Legs are broken. Occasionally, someone is killed. But this is not too bad. Without some risk, it all becomes "child's play," too transparent to take seriously. The far greater danger is that the play will be "corrupted." That is, that what was once spontaneous and voluntary action will become as compulsory and routinized as the casual jobs that *yankii* and *bosozoku* endure to earn enough money to buy their vehicles and decorate both themselves and their machines. At the moral frontier the rules are not that clear, and occasionally someone goes over the edge, burning his or her (for there are *boso* and *yankii* girls too) bridges and spoiling for others as well the impression that it was "just play." The worst fate is to fall victim to the mixture of blandishments and intimidation of organized criminals, the *yakuza,* who must defy the police out of duty and for little compensation. Almost as fateful is the humiliation and estrangement from one's parents following a conviction after the age of twenty. And some individuals just seem unable to withdraw from the amphetamines, glue-sniffing, and nighttime highs that have captured them. Even in the tight Japanese labor market, employers are leery of *yankii* well into their twenties. Fortunately, most *bosozoku* and *yankii* are able to graduate. They often do so ceremonially, at a *sotsugyo,* where they hand over to the police some of the more "fiendish" of their group emblems.

But I do not want here only to condense Sato's tale and entice the reader further into it. He does that quite well by himself. What I want to do is draw out some selected doubts about our own more familiar images of youth and delinquency. It seems to me that the Japanese case is just sufficiently exceptional that it risks being dismissed as only an exception. After all, glue-sniffing, girl-chasing, and joyriding are pretty tame stuff as compared to what goes on in American and British youth culture and delinquency. But the value of comparative studies is exactly their exceptional findings, because they confound our own most familiar and accepted self-reflections.

Perhaps the most obvious thing that will puzzle American and British observers is the absence of much attention to social stratification or social class. Sato's boys and girls are so clearly blue-collar workers between the ages of fourteen and twenty that one wonders, "Aren't they really just like the gang kids in Birmingham or Chicago except that they mature out of street life somewhat earlier and more decisively?" The British with their ethnographic approach and sharply defined class boundaries and the Americans with their more actuarial approach and socioeconomic dimension will want to see here a kind of reduced version of their own findings. This, I think, would be a serious misreading of the Japanese case. Both the Americans and the British may have put the cart before the horse. As Sato reminds us, you do not have to start at the bottom of the class structure to reach the bottom. What may matter most is not one's class or socioeconomic origins but one's anticipated class or socioeconomic destination. In Japan the school is still a rather robust institution which stands more fatefully between family origins and the work place. Sato's *bosozoku* and *yankii* are apparently a rather diverse lot in terms of their origins. What distinguishes them is that they have found school too boring, or too much like the employment already available for them, to pursue it further.

"So what?" you may say, "It's still all class or socioeconomic status." But the story does not end there. The Japanese seem to have a variant conception of their own social stratification and it is at least as distinct as the British conception is from the American one. Part myth and part substance, the Japanese view is still one of themselves as a single people rising on a common tide of prosperity. Until recently there was relatively little in the way of accumulated wealth, and wage differences remain comparatively small. Everyone, including *bosozoku* and *yankii*, can see themselves as a little bit upwardly mobile. That, of course, is one of the "advantages of comparative backwardness." *Bosozoku* and *yankii* are just lucky.

But it is not all luck. The British, especially the intellectuals among them, seem to have worked so long and so hard to codify the markers of class boundaries that upward mobility is almost as disagreeable to them as the reverse. Americans, with their conception of mobility as a sort of individuated lottery, show little bitterness, whether they go up or down. It is just that they never quite know if they have arrived. Birmingham boys, then, seem an embittered lot while Chicago boys act as if childhood was endless. Sato's boys, in turn, seem to have at least a liminal glimpse of where they are going, and their self-mockery and profanation of self may make it a little easier for them to come down from the adolescent fantasies of celebrity.

Japanese exceptionalism extends in yet another direction that may leave others reluctant to see any implications in Sato's study for their own societies. The Japanese family remains a remarkably stable institution, surviving with little change a world war, near starvation, and now unprecedented prosperity. Surely this sort of fixity must be owing to something peculiarly Japanese. But what is most revealing in Sato's account is the way the Japanese family, for the most part, still fits into the world of work and consumption like the adjacent pieces of a jigsaw puzzle.

It is sometimes said of American corner boys that they are so poorly trained that they are suitable only for "dead end" jobs insufficient to support a family of procreation. British corner boys, in turn, are said to be too well trained for the menial jobs that humiliate them and their families and deny both a sense of "industrial citizenship." The Japanese boys take the jobs the American boys spurn and their families protect them from the humiliation the British boys experience.

Would British vocational training prompt the American boys to establish stronger families or adoption in an immigrant Japanese family shelter the British boys from humiliation? *Ceteris paribus,* I doubt it. One point that Sato does not sufficiently emphasize is that much of the recent prosperity experienced by the Japanese has gone into collective accumulation: Washing machines and refrigerators "for the home" and a great deal of savings "for the future." In terms of "capital goods" and wealth, the Japanese are still "catching up" and family members still participate in the labor force as unequals while they consume jointly. But as Japanese firms continue to differentiate their product lines by age and sex and as they respond to American and European insistence that they save less and buy more, will the Japanese family remain so single-minded? Or will each member go hunting for a separate bluebird of romance? The more general alarms over youthful extravagance that Sato reports may be inarticulate, but they are not groundless. Ah, if we could only produce and save at the same time!

Now what does all this have to do with locomotion? As I ask this question I get up and pace about trying to find the words that will allow me to go beyond the point at which Park and Sato have left it. Staring at my feet I finally realize that I have somehow created the illusion of going somewhere, of having a destination and of making headway toward it. The illusion broken, I sit back down at the typewriter, more vegetative, more contemplative.

Movement through time and space seems to provide us with a kind of ultimate prototype of purposeful action in which means and ends are commensurate to one another. We can and do build narratives about this prototype and, once we have a narrative, we can appoint to it a moving persona along with the landscape or props that mark the persona's passage and give credence to his progress. All our games seem to have in them some such bodily or simulated movement. Fictional accounts rely on this prototype, most obviously the pilgrimage, but all other accounts do too. So far as I know, no one has yet written a book beyond the length of a palindrome that you can read backwards as easily as forwards. Poets and physicists may play with this prototype, but only to confound us and violate intuition. All our fantasies, if not our nightmares, seem to be ordered in this fashion.

But is this equally true of real life, of school, of work, of rearing children? Is it possible that much of life consists of bits and pieces of behavior, a kind of litter of disjointed acts, which we can reassemble as narrative only with effort and invention? Sometimes we do complain of this when, for example, we say that bureaucracies are "mindless" or that our behavior is only "mechanical." More often, by some stretch of the imagination, we manage to impose, perhaps retrospectively, some narrative on our conduct. And there are usually others around, still more imaginative, who will be still more inventive.

This is the old problem of complex societies whose purposes seem to be other than that of their members. Durkheim puzzled over it before Park did, although he called them "organic societies." Both, however, seemed to hope that at some point we could go beyond improvised fantasy and arrive at less vulnerable inventions. There are many similarities in their aspirations but the differences are more interesting. Park recommended a return to the local community where we might "encourage men to seek God in their own village." Durkheim was more ambitious, thinking that occupational associations might provide a more secular and more responsive intelligence by which to understand and make narrative out of our behavior.

As between the two, I might prefer Durkheim, but in fact both appear to have lost out. When half-literate boys and girls on the street corners can puncture the best of our shared fantasies and replace them with their own, something is very wrong with our occupational groups, our local communities, and our collective representations. It is not that their fantasies are more accurate but that they are apparently more fun, more able to create the behavior they prefigure.

The attraction of these fantasies is not limited to the street corner. They provide a terrific market for the music, entertainment, clothing, and news industries. An increasing number of us go about in "low drag," costumed as someone else. A more mobile sound technology helps to drown out any peripheral doubts. Logos mark our person as if a walking billboard, free for use. On the weekends we live and locomote. On the weekdays we vegetate. We have created our own fun house, only it is out in broad daylight and without mirrors.

There are some who see in all this a political statement. Economists give up their weekends to find new reasons and a sober plot-line for such conduct. These are imaginative fantasies indeed. Sato has punctured some of these fantasies, although I am sure that others lie in wait. His fantasy, and mine, is that we are just more earnestly hunting the bluebird of romance, only now it has become a duty in the consumer society. One can be sure that it will take something more than additional consumerism to bring self and locomotion into stride.

Durkheim, no doubt, would have been disappointed that we have come no closer to merging individual goals and collective restraints. Park would be disappointed too, but I doubt if he would have been much surprised. He never really took to village gods himself. After his twenty-year detour at the University of Chicago, he resumed his ramblings and the question Walt Whitman asked him.

"What do you suppose will satisfy the soul, except to walk free and own no superior?" (quoted in "The Mind of the Hobo," p. 160).

GERALD D. SUTTLES

Acknowledgments

I have received much help and kindness throughout my study of *bosozoku* and the writing of this volume, which began as a doctoral dissertation submitted to the University of Chicago. The following institutions provided financial support during my field research: The Center for Far Eastern Studies and the Committee on Japanese Studies at the University of Chicago, the Toyota Foundation, the Japanese Society for the Promotion of Science, and the Japanese Association of Social Psychology. Their help made it possible for me to concentrate on my research for over a year without any financial burdens.

For assistance of another, no less tangible, sort I am indebted to the many experts who so generously gave me advice and encouragement during the time I did my research and wrote this volume. First, there are the members of my dissertation committee, Professors Gerald D. Suttles, Mihaly Csikszentmihalyi, and Harry Harootunian. Professor Suttles, who generously provided the Foreword, not only gave me a lead in field research through his perceptive works on urban sociology but also provided me with many invaluable theoretical and editorial suggestions. In particular, his comments on Japanese consumerism alerted me to the role of material affluence and the mass media as a general background to motorcycle-gang activity. My description and interpretation of the subjective experience of the *bosozoku* drive owes a great debt to Professor Csikszentmihalyi's studies on psychological "flow" and his provocative class on adolescent life. Professor Harootunian led me to consider the revolutionary potential of playlike activity and called to my attention the political implications in *bosozoku* "play" and in the "official" and the scholarly definitions of this play—implications that I tended to overlook.

I would also like to offer special thanks to Professor Gary Fine at the University of Minnesota and Professor Takekatsu Kikuchi at Tohoku University for their invaluable support and encouragement. Professor Fine gave me detailed criticisms and insightful suggestions on the earlier drafts, particularly on the use of ethnographic data. During my stay in Kyoto, Professor Kikuchi, then at the Kyoto University of Education, offered me office space and encouraged me to persevere in my work, especially when my initial attempts to contact the *bosozoku* failed several times.

I also am grateful to two anonymous reviewers of an earlier draft of this volume. They alerted me to the possible gap between Japanese and Western readers in understanding the class situation in Japan.

The University of Chicago encourages an interdisciplinary approach to research. During my four years there, I greatly profited from intellectual exchange with many faculty and students from various departments and schools. I would especially like to thank the faculty and staff members of the Department of Sociology; they provided me with an ideal setting to prepare for and to complete this study. I would also like to express my thanks to my friends John Broadus, Martin Pauly, Leslie Pincus, Natalie Silberman-Wainwright, and Julian Harris, who patiently corrected various manuscript versions of this volume.

Last, but not least, I wish to express my profound gratitude to my *bosozoku* and non-*bosozoku* friends in Kyoto. Although their identities must remain anonymous, I owe my greatest debt to my "Yankee" informants, whose hospitality, friendship, and tolerance made it possible for me to complete this study. To witness and occasionally to participate in the process of their transition to adulthood aided my own growth. Indeed, they in no small way helped me to negotiate the passage from adolescence to adulthood, which in my case had to wait until I was in my early thirties.

Introduction

On weekend nights in the summer, the most popular and congested streets in Japanese metropolises explode with sounds that startle and deafen pedestrians. Tens, often hundreds, of *bosozoku*, members of Japanese motorcycle gangs, terrorize the cities. Massed automobiles, their original appearance modified beyond recognition, and souped-up motorbikes roar down the streets at speeds twice those posted and three times those most Japanese drivers manage in Japan's urban congestion. The automobiles that *bosozoku* use look like those used by "low riders" or "hot-rodders" in the U.S. Some motorcycles resemble "chopped hogs," the customized Harley 74s that the Hell's Angels ride. Yet, otherwise, *bosozoku* do not at all resemble American gang members. Young, well-groomed, and carefully dressed in elegant if bizarre costumes, including some resembling kamikaze party uniforms, they live for *boso*—high speed and high-risk driving on city streets. That is why the Japanese public gave them the name *bosozoku*, the tribe (*zoku*) of those who devote themselves to unlawful and often fatal racing.

Americans may be taken aback and offended if they know that the members of this speeding tribe are also called "Yankees," once they are out of their vehicles and hanging around street corners. With their permed hair and shaved eyebrows and hairlines, Japanese Yankees look like *yakuza*, criminal gangsters. They prowl the streets in groups and seek "action," including occasional gang fights.

One could frequently witness a scene such as the above in the mid-1970s through the early 1980s. *Bosozoku* were one of the major youth problems in Japan. The 1981 edition of the *White Paper on the Police* included a feature article on *bosozoku*. This article, occupying about one-sixth of the issue, treated *bosozoku* as the first reserve of *yakuza*. A 1981 article in a major Japanese newspaper reported, erroneously, that *bosozoku* committed one-fourth of all criminal offenses

1

in Japan and made that year's record of juvenile delinquency the worst in the country's history.[1]

The information about the size of the *bosozoku* population was enough to cause moral hysteria. In the ten-year period between 1973 and 1983 the number of youngsters associated with motorcycle gangs rose from about 12,500 to about 39,000, involving about 24,000 vehicles. During the same period, the number of arrests for *bosozoku* activity increased from some 28,000 to 54,819 cases, including 48,278 traffic and 6,541 criminal citations.[2]

As one might guess, *bosozoku* were a tempting subject for the mass media, and the social scientists were not far behind. Numerous articles and books were written about motorcycle gangs. But virtually none of them could provide a satisfactory explanation for a crucial aspect of the gang activity: playfulness.

"Fun" in Doing Evil

One of the apparent characteristics of the *bosozoku* activity (and their behavior on the street as "Yankees") is its extreme expressiveness and playfulness. Along with high-speed *boso* driving on the city streets, the racing tribe show off its bizarre and flashy costumes called *tokkofuku* (the uniform of suicidal kamikaze bombers) or *sentofuku* (combat uniform), whose colors include pink and white as well as black and dark blue. The accounts provided by gang members include many statements referring to "play," "thrills," and "kicks" in gang activities. The majority of those who participate in gang activities are from middle-class families, and gangs are rarely involved in illicit underworld activities as groups. It seems obvious that most *bosozoku* youths are engaged in gang activities for the pursuit of excitement and thrills rather than from considerations of gain and profit.

Most Japanese criminologists were aware of the "playfulness" of *bosozoku* activity. Some included this gang activity among *asobigata hiko* (playlike delinquency), a crudely descriptive term given to an emergent delinquent pattern since the late 1960s, which was not apparently related to hardships of life. Few scholars, however, gave more than cursory attention to the playfulness. Instead, in their attempt to make sense out of the senseless violence of motorcycle gangs and to impute some motive to the gangs' seemingly motiveless malignity, they mentioned some sort of psychological strain as the "real cause" or "hidden motive" behind the apparent playlike activity. Such an interpretation was also predominant among the mass media reports and in the public conception of *bosozoku*. Scholars and journalists alike characterized *bosozoku* and Yankees most frequently as dropouts from the *gakureki shakai* (academic-pedigree-oriented society) or as victims of a managed, meritocratic society. It was argued that they vented their pent-up feelings, arising from their inferior academic attainments or inferior social positions, through the gang activities.

There is, then, a strange gap between the apparent playfulness of the *bosozoku* activity and official and public representations of motorcycle gangs. This is partly due to the relatively slow development of so- ciological theory which can take account of playlike qualities of deviant behavior. It is not only the Japanese scholars and mass media who are reluctant to acknowledge the fun in doing evil. In fact, the three dominant theoretical perspectives regarding crime and delin- quency (the cultural-deviance model, the strain model, and the control model), especially in their recent versions,[3] include few as- sumptions appropriate for analyzing playlike aspects of delinquency.

According to the strain theorists (e.g., Merton, Cohen), deviance is a behavioral expression of frustrated wants and needs, resulting from in- congruity between culturally induced aspirations and socially distrib- uted legitimate means. In this model, the delinquent is not playful but obsessive and desperate. It is this type of theory, either folk or academ- ic, which was most popular in Japan for the explanation of *bosozoku* activity.

The cultural deviance theorists (e.g., Sutherland, Sellin, Miller) ex- plain deviant behavior in terms of conformity to a set of (sub)cultural standards, which are not accepted by a larger or more powerful society. In this formulation, persons are often treated as cultural automatons who translate cultural imperatives into behavior. Delinquency appears obligatory rather than spontaneous and playful.

The social control theorists (e.g., Hirschi, Nye) explain deviant be- havior in terms of the balance between motive forces for deviance and the pressure of various social-control mechanisms which counteract the tendency toward deviance. If we regard "play" as the reign of hedonistic impulse liberated from any kind of control, this theory may seem the most adequate for the analysis of the playlike quality of delin- quency. Yet, as the literature on play shows, play presupposes a set of rules and goals and is not synonymous with total anarchy and chaos, which lead to dread and anxiety rather than enjoyment.

It seems, then, that the existing criminological theories are not of much help in the understanding of *bosozoku* and Yankees.

ATTRACTION THEORY OF DELINQUENCY

Although the existing theories of delinquency, especially those constructed by observers without firsthand experience, cannot elucidate the playlike quality of deviance, there is a tradition, one that has often been interrupted, of "attraction theory" (as against "reaction theory) on delinquency.[4] We can draw a number of clues for interpreting and understanding the playlike qualities of activities of *bosozoku* and Yankees from the works in this tradition. The sociologists who are attracted to the attractiveness of delinquency include, among others, Thrasher, Matza and Sykes, Downes, and most recently Katz.[5] These sociologists, especially Thrasher and Downes, base their theories on detailed observation of youths on the street and provide thoughtful answers to the question, "Why and how can evil be fun?" Though not necessarily exclusively focused on the problem of delinquency, a number of urban ethnographies treating active pursuits of adolescents also offer important insights for the understanding of "fun" in evil. The authors of these ethnographic monographs (e.g., Gans, Suttles, Hannerz)[6] made firsthand observations of youngsters whose life-styles evolve around the pursuit of "action." The ethnographers also analyzed the relationship between the youthful action and the wider sociocultural background.

A common thread running through the attraction theories of delinquency and the urban ethnographies is an assumption that persons are endowed with the ability to create their own versions of the "definition of the situation."[7] Delinquents, then, do not merely translate subcultural imperatives into action, nor are they merely prodded by turbulent emotions or hedonistic impulses. They can control their emotions and impulses by creating and revising their own individual and collective definitions of the situation. The control capability of the definitions is not unlike that of emergent rules in social play. The attraction theory of gang delinquency offered in this work on *bosozoku* and Yankees is, therefore, a sort of rehabilitated control theory. While control theories of delinquency, especially their recent versions, discount the significance of "personal control"[8] in deviant behavior, this study tries to show how social (and societal) control and personal control are interwoven in gang delinquency. I will try to elucidate how *bosozoku* and Yankees, through their expressive behavior and symbolism, attempt to impose meaning and order on their adolescent lives when conformity to predominant standards makes their lives extraordinarily boring and purposeless.

The whole volume evolves around a contrast between this interpretation of *bosozoku* activity in terms of attraction theory and the popular interpretation of gang activity in terms of psychological or structural strain. In other words, I will show that the metaphor of *bosozoku* activity as play makes far more sense than the popular metaphor of *bosozoku* activity as personal or societal malaise does.[9] I will show that those who present pathological interpretations of *bosozoku* fail to provide any convincing evidence for the prevalence of psychological or structural strain among the gang population. By adducing strain or "real motive" from their cursory observations of expressive and deviant activities of motorcycle gangs, they provide arguments which are basically tautological. The failure of the pathological metaphor suggests limitations of strain as explanation for crime in general as well as for *bosozoku* activity.[10]

THE TEXT AND CONTEXT OF "PLAY"

As is obvious from the foregoing discussion, this study treats the playlike definitions of *bosozoku* as symbolic construction by the youths themselves. I regard the playlike definitions as a manifestation of the youths' attempt to order their lives with a set of rules and goals. To reveal this symbolic construction as a "text" of play, however, one must place this "play world" in contrast to its sociocultural contexts or the primary reality. The alternative or counter reality which *bosozoku* and Yankees try to create through expressive behavior and symbolism cannot but reflect their sociocultural backgrounds, or the primary reality. It should be noted that the play world may also give a "metasocial commentary" upon its backgrounds.[11] Imaginative play not only reflects its contexts but also "reflects upon" them by selectively incorporating cultural themes and combining them in a unique way within a play context.[12]

At one level, the symbolic construction or playlike definitions of the situation by *bosozoku* may provide critical commentary on the predominant and official definitions such as mainstream values, norms, and cognitive frameworks. At another and deeper level, however, they may add only minor twists to or constitute a second-rate parody of codes which are culturally given. In such a case, the symbolic construction ultimately merely reflects or even serves to affirm predominant patterns, thus becoming a semi-institutionalized deviance or another "safety valve" for society. (In many cases, then, we have to qualify the Thomas dictum: "If men define the situations as real, they are real in their consequences"—*but only to a certain extent*.)[13] This work treats these complex relationships between the text and the context of *bosozoku* play.

Chapters in Part I deal with the text of *bosozoku* social play and evolve from three modes or genres of play derived from the general metaphor of *bosozoku* activity as play. They can be described in terms of the following questions:

1. Speed and Thrills (chapter 1)
    a) What are the motives for the youths' engagement in *boso* driving?
    b) What are the phenomenological characteristics of *boso* driving?
    c) What kinds of physical, psychological, and social characteristics of *boso* driving make the experience in that driving possible?
2. Fashion and Style (chapter 2)
    a) What do the extreme conversions of vehicles, "grotesque" group names, and flashy or intimidating costumes mean?
    b) Is the seeming peculiarity of symbolic expressions in subcultural artifacts of *bosozoku* really a manifestation of psychological eccentricity in *bosozoku* youths?
3. Drama and Dramatization (chapter 3)
    a) What kinds of dramaturgical characters do *bosozoku* youths attempt to project through the mass media?
    b) What types of plots and themes are implicit in the dramaturgical presentation?
    c) How are the dramatized images of *bosozoku* and the self-image of *bosozoku* youths related?

In answering these questions, I will describe *bosozoku* activity as a type of "make-believe play" or "pretend play."[14] The three genres of play correspond roughly to three components of pretend play: performance, props, and script. I will show how the playlike definitions of the situation included in the three genres of *bosozoku* play provide Japanese youngsters with the means of organizing and structuring their life and constructing gratifying personal and social identities.

In constructing this "ludic" illustration of *bosozoku* activity, I draw on three sets of studies in addition to the existing attraction theories and urban ethnographies. The first set is psychological studies of "intrinsic motivation." They offer us concepts with which to describe and analyze motives for play and phenomenological characteristics. The second set of studies is often called "symbolic anthropology," in which the symbolic meanings that underlie play, game, ritual, and carnival are analyzed. Sociological studies closely related to the tradition of symbolic interactionism, especially those called the "dramaturgical" and "dramatistic" approaches, form the third set. They provide important clues for analyzing the relationship between symbolic meanings of playful activities and social interaction.[15] (It should be noted that the three sets of studies do not necessarily correspond to the three groups of questions mentioned above.)

Parts II and III deal with various contexts of *bosozoku* play. In Part II, I will examine the natural history of Yankee life on the street as a proximate context of *bosozoku* social play. Spectacular performances and the outrageous paraphernalia of *bosozoku* are dramaturgical presentations of the Yankee action-seeking life-style. Through the presentation of the image of tough-minded, intractable, manly, or "mean" motorcycle-gang members, Yankee boys dramatize and romanticize their self-identity and can dispense with the self-image of petty hoodlum. For most Yankee/corner boys, however, *bosozoku* is nothing but a temporal phase in their action-oriented life, which itself lasts for only a few years of their adolescence. Although *bosozoku* activity and style provide Yankee youths with intrinsic enjoyment, a heightened sense of reality, and a sense of self-worth, the style and activity are also defined essentially as "kid stuff" or "just play" by the youths themselves. In other words, the youths themselves use their own ludic metaphor in justifying their misbehavior: "Our wrongdoing is just child's play, not a serious offense." The metaphor serves to neutralize negative implications of the "diabolical" characterization of *bosozoku* as criminals or as devils. (This diabolical metaphor coexisted with the pathological and pathetic metaphor in the heyday of gang activity, as we will see in chapter 7.)

In their late teens or early twenties, most Yankees disengage themselves from association with peers—the association that facilitated their participation in deviant activities—and "settle down" to become *ippan shimin* (ordinary citizens). This typical career line of the Yankee youth is reflected and romanticized in the theme of "death and rebirth" included in the dramaturgical script shared by *bosozoku* youths and disseminated by the mass media.

In Part III (chapter 7), I will examine the societal backgrounds of the emergence and development of *bosozoku* and of the social reaction against them. We will see that developing affluence and consumerism have led to the proliferation of experimental and spectacular life-styles among Japanese youths, including decidedly unconventional ones like *bosozoku* and Yankees. Societal reaction against *bosozoku* reflects public anxiety about increased age-segregation that leads to "delinquency amid abundance and affluence," a concept quite unfamiliar to older generations. In a broader context, the reaction also reflects anxiety about the future of Japanese society which has now "caught up" with Western nations and is groping for its own future.

The concluding chapter extends the findings of my case study of *bosozoku* play and its context in order to construct a more general conceptual scheme for the understanding of the relationship between crime and play. In other words, I will explore the possibility of a general attraction theory of crime, or a general metaphor of crime as play. Drawing on ethnographic studies of "action," I will show that playlike deviance is inseparably related to the problem of reality construction and identity for modern people in general.

As we have seen, the whole discussion proceeds from micro to macro; from the play world of *bosozoku,* to the life-style of Yankees, and then to Japanese society as a whole. Similarly, most chapters, especially the three in Part I, start with descriptive material and then provide interpretations for the description and its context. In most parts, except chapter 7, I use the "ethnographic present." Some readers may find this ordering of materials and the use of the present tense too journalistic. Their impression is partly correct because the subject matter itself has abundant journalistic possibilities and my approach to my informants resembled that of a journalist.

METHODS

I conducted field research in Kyoto for fifteen months (from May 1983 to August 1984) and contacted approximately seventy *bosozoku* members belonging to a gang confederation called the Ukyo Rengo. Research techniques included participant observation, interviews, and questionnaires. Various censuses, official documents, mass media reports, and scholarly publications were also examined in order to analyze sociocultural backgrounds of *bosozoku* activity and to explore the process in which official definitions are imposed upon deviant behavior (for details of the techniques used, see appendix A). My approach may be characterized by what Suttles calls that "shameless eclecticism" which distinguishes urban ethnography.[16]

In many cases, the participant observer has to continuously negotiate his role.[17] This was especially difficult in the case of research with *bosozoku* because one of their major concerns is self-dramatization. My contact with my informants aroused their interest in the publication of a book, which they hoped would include numerous pictures. While I tried to persuade them that my book would be academic and low-keyed rather than journalistic and "sensational," my Yankee/*bosozoku* informants tended to define my role as "reporter" or "cameraman." Even after most informants came to call me *occhan,* "old man" in the Kansai dialect, I had to explain my role every time I met a new informant.

My participation in the scenes of *bosozoku* action probably cannot compare in depth with Hunter Thompson's in his fascinating research with the Hell's Angels. I never had an impression like his, that I was "no longer sure whether I was doing research on the Hell's Angels or being slowly absorbed by them."[18] Still, however, I could frequently participate in their activities. I visited Yankee/*bosozoku* informants in their hangouts, joined in their weekly meetings, and was invited to their parties, including a Christmas party, a year-end party, and two birthday parties. On several occasions I drank, chatted, and gossiped with them until dawn. Fortunately—or unfortunately—I never had to leave the field because, as in the case of Thompson, I had been stomped by my informants. Instead, some of my informants, who by then had already retired from gang activity, held a farewell party for me shortly before I left Kyoto. On our way to the party, they raced each other, in a Mazda Cosmo, a Mazda Familia, and a Nissan Bluebird, zigzagging on the city streets of Kyoto as they used to do in *boso* driving on a much grander scale.

I   *The Text of Play*

1   Speed and Thrills: Flow Experience in *Boso* Driving

> I . . . I understand something, when all of our feelings get tuned up. . . . At the start, when we are running, we are not in complete harmony. But if the *boso* drive begins going well, all of us—all of us—feel for each other. How can I say this? When we wag the tail of the band [hinder pursuit by the police by driving zigzag] . . . when our minds become one. At such a time, it's a real pleasure. . . . When we realize that we become one flesh, it's supreme. When we get high on speed. At such a moment, it's really super.
>
> —Personal interview

WHAT IS *BOSO* DRIVING?

What *bosozoku* call a *shinai boso* includes both driving at breakneck speeds and showing off before passersby or curiosity-seekers on the busiest streets of Japanese cities.[1] A *boso* drive starts from a certain assembly point, usually a city park or a parking lot. Members of a *bosozoku* group or several *bosozoku* groups come together at an appointed time. They have made these arrangements at the last *boso* drive or at a conference of leaders called for that purpose. Although they make every effort to conceal the arrangements from the police, the information often leaks out, so that they have to change their plans. The number of participants in a *boso* drive varies from ten to over a hundred. Quite often the size of a drive expands in the course of the night by recruitment of the vehicles of observers.

A *boso* drive during one night consists of several sessions of high-risk races broken by intermissions. The length of each session varies from

This chapter is adapted from my *"Bosozoku: Flow in Japanese Motorcycle Gangs,"* in *Optimal Experience,* ed. Mihaly and Isabella Csikszentimihalyi (New York: Cambridge University Press, 1988), 92–117, by permission of the publisher. Copyright 1988 by the Cambridge University Press.

one to two hours. The speed of a *boso* drive depends on several factors, such as the density of traffic and the condition of the road. Speeds will usually vary from 70 kilometers an hour (44 miles an hour) to 100 kilometers an hour (63 miles an hour), while the speed limit on the city street is usually 40 or 50 kilometers an hour. Although the course of a *boso* drive is decided beforehand and then transmitted to the participants, it is frequently changed because of the numerous contingencies that tend to affect such a drive: e.g., an unexpected number of police cars or the exceptional density of traffic. Changes in the course are indicated by the *sento sha* (front vehicle), the vehicle at the head of the band. The leader of the *bosozoku* group fills this role. When several groups join in a *boso* drive, the leader of the group sponsoring the drive fills the role. A group flag flying from a motorcycle or a car has on it the name of the host group. The member who holds the flag is called the *hatamochi* (flag holder).[2]

Several measures are taken to prevent the band from becoming disorganized and to cope with various risks. While the participants are free to race each other, none of them is supposed to pass the front vehicle. Also, a few automobiles are in charge of *shingo heisa* (intersection blocking), in which they block the traffic intersecting the course of the *boso* driving by making loud exhaust noises and sounding their horns. Automobiles at the head of the band also clear out the course of the drive by intimidating ordinary motorists with exhaust noises and horns. Motorcycles at the rear of the band engage in *ketsumakuri* (tail wagging) to hinder pursuit by the police. When the police cars reach the rear of the band, the motorcycles fall back and zigzag until the band gains sufficient distance on the police.

If there is no emergency, *bosozoku* youths exhibit several types of acrobatic driving techniques to their fellows, passersby, or curiosity-seekers. The techniques include *yonshasen kama* (zigzagging across four lanes), *hanabi* (fireworks, or making sparks by striking the asphalt pavement with the kickstand of a motorcycle), and *raidaa chenji* (rider change, or interchanging riding positions while driving a vehicle).

Intermissions are necessary because *boso* driving requires a high level of concentration and tension. Although resting places are agreed upon beforehand, they are frequently changed according to need. At each resting place, the leaders and executive members collect information about traffic accidents and arrests which have occurred during the preceding portion of the drive. The other members lounge about and chat, and those who have fallen behind the band catch up with it. (Even if the resting place is changed, they can easily catch up because several specific places are routinely used as alternative resting places.) When most participants have assembled at the resting place and after some consultation, the leader of each group takes a roll call and announces the opening of the next session of the drive.

At the end of a *boso* drive, participants reassemble in a designated place. When the drive has included several groups, the groups reassemble in different places in their respective territories. Not all participants get to the reassembly points. Some may have gone home early and some may have been arrested during the drive. Among those who have come to the reassembly point, some fall asleep as soon as they get there and some continue to engage in acrobatic performances or drag races. In the meantime, the leader of the group announces that it is time to break up. The youths go home in the light of dawn.

WHY DO *BOSOZOKU* JOIN IN *BOSO* DRIVING?
Two Answers

"Why do young Japanese males and females join in a *boso* drive?" The question itself usually presupposes their irrationality and implies the further question: "Why do they join in *boso* driving in spite of the high risk and lack of material reward?" Two types of answers have been provided.

One is to look for ulterior motives "behind" the *boso* driving. In this case, the driving is treated as a means of satisfying a pressing need to overcome a sense of frustration or inferiority. Another alternative has been to say that *bosozoku* youths are simply "driven" to express frustration or inferiority. The *boso* driving becomes an "outlet," or an enactment of one's emotions rather than an evasion of them. We can find many instances of each answer in the mass media and in scholarly treatments of *bosozoku*. For example, an editorial in the *Mainichi Shimbun* (a major Japanese newspaper) asks:

> What would be the causal relationship between the onset of the rainy season and the stirring up of *bosozoku? Many scholars* point out that the proliferation of *bosozoku* is caused by "frustration" and "desire to show off." Is it because people's frustrations accumulate before and after the onset of the rainy season, when it is so muggy?[3]

Kaneto, a psychologist and the chief social investigator of the Family Court of Toyama, is more direct on this point. After mentioning five categories of pathology leading to *bosozoku* activity (pathology of adolescence, family, school, workplace, and society as a whole), he says:

> They are self-conscious as dropouts and try to satisfy by the *boso* driving the desires for self-assertion and recognition, which are not satisfied in school or at the workplace. Their attachment to cars seems to me even abnormal.[4]

PLATE 1. BOSO DRIVING. Motorcycles clear the way for automobiles during a *boso* drive. The flag held by the boy on the pillion seat of a motorcycle indicates the name of the *bosozoku* group. A boy and a girl are sitting on the doors of the automobile. This riding style is called *hakonori* (box-riding). See fig. 3.7.

Similar arguments are abundant in the studies attributed to "many scholars."[5] However, neither the statements by the mass media nor the reports of academic studies have substantiated any of their arguments with empirical investigations. Most of the studies take the existence of frustration for granted and merely guess about the characteristics of the *boso* driving without convincing empirical data. And they footnote each other.

The results of preliminary interviews with my informants, as well as a review of the literature on *bosozoku,* suggest that the second category of answers is more plausible than the first. In this case, *boso* driving is treated as *asobi* (play), that is, an intrinsically enjoyable activity. While the irrationality of the actor is the focus of argument in the first category of answers, *non*rationality of activity becomes crucial in the second category. Two words, *spido* (speed) and *suriru* (thrills), frequently appear in this approach. For example, in a questionnaire administered to 1,224 *bosozoku* youths, "speed and thrills" was the most frequently chosen reason given for participation.[6] "Speed and thrills" also frequently appear in interview records compiled in numerous journalistic

PLATE 2. INTERMISSION OF A BOSO DRIVE. During an intermission, the leaders and executive members collect information about traffic accidents and arrests which have occurred in the preceding session of the *boso* drive.

books. While "frustration" and "inferiority complex" are motives which are inferred or imputed by outside observers, "speed and thrills" are "native categories" of motivation and experience involved in *boso* driving.

It is unfortunate that neither academic nor journalistic accounts have tried to explore thoroughly the implications of the native categories. Academic studies mention speed and thrills as "only" the *bosozoku* youths' own words, but they do see the *boso* driving as an instance of play or "vertigo."[7] But there is no further analysis of the conditions for "vertigo" or "speed and thrills" in the *boso* driving or of its phenomenological characteristics.

We cannot, of course, expect much from journalistic accounts. They seek, essentially, to attract readers by presenting impressionistic interviews that are full of onomatopoetic expressions and instances of bravado.[8]

Boso Driving and Flow

One concept particularly appropriate for the exploration of the motivation and experience of "speed and thrills" is the "flow concept."

Csikszentmihalyi and his associates have investigated the common structure and characteristics of autotelic (intrinsically enjoyable) activities by means of intensive interviews and questionnaires.[9] On the basis of his analysis of diverse autotelic activities (e.g., chess, mountain climbing, rock dancing), Csikszentmihalyi found that those who are engaged in these activities often experience a peculiar dynamic state, which he calls "flow." According to him, flow refers to "the holistic sensation that people feel when they act with total involvement":

> In the flow state, action follows upon action according to an internal logic that seems to need no conscious intervention by the actor. He experiences it as a unified flowing from one moment to the next, in which he is in control of actions, and in which there is little distinction between self and environment, between stimulus and response, or between past, present, and future.[10]

Preliminary interviews with my informants suggested that the "speed and thrills" of *boso* driving can indeed be characterized as an experience of flow. A more systematic investigation, including semi-structured interviews and a questionnaire, supports this interpretation and allows us to compare *boso* driving with other flow activities.

CHARACTERISTICS OF EXPERIENCE IN *BOSO* DRIVING

According to Csikszentmihalyi, flow experience has the following phenomenological characteristics:
  1. merging of action and awareness
  2. centering of attention on limited stimulus field
  3. loss of ego (or transcendence of ego)
  4. feeling of competence and control
  5. unambiguous goals and immediate feedback
  6. autotelic nature[11]
The results of interviews and questionnaires show that *boso* driving includes opportunities for experience characterized by these six features. But the *boso* driving also has some peculiar characteristics when compared to other flow activities.

Centering of Attention

During a *boso* drive, *bosozoku* youths enter into a context of activity which is clearly bracketed off from everyday life. Numerous components of *boso* driving contribute to the creation of this bracketed context. They include a definite timing of the *boso* drive, the sudden burst of noise from motorcycles or cars without mufflers, or with altered mufflers, the sounds of horns, the beams of headlights crossing each other in the midnight darkness, and the spectacular massed presence of a great number of vehicles. Informants use the words *(o)matsuri* (festival) or *kaanibal* (carnival) to describe the atmosphere of *boso* driving. The "carnivalesque" atmosphere seems to contribute to the youths' engrossment in the *boso* driving.

Informants' comments on the excitement of such a carnivalesque atmosphere describe it with many onomatopoetic and mimetic expressions.

> My heart makes a sound like "Don-don! Don-don!" It's pounding. It's almost painful. [I say to myself,] "Oh! Here we go again!"
> So many cars! So many people! My heart sounds like "Ban-ban! Been! Doki-doki!" Like being stricken with polio. . . . I cannot say it in words. I just cry, "Eyaooo!"

It seems that onomatopoetic expression is a convenient tool to describe "action-type" behavior which by nature tend to defy reconstruction in articulate verbal form. Onomatopoetic expressions are also frequently used in the informants' daily conversation, when they, as Yankee/corner boys, recount and dramatize their experience in such activities (e.g., rape, gang fighting). The close connection between action-type behavior and its reconstruction in terms of onomatopoetic and mimetic expressions suggests the possibility that the expressions themselves become a factor which programs future action-type behavior.[12]

The darkness of night reduces distraction from peripheral vision. Uniforms, headbands with the image of a rising sun, and group flags can be seen directly ahead in the vehicle's headlights. They are important stage props which dramatize the scene and create a theatrical "frame."[13] Before starting, some participants inhale paint thinner, apparently to limit their field of awareness. But it is, above all, the loud sounds that engross the youths in the *boso* drive. This, at least, is what they most frequently report. In addition to those youths who make exhaust noises and honk their horns, those who are in cars play their stereos at full volume during *boso* driving. They even open windows in mid-winter to expose themselves to the surrounding noise. While outside observers may regard these high-volume sounds as incoherent or random "noise," *bosozoku* report that they sound like music with a regular beat. As we shall see later (table 1.2), "listening to good music" is frequently likened to the subjective experience of *boso* driving.

Feeling of Competence and Control

Considerable danger is involved in *bosozoku* drives. In 1983, a total of 6,711 *bosozoku* were arrested for "collective dangerous behavior."[14] A police report lists eighty-nine youths who were accidentally killed during *boso* drives in 1980 in Japan, and eighty-seven youths in 1981, while the number of those who were injured was 1,097 in 1980 and 841 in 1981.[15] At least three members of the *bosozoku* group I studied were killed in accidents during *boso* driving in the course of some three years. (The number of members killed during *boso* drives varies, depending on how one defines the group boundary. Some informants mention five members killed; others mention three.) Many of my informants had been injured and some were crippled.

Yet, physical danger is among the important factors that seem to focus the youths' attention on the immediate situation. They even increase their risks by acrobatic driving. Bike riders rarely use protective gear such as leather gloves, boots, or a helmet. Even those who have just left the hospital and are still wearing plaster casts on their legs ride on motorcycles without this kind of protection.

This willingness to take risks seems irrational and pathological. And, indeed, *bosozoku* youths themselves often actively present themselves as risk-loving daredevils. Conversation among informants contains much boasting about the risks they have taken. Once out of their cars and bikes, they define themselves as "Yankee," a social type of street-corner boys whose life-style evolves around the pursuit of thrills, kicks, and "action." At the same time, however, some measures are taken to avoid particular dangers: e.g., "intersection blocking" to avoid cross traffic, "tail wagging" to avoid easy arrests. Informants almost uniformly say that danger itself is not enjoyable. Danger is not pursued for its own sake but is regarded as something which should be overcome by one's own skills and used to manufacture "thrills."[16] Risk is necessary to present a challenge to skill, but this challenge should be met. Insurmountable challenges to skill, or risks (e.g., easy arrest) that might not allow one to demonstrate skill, are to be avoided. During a *boso* drive, feelings of competence and control overcome the awareness of danger. The following is a typical answer about this aspect of *boso* driving experience:

> No. I don't think it's dangerous. I rather think about going ahead as far as I can.

Awareness of danger, however, does rise to the surface of consciousness shortly before the beginning of a *boso* drive or when *bosozoku* youths reflect upon the drive afterwards:

> Sometimes, shortly before we start, I think that it may be dangerous. . . . Sometimes, I get nervous before the start. But once we start, I forget [the danger]. . . . And after getting back, I say to myself, "What did I do at that moment!" I get scared when I think back on it. . . . I think "How could I do that!" after a *boso* drive. But once we start. . . .

Being pursued by the police in squad cars means not only physical danger but also the risk of apprehension and detention. The police thus constitute a persistent challenge which is not easily overcome. Outwitting the police, nonetheless, leads to feelings of competence and control:

> Once we start, it's fun to be chased by police cars.

> It's so delightful to be chased by patrol cars.

> Well, the most exciting thing is to get away from the pursuing police cars.

Police cars also seem to symbolize the general power and authority of the Japanese police. While they are overwhelming and unchallenged in everyday life, they can be beaten and mocked within the bracketed context of a *boso* drive:

> Another thing is defiance. How should I say this? The thrill of defying the police, or the fun of matching them. It's really fun.

The feeling of control is derived also from the recognition that one has transformed a city into one's own playground. An ex-leader of a *bosozoku* group writes in his manuscript:

> We start a *boso* drive by putting the bike party at the tail of the band. *Hoon! Guaan!* [onomatopoetic expression of exhaust noise]. Seventy to one hundred vehicles start their engines all at once. We can hear nothing but the exhaust noises. Nobody, not even the police, can stop us. . . . The moment the engines are started, this disorderly crowd becomes a big monster. It's really overwhelming. We speed down the middle of the road. Who cares about police cars! When I see the band from in front, it's like a tide of headlights devouring the city.[17]

Kawaramachi Avenue is the main street of Kyoto (see figure 5.2). This street is (or has to be) almost always included in the course of a *boso* drive in that city, not only because a large audience is to be found there but also because the street is a major symbol of the city.

> "Let's go and beat Kawaramachi!" . . . We say "go and beat" [*iwasu*] when we play around and make lots of noise there.

> I feel that "This [Kawaramachi] is my street" [during a *boso* drive].

> You know, we go up and down Kawaramachi again and again. At such a time, I feel that Kawaramachi's the place for *bosozoku*.

The significance of overcoming physical danger in a *boso* drive is not unlike that in rock climbing, reported by Csikszentmihalyi and Mitchell.[18] But the risks taken in *boso* driving are far more unpredictable and unmanageable than those of rock climbing. In fact, some rock climbers in Csikszentmihalyi's study regarded driving a car or walking down the street as more dangerous than rock climbing.[19] *Bosozoku* would not say this about *boso* driving. It is also said that many professional racers regard driving a car on the street as more dangerous than racing on a racetrack. While the danger of a mountain and of a racetrack might be calculated beforehand and carefully matched to one's skills to a considerable extent, a *boso* drive includes many uncontrollable contingencies. Even those *bosozoku* youths who do intersection blocking run the risk of some cars rushing past them into the intersection. Moreover one cannot predict exactly the number of police cars or their movement.

One of the important characteristics of flow activity is that it follows ordered rules which make action and the evaluation of action automatic and unproblematic.[20] Actors seem to predict and cope with events in the activity on the basis of the implicit rules and long-term practice. There seems to be such a set of rules in *boso* driving as well, which is assumed to regulate events in it. For example, the *bosozoku* youths assume that police cars will not cut into the band if they do "tail wagging." They also assume that ordinary cars will not rush into an intersection once the drivers hear the exhaust noises from the cross street. These assumptions are, of course, "rules" only for the *bosozoku*. Occasionally, police cars do cut into the band or ordinary cars rush into the intersection. Even if policemen and ordinary cars move in ways which are anticipated by the "rules," it is not because they share the rules but because they have to move in such ways for their own safety. The "rules" are imposed upon policemen and ordinary cars. Although an informant characterized the *boso* driving as a "game in which life is at stake," it is a rule-ordered "game" only for *bosozoku* youths. Many informants have actually experienced situations in which their lives were at stake.

These unpredictable and uncontrollable factors in a *boso* drive sometimes disrupt the feeling of competence and control:

Even if I get high on a *boso* drive, I feel somehow scared. Yeah, I definitely think so. Often, during a *boso* drive, I think, "Will I go home alive?"

Oh, it's dangerous. But it [the chance of having an accident] depends wholly on luck.

We shall see later how this aspect delimits the quality of flow in *boso* driving.

Unambiguous Goals and Immediate Feedback

In the clearly bracketed context of *boso* driving, means-ends relationships are simplified. One clearly knows what is right and what is wrong. High speed and extreme physical danger are prerequisites for the unambiguous and immediate feedback of *boso* driving. To fall behind the band or to fail in one's encounter with pressing danger are clear signs that one did something wrong. Facial expressions, gestures, and moves of fellow participants serve as important forms of feedback. They confirm and maintain the "frame" of *boso* driving, and they heighten excitement and involvement in the driving:

Any difference between solo driving and driving in a group? Of course! They're totally different. Because there's no mirror [in the case of solo driving]. How can I say this? Is it awkward to say, "I can feel people's eyes"?

There're some guys who get really high. . . . They race engines with a really loud roar, like *hohohohohoon!* If I see such a guy, I think in my mind, "I have to do it, too. I have to keep up with that guy!"

In other words, fellow participants become amplifiers as well as "mirrors" for the feedback. But the mirror or amplifier is sometimes defective and gives a dampening feedback:

I think the [reaction of a] partner on the pillion seat is crucial. . . . If he's a stupid novice, it's so miserable. . . . Such a guy says nothing [to stir me up]. If he's a smart guy and says, "Oh, K! You're great!" or "Let's go! K! Let's make fun of the police car!" I'll be really excited.

When riding on a bike, the guy on the rear seat is really important. . . . When a squad car's coming close to us, one stupid guy always hurries me by saying "It's coming! It's coming! A police car's coming!" Then I completely lose my high.

Passersby and curiosity-seekers also provide important feedback, especially in busy areas like Kawaramachi Avenue. *Medatsu* (being seen, looking conspicuous) is the word which is almost always used to describe the importance of the feedback from an audience:

> Because, you know, Kawaramachi is the main street of Kyoto. That's why we always went there. . . . If we could not be seen [*medatsu*] in Kawaramachi, we would have to drive somewhere else. Kawaramachi is so narrow. Who would go to Kawaramachi, if there were not a lot of people there?

The notion of *medatsu* is crucial in understanding the enjoyment of *boso* driving. I shall explore the implications of this concept later.

Merging of Action and Awareness— Loss of Self-consciousness

When an actor is completely involved in the immediate demands of action, he loses awareness of his self as a separate "observer." One's "ego," which may intervene between self and environment, disappears temporarily in the flow state.[21] In the case of *boso* driving, extreme physical danger and the rapid sequence of perceptions, decisions, operations, and movements seem to lead to this loss of ego. Participants forget themselves and feel as if their bodies moved automatically:

> Instinct. My body moves instinctively. It moves without any thought. I forget myself.

> I think about nothing. Really. I think about nothing but my driving.

> On a *boso* drive, I forget everything. I feel I am running with "all my heart and mind and strength."

Closely related to the state of loss of ego is the feeling of being merged with the world of *boso* driving. At the climax of the drive, *bosozoku* youths feel that they get totally "tuned into" the rhythm of *boso* driving. Informants frequently use *moetekuru* (burning like a fire), *shibireru* (being paralyzed), and *nottekuru* (getting high) in describing this feeling. When one gets fully engrossed in *boso* driving, even subtle cues are enough to "burn one like fire":

> I lose myself completely when I hear exhaust noise.

> We can be burning like fire just from the exhaust noise.

Some who are in automobiles start moving their bodies in order to get tuned into the rhythm:

> Steering wheel. When I am burning, it appears in my handling of the steering wheel . . . [he moves his body rhythmically]. I get

myself tuned into the rhythm. Yeah, anyone who is skillful at driving does this.

When one loses self-consciousness, he also loses the usual sense of time. The temporal framework in *boso* driving is different from that in ordinary life:

> How can I know that [lapse of time]? I say, "Really? It's time already?" I say to myself, "Really?" It will be dawn in a moment.

> Time passes so fast. . . . Well, no. I forget time. I say, "Really! Is it time to go already?" or "Oh! I didn't notice that!" I don't mind at all about such a matter as [lapse of] time. The only thing we have to keep in mind is the assembly time.

In the state of psychological flow, one loses track of time in the usual sense of the word. Reflecting afterwards, one cannot grasp it by means of the time sense and the memory for time used in everyday life. The feeling of "collective effervescence"[22] that participants in *boso* driving experience is also related to the loss of ego. It will be discussed later.

The Autotelic Nature of *Boso* Driving

Like other activities which are usually called "play" or "games," the major enjoyment in *boso* driving is found in the activity itself. In this regard, a *boso* drive is qualitatively different from those activities which are carried out mainly for the sake of extrinsic rewards such as money or fame, although the latter does figure into the broader range of *bosozoku* activities. As Csikszentmihalyi has shown in detail, autotelic activities differ somewhat from each other with regard to types of intrinsic rewards and the quality of flow experience. Questionnaire responses and interviews indicate that *boso* driving has its own peculiar characteristics as an autotelic activities.

The questionnaire included a rating scale which required respondents to evaluate the relative importance of nine reasons for enjoying *boso* driving: "friendship, companionship," "competition, measuring oneself against others," "development of personal skills," "*medatsu koto* [being seen]," "the activity itself, getting involved in the world peculiar to *boso* driving," "*sukatto suru koto* [emotional release]," "prestige, regard, glamor," "experience of speeding, use of driving skills," "challenging one's own limitations and/or ideals" (see appendix C). Eight of the nine reasons were adopted from the questionnaire used by Csikszentmihalyi. The eight reasons have been found to "represent exhaustive and nonredundant incentives for participating in activities which lack conventional reward."[23] The other reason, i.e., *medatsu koto* (being seen, looking conspicuous) was added to the ques-

TABLE 1.1 Ranking of Mean Scores, Reasons for Enjoying Activity, by Groups

Reason	Rock Climbers N = 26	Composers N = 22	Dancers N = 27	Male Chess Players N = 28	Female Chess Players N = 20	Basketball Players N = 35	Bosozoku N = 45
1. Enjoyment of the experience and use of skills	1	1.5	1.5	1	1	4	5*
2. The activity itself	2	1.5	1.5	2	2	3	3.5
3. Friendship, companionship	3	6.5	6	4	4.5	1	1
4. Development of skills	4	3	3	3	3	5.5	6.5
5. Measuring self against own ideals	6	4	5	6	6.5	5.5	6.5
6. Emotional release	5	5	4	7	6.5	2	2
7. Competition	7	8	8	5	4.5	7	8
8. Prestige, regard, glamor	8	6.5	7	8	8	8	9
9. Medatsu	—	—	—	—	—	—	3.5
Total autotelic rank	3	1	2	4	5	6	—

Source: Mihaly Csikszentmihalyi, *Beyond Boredom and Anxiety* (San Francisco: Jossey-Bass), table 2.
*This column includes the enjoyment of *medatsu*.

tionnaire because the preliminary interviews had suggested that public display constitutes an important component in the enjoyment of *boso* driving.

Table 1.1 juxtaposes the responses of my informants and those of Csikszentmihalyi. All other groups except basketball players rank "enjoyment of the experience and the use of skills" and "the activity itself" highest, while *bosozoku* youths rank these two reasons fourth and third. "Total Autotelic Rank" in the bottom line of the table indicates the relative importance of intrinsic rewards for the various groups. Among all the groups, aside from basketball players, *bosozoku* youths rank the autotelic component lowest. These results presumably indicate internal differences among autotelic activities. They support the notion that *boso* driving is motivated primarily by intrinsic reward but suggest that, compared to other activities like chess or rock climbing, the intrinsic rewards are relatively less salient. It should be also kept in mind that the interview records strongly indicate that the youngsters do see the activity itself as enjoyable.

Follow-up interviews also show that different types of enjoyment come into play at different phases of a *boso* drive. On broad streets like Gojo Street or Horikawa Street, where traffic is light at midnight and the youths can speed at will, "the enjoyment of the experience" (i.e., enjoyment of the experience of speeding) and "the activity itself" become the primary gratifications. On the other hand, on Kawaramachi Avenue where there is a large audience, the enjoyment of public display, namely, the enjoyment of *medatsu koto* becomes important. "Friendship and companionship" is most important in jovial mock fights during a *boso* drive, and lively sociability during an intermission.

"Emotional release" mainly refers to the cathartic feeling one experiences shortly after each session of *boso* driving. *Sukatto suru* ("feel completely satisfied," "completely refreshed") is the phrase that usually describes this experience. This phrase also frequently appears in daily conversations among informants and in journalistic accounts. Indeed the *bosozoku* youths' emphasis on the cathartic function of *boso* driving misled journalists and scholars into regarding it only as a means of compensating for their inferiority complex and of venting their frustration. But as we have seen and as we shall see in detail in the next section, *boso* driving includes various kinds of enjoyment. The cathartic experience is merely one of them.

MEDATSU, COMMUNITAS, FLOW
Medatsu

Table 1.1. shows that *medatsu koto* (being seen) was ranked as important as "the activity itself" among reasons for one's enjoyment.

Medatsu is the category which informants use when they emphasize the importance of feedback from the audience. For example,

> If I drive a motorcycle alone, it sounds like *pahn!* [But during a *boso* drive] It's like *Guwa, Guwa!* Everybody directs attention to us. We carry out a *boso* drive absolutely because we want to be seen [*medachitai kara*].

The word *medatsu* is also frequently found in interviews recorded in academic and journalistic publications. *Medatsu* is also used when *bosozoku* youths explain the motives for using "bizarre" and "grotesque" costumes and making extreme modifications to their vehicles.[24] *Medatsu* extends to their choice of life-style as "Yankees" in general.[25]

Japanese scholars as well as journalists usually account for the youths' desires to make themselves conspicuous (*medatsu*) in *boso* driving, or to show off their belongings, in terms of *jiko kenji yoku* (desire for showing off, desire for self-assertion). The phrase is fine if used as a simple descriptive term, but it becomes circular if used as an explanation. Little evidence is given on the relative intensity of this desire among *bosozoku* youths. Nor do they have detailed descriptions of the ways in which the youths try to make themselves and their belongings seen. The results of my research suggest that *medatsu* is not a straightforward expression of individual desires but something more complex. One of the keys to understanding *medatsu* is the nature of the audience's feedback. Note the different ratings of the two very similar activities included in the *medatsu* dimension in table 1.2. While "playing a theatrical role before a large audience" was ranked fourth, "appearing in a TV program" was ranked twelfth among twenty activities with regard to their similarity to *boso* driving. Informants almost uniformly mention the difference in the intensity and directness of audience response in accounting for the differences in these two rankings. Many also argue that *boso* driving is far more thrilling and full of unexpected events. One informant said,

> Vividness [is different]. . . . We can repeat it again on a TV program, if the director says, "This is not good." But, this [*boso* driving] is totally different. . . . When I zigzag and crash, who would say, "N.G." or "Cut!"? It's a miserable accident.

Another key is the difference between *medatsu* and "prestige, regard, glamor." Table 1.1 shows that while *medatsu koto* was ranked third, "prestige, regard, glamor" was given the lowest rank. *Medatsu* is akin to "prestige, regard, glamor" in that both of them require an audience for one's performance or appearance and that the performance or ap-

Table 1.2 Ranking of Similarity-of-Experience Items within Each Autotelic Activity

Factors	Rock Climbers N = 26	Composers N = 22	Dancers N = 27	Male Chess Players N = 28	Female Chess Players N = 20	Basketball Players N = 35	Bosozoku N = 45	Bosozoku N = 45
1. Friendship and Relaxation								
Making love	6	6.5	4.5	16.5	17.5	14	16	18*
Being with a good friend	3	9	4.5	9	14.5	8	3	3
Watching a movie	15.5	5	9	12	17.5	6	12	14
Listening to music	6	3	2	10	12.5	3	4	5
Reading a book	8	8	6.5	5	12.5	15.5	13.5	15.5
2. Risk and chance								
Swimming out on a dare	13	13.5	15	14	7	17.5	10.5	12
Exposure to radiation**	17	10	12	12	10	9.5	5.5	6.5
Driving fast	10	16.5	12	12	10	6	1	1
Taking drugs**	10	13.5	15	15	14.5	9.5	9	10
Playing a slot machine**	18	18	15	18	16	17.5	10.5	12
Entering a burning house	13	11	12	16.5	10	4	13.5	15.5
3. Problem Solving								
Math problem**	4	2	9	1.5	2	12	17.5	19.5
Assembling furniture	13	6.5	17	7.5	7	15.5	17.5	19.5
Exploring strange places	15.5	13.5	18	6	5	12	7.5	8.5
Playing poker	15.5	13.5	18	6	5	12	15	17
4. Competition								
Running a race	6	16.5	9	7.5	7	2	2	2
Competitive sport	10	13.5	6.5	1.5	3	1	5.5	6.5
5. Creative								
Designing, discovering	2	1	1	3	1	6	7.5	8.5
6. Medatsu								
Appearing on a TV program	—	—	—	—	—	—	—	12
Playing a theatrical role	—	—	—	—	—	—	—	4

Source: Mihaly Csikszentmihalyi, *Beyond Boredom and Anxiety* (San Francisco: Jossey-Bass), Table 3.
*This column includes the enjoyment of *medatsu.*
**For wording of these items, see Appendix C.

pearance should attract the attention of the audience. The most important difference between the two is that while "prestige, regard, glamor" presupposes a shared value judgment, *medatsu* does not. *Bosozoku* enjoy being watched by people, even if the spectators express shock and outrage. What really matters is the attention of others, regardless of any moral implications of that behavior. It is obvious that "prestige, regard, glamor" is seen as a more conventional or consensual accomplishment.

Csikszentmihalyi comments on this point so as to clarify the issue and make explicit the relationship between the enjoyment of *medatsu* and genuine flow experience. After pointing out that *medatsu* can be regarded as the "basic, primitive *ur*-form of the motivation out of which more abstract social forms of 'prestige, regard, glamor' evolve," he mentions two ways to maintain the self strong and ordered. One is to invest one's attention in goals and getting feedback that confirms one's intentions. The other is to get the attention of others to recognize one's existence and one's intentions. Csikszentmihalyi suggests that *medatsu* is a way of getting this second type of feedback. He then points out that the pure "flow" activities mainly provide feedback based on personal achievement and thus also strengthen the sense of self, but this is an unintended consequence and not the main goal of the activity.[26]

As the phenomenon of "stage fright" suggests, feedback from an audience may interfere with the feedback provided by the concentration on the activity in a flow activity itself. For instance, heightened self-consciousness due to the presence of bystanders may disrupt the flow experience of rock dancing.[27] By contrast, both types of information—feedback from the use of one's skills, and feedback from the audience—are combined in the "ideal" *boso* driving. This is probably not unlike the experience of an actor at the peak of his theatrical performance. In both cases, the audience response does not evoke a monitoring ego but becomes a "mirror" which transmits immediate and unambiguous feedback. As we shall see in chapter 3, *bosozoku* can be characterized as picaresque heroes, that is, strange combinations of picaro (rogue) and hero. *Boso* driving is essentially a theatrical stage on which the themes and plots implied in the character image of *bosozoku* are activated and organized into "performance," not just a scheme of action written in a script. The character image of *bosozoku* includes many contradictions and inconsistencies, and includes especially the traits of hero and rogue. But the performance is staged as though it were based on a script with coherent themes and narrative plot with a hero. The aspect of the social drama about *bosozoku* as hero is clarified by the emergent quality of the "performance."[28] The immediate demands of the ongoing action pare away the contradictions and inconsistencies implicit in the character of *bosozoku*. The script of this hero narrative becomes a set of game-rules which make it possible for *bosozoku* youths to construct their dramatized self-image in an orderly manner. However temporary the performance, and no matter whether the audience shares the heroic image of *bosozoku*, the youths can act as heroes of an ongoing drama.[29]

Communitas

"Friendship, companionship" was rated highest among the rewards that provide the most enjoyment in *boso* driving (table 1.1). "Being with a good friend" also ranks third among the twenty activities with regard to its similarity to a *boso* drive (table 1.2). Many informants emphasized the enjoyment of vivid and unmediated sociability. Two informants described the interaction and mock fighting during *boso* driving:

> M.: . . . Yeah. All of us are so happy. Everybody looks so cheerful. Really.
> E.: When passing each other, we wave and exclaim, "Wow!"
> M.: When driving side by side, we exclaim, "Peace!" and make the V sign. We get really high.
> E.: If we drive side by side with some guy we know, we may zigzag [but] playfully.
> M.: I may zigzag and kick his bike [as in a playful mock fight].

In considering the significance of "friendship and companionship" in the context of *boso* driving, we have to take account of the contrast between the pattern of interaction among these youths in their hangouts, where they become "Yankees," and the interaction pattern in *boso* driving, where they become *bosozoku*. Informants, as Yankee/corner boys, spend most of their leisure time talking and gossiping in their hangouts. Roles are undifferentiated in these interactions, and there is ambiguity about who should take the initiative. Although "Yankee" implies an action-seeking youngster, the character image includes much more ambivalence and confusion than that of *bosozoku*.[30] An intransitive verb, *tamaru*, is used in describing such a pattern of unstructured interaction among Yankees. The typical answer given to my question, *Nani shiten noya?* (What are you guys doing here?) was *Nani mo shitehen. Tamatteru dakeya.* (Nothing. We're just gathering.) *Tamaru* is commonly used to refer to stagnant water or puddles that have formed on the road. And a Japanese word used for "hangout" is *tamariba*, a place where a group of people gather, like water gathers in a puddle.

In clear contrast to *tamaru*-type interaction, the interaction in *boso* driving is ordered, exciting, and organized. During a *boso* drive, roles are differentiated, the flow of time is synchronized, and resources are structured for the sake of a single, simple, clear-cut purpose. Youths join in the *boso* drive voluntarily. They share situation-specific and playlike definitions of the character image of *bosozoku*—an almost idealized action-type hero.[31] They also share themes and plots of the *boso* driving. Synchronized movements of youths and vehicles present the "beauty of massed gymnastics." Youths experience a sense of self-transcendence and feel that they belong to a more powerful system.[32]

The enjoyment of "friendship, companionship" or that of "collective effervescence" derives from a sense of unity in the ordered collective undertaking in which the youths participate voluntarily. In the carnivalesque atmosphere of *boso* driving, the rules governing interpersonal interaction in everyday life are temporarily suspended; vivid and unmediated sociability becomes possible. A female informant described her experience of euphoria as follows:

> I . . . I understand something, when all of our feelings get tuned up. . . . At the start, when we are running, we are not in complete harmony. But if the *boso* drive begins going well, all of us—all of us—feel for each other. How can I say this? When we wag the tail of the band . . . When our minds become one. At such a time, it's a real pleasure. . . . When we realize that we become one flesh, it's supreme. When we get high on speed. At such a moment, it's really super.

The enjoyment of "friendship, companionship" derives from what Victor Turner called "communitas," namely, "a total, unmediated relationship between person and person,"[33] which can be found in the liminal phase of society such as rituals, festivals, and initiation rites. The roles differentiated in the performance of *boso* driving are not those which segmentalize or separate people. On the contrary, they can be compared to roles in a "pretend play" which make it possible for participants to liberate themselves from the social roles of everyday life and to present an alternative model of human association. As Turner says about the hierarchical organization of the Conservative Vice Lords (a gang of adolescent black youths in Chicago) and Hell's Angels, *bosozoku* youths are "playing the game of structure rather than engaging in the socioeconomic structure in real earnest."[34] Resources in this game are not allocated against the participants' wills. Nor is time synchronized coercively. Both are aimed at creating and maintaining the playlike, purely voluntary definition of *boso* driving, to which the participants willingly subscribe.

Flow: Skills and Challenges in *Boso* Driving

While *medatsu* and communitas are those forms of enjoyment which presuppose feedback from others on one's own actions, the enjoyment of high-speed driving does not invariably require such a response. The enjoyment of "speed and thrills" affords the opportunity for genuine flow experience, an experience in which the actor gets feedback which confirms his intentions by engrossing his attention in immediate goals. Results from the questionnaire, interviews, and field observations all indicate that the range of this genuine flow in a *boso* drive is quite limited and that the limitation is based on the peculiar nature of skills and challenges in *boso* driving.

Csikszentmihalyi regards the matching of skills to challenges as the essential feature of flow. He argues,

> [A]ctivities that reliably produce flow experiences are similar in that they provide opportunities for action which a person can act upon without being bored or worried. . . . when a person is bombarded with demands which he or she feels unable to meet, a state of anxiety ensues. When the demands for action are fewer, but still more than what the person feels capable of handling, the state of experience is one of worry.[35]

His idea is illustrated in figure 1.1. In his discussion of this theoretical model of psychological flow, Csikszentmihalyi shows two ways in which people in a state of worry return to flow. One is by decreasing challenge. Another is by increasing skill. The latter is closely related to an integral aspect of psychological flow. As the high rankings given to the items under "Creative" and "Problem Solving" in table 1.2 suggest, flow activities provide a certain degree of uncertainty and novelty. The uncertainty and novelty can be overcome by the actor if he expands his capacities to include new dimensions of skill and competence. In this way, flow activities provide people with an opportunity to surpass their own limitations. Flow activities not only provide opportunities of matching skills to challenges but also present the possibility of elevating a existing skill-challenge balance to a higher level. The higher the level of the skill-challenge balance, presumably the deeper the flow experience will be. Flow activities like rock climbing are characterized by indefinite sets of skill-challenge balance and thus a broad range of "flow channels" (bands of skill-challenge balances—figure 1.1).[36]

Boso driving is a limited flow activity in this sense. This can be seen in the *bosozoku* youths' evaluation of the components of autotelic activities. Table 1.2 shows that *bosozoku* youths gave comparatively lower

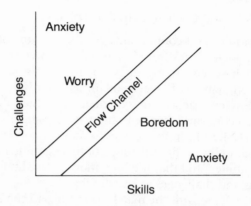

FIG. 1.1. Flow Model. (Reprinted, by permission, from I. Sato, *An Ethnography of* Bosozoku [Tokyo: Shin'yosha, 1984], 72, where it was redrawn from Mihaly Csikszentmihalyi, *Beyond Boredom and Anxiety* [San Francisco: Jossey-Bass, 1975], fig. 1.)

scores to the activities in "Creative" and "Problem Solving" components in comparing them with *boso* driving. They also describe *boso* driving as involving more risk than the activities in any of the other six groups; they give the highest total scores among the seven groups of respondents to the activities in "Risk and Chance." The peculiar characteristics of "skills" and "challenges" in *boso* driving underlie this atypical rating pattern.

The first reason for this would seem to be that the challenges in a *boso* drive are to a considerable degree unpredictable and uncontrollable. *Bosozoku* youths cannot easily match skills to challenges. Extreme physical danger is a prerequisite for several characteristics of flow experiences both in rock climbing and *boso* driving. But as compared to rock climbing, physical danger in a *boso* drive is more contingent upon situational factors which are unpredictable and difficult to control and may intrude upon full psychological involvement. One is frequently drawn "back to reality." Excessive physical danger, then, leads to disruption of the skill-challenge balance and sometimes to injury or even death. This makes it difficult to upgrade the skill-challenge balance beyond a certain point.

This difficulty is illustrated by the changes in the types of vehicles that *bosozoku* youths use at different stages of their careers. As shown in figure 1.2, the youths tend to use larger motorcycles as they become more skilled in *boso* driving. The larger the motorcycle one uses, the deeper flow he can experience (or the greater the enjoyment of "speed

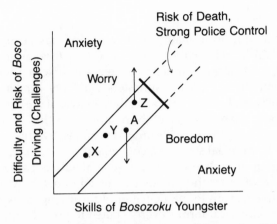

Fɪɢ. 1.2. Flow Channel of *Boso* Driving: X, *Boso* Driving on Small Motorcycles; Y, *Boso* Driving on Medium-size Motorcycles; Z, *Boso* Driving on Large Motorocycles; A, *Boso* Driving in Automobiles. (Reprinted, by permission, from I. Sato, *An Ethnography of* Bosozoku [Tokyo: Shin'yosha, 1984], 72.)

and thrills"). But the deepest flow (represented by Z in figure 1.2) easily collapses and leads to worry and anxiety, because it is based on a quite precarious skill-challenge balance and is exceptionally vulnerable to unpredictable hazards. *Bosozoku* youths graduate to automobiles from the largest motorcycles.[37] Although the use of a car makes it possible for them to ensure greater safety for themselves, it often results in a shallower flow experience and in boredom.

The nature of skills as well as of challenges sets a limit to the quality of flow in *boso* driving. "Skills" in *boso* driving refer mainly to physical skills, especially one's reflexes. In this respect, *boso* driving stands in contrast to rock climbing, which requires a high level of both intellectual and physical skills in order to manage risks. The combination of the two kinds of skills makes it possible to maintain intense concentration in rock climbing, which in turn leads to complex and deep flow.[38] This is probably why "Problem Solving" and "Creativity" were rated high and "Risk and Chance" was rated low by rock climbers. As the contrastive rating pattern of *bosozoku* youths in table 1.2 shows, a *boso* drive is not thought to resemble other activities that require intellectual skills and it tends to be characterized by a narrow flow-channel. Although some of the youths may exhibit acrobatic driving, the participants' choices are severely restricted. It is mainly the leaders who decide the details of a *boso* drive and it is they who use intellectual skills.

CONCLUSION

The seeming irrationality of *boso* driving has been explained conventionally as being either a way of evading frustrations or a way of expressing frustrations inherent among dispossessed youths. The overrepresentation of those youngsters with low academic attainments in the *bosozoku* population and the life-style of the core members as corner boys (Yankees) have given support to this "pathetic" interpretation of *boso* driving. Like other deviations, psychological strain originating from social strain is a convenient way of making sense of *boso* driving, or of explaining it to the general public. This chapter has shown, however, that the activities involved in *boso* driving provide strong positive reasons for participation. *Boso* driving turns out to be a creative dramaturgical form cleverly crafted to provide a temporarily heightened sense of self among the participants. *Boso* driving, then, allows the enactment of a heroic role before the public and, through the use of skills and disciplines, the experience of limited psychological flow. *Boso* driving also provides a sense of belonging to a community and a shared experience of collective effervescence. Finally, participation in a *boso* drive provides autotelic experiences by structuring the activity in a play-form that allows the pitting of personal skills against relevant challenges, and that produces clear goals and unambiguous feedback in a setting that cuts out most ordinary stimulation while forcing concentration on a narrow range of stimuli.

Despite these positive characteristics, *boso* driving, like all play-forms, has its limitations. It involves many risks without allowing for the development of a great number of skills. Intellectual challenges are almost nonexistent. One informant, whose driving techniques as a bike rider were well-recognized among his fellows, said, self-deprecatingly, to me,

> Those who are not good at driving become *bosozoku*. If they are really good at it, they will go to Suzuka [an official racetrack] or some other place to race. . . . *Boso* driving is, after all, mere *asobi* [play].

The enjoyment of *boso* driving is not the sole element of "play" in *bosozoku* activity. As stage props are no less important than the performance of the actors in a theatrical play, the cultural artifacts of *bosozoku* (e.g., costumes, vehicles) constitute an important component of the gang activity. They help to create a playlike definition of the situation or "frame," and are prerequisites to the enjoyment and engrossment in *boso* driving. In the next chapter, I shall deal with this genre of play in *bosozoku* subculture and activity, which conveys and confirms the (meta) message "This is play."

2   Fashion and Style: Meanings of Outrageous Paraphernalia

> With rare exceptions, the outlaw bike is a Harley 74, a giant of a motorcycle that comes out of the Milwaukee factory weighing seven hundred pounds, but which the Angels strip down to five hundred. In the argot of the cycle world the Harley is a "hog," and the outlaw bike is a "chopped hog." Basically it is the same machine all motorcycle cops use, but the police bike is an accessory-laden elephant compared to the lean, customized dynamos that Hell's Angels ride. The resemblance is about the same as that of a factory-equipped Cadillac to a dragster's stripped-down essence of the same car. The Angels refer to standard 74s as "garbage wagons," and Bylaw Number 11 of the charter is a put-down in the grand manner: "An Angel cannot wear the colors while riding on a garbage wagon with a non-Angel."
>
> —Hunter Thompson, *Hell's Angels*

At first sight *bosozoku* do not at all resemble American motorcycle gangs, especially Hell's Angels. While many Angels are in their thirties, most *bosozoku* are either teenagers or in their early twenties. In contrast to the Angels' long and unkempt hair, most *bosozoku* have permanent waves, which are also a hallmark of Yankees. *Bosozoku*/Yankees frequently and meticulously comb their permed hair with brushes. While many Angels affect beards, few *bosozoku* are bearded. Some *bosozoku*/Yankees have mustaches and are quite meticulous in keeping their mustaches trimmed. *Bosozoku* uniforms look far more elegant than those Hell's Angels wear. *Bosozoku* costumes are usually made by tailors and are of various colors, including pink and white as well as black and gray. The costumes rarely exude a powerful stench as the crusty and grease-permeated Angels' uniforms often do.[1]

There is, however, a fundamental similarity between *bosozoku* and Hell's Angels: the outrageous nature of their paraphernalia. *Bosozoku* automobiles and motorbikes are heavily decorated with accessories and are modified beyond recognition from their original condition. The earsplitting noise from the modified exhaust systems and the horns of the vehicles deafen pedestrians. Pedestrians and onlookers may also be shocked by the flashy costumes *bosozoku* wear. *Bosozoku* sometimes call the costumes *tokkofuku,* the uniform of suicidal *kamikaze* bombers. On the costumes and uniforms are embroidered group names in bizarre Chinese characters such as 武羅悪区　江無屁羅 (Black Emperor) or 地獄族 (Hell Tribe). Phrases with nationalistic and fanatic implications—e.g., 国士無双 (Patriot), 護国尊皇 (Protection of the Nation and Respect for the Emperor)—are also often sewn or painted on the costumes or on national flags *bosozoku* use as their group flag. These items shock and outrage the general public and make them suspect the motives behind the use of such paraphernalia.

Why Do *Bosozoku* Use "Unnatural" Symbols? Two Answers

As with the motivation for the *boso* driving, two explanations have been provided by scholars for the outrageous and "unnatural" symbols associated with *bosozoku.* The first presupposes that *bosozoku* are eccentric or pathological. For example, Kikuchi regards the "perverse desire for self-assertion" as the background of extreme modification of *bosozoku* vehicles:

> They [*bosozoku* youths] acknowledge themselves to be dropouts who have seen ordinary youths "open up a big lead" in the competition for academic achievement and occupational status. They are eager to surpass ordinary youths in other matters. This perverse desire for self-assertion drives them to add more and more extreme modifications to their vehicles.[2]

Similarly, Tazaki considers *bosozoku* group names "manifestations of infantile desires for self-assertion which are based on undifferentiated mentality." Chiba refers to the costumes of *bosozoku* as "exhibitionistic" and "frivolous."[3]

These interpretations are rarely substantiated by detailed empirical analyses. In most cases, the authors merely present their own values in "interpretations" based on impressions. Some attempts have been made to corroborate their arguments by empirical observation. But their selection and categorization of empirical instances are quite arbitrary and impressionistic.[4]

The second explanation, cited by fewer authors as compared to the first one, views the use of subcultural artifacts and symbols as "play [*asobi*] of mimicry" or "disguise play."[5] For example, Tamura and Mugishima state that:

> Driving a car is, according to Caillois's characterization, "playing with vertigo." *Bosozoku* [activity] also includes "play of mimicry" in that rebellious names such as those mentioned above are frequently used. When they [*bosozoku* youths] assume an aggressive stance toward society, they imitate [the themes and plots in] the fictional worlds of cartoons, television, and movies.[6]

As with the concepts of abnormality and eccentricity in the first explanation, the concept of "play" (*asobi*) is imputed to members of a subculture by outside observers. It is not based on *bosozoku* youths' own accounts of the use of symbols and paraphernalia. The scholars who use the concept of "play" rarely present the participants' own accounts. Nor do they use empirical cases to substantiate their arguments.

In marked contrast to these academic studies, popular works by journalists include many empirical accounts of the use of *bosozoku* paraphernalia as well as *bosozoku* youths' own statements about such items. Such works include extensive lists of group names with numerous pictures of vehicles, costumes, and insignia.[7] Some accounts also contain interview transcripts which refer to the significance of subcultural items.[8] Though not derived from systematic inquiry, the pictures and lists of group names may be utilized as raw material for further analysis. The word *medatsu* (being seen) is frequently found in interview transcripts. Although the journalists do not elaborate on the significance of *medatsu* in *bosozoku* symbolism, the word suggests a close relationship between unnatural symbols and the enjoyment of self-display. Indeed, the materials in the journalistic works strongly suggest that the second answer, in terms of play, is more plausible than the pathological interpretation. It should be noted, however, that the play shown through motorcycle gang artifacts includes more than what "mimicry" or "disguise play" implies.

Subcultural Items and Playlike Definitions of the Situation

It is widely acknowledged that *bosozoku* vehicles are modified according to similar patterns found throughout Japan. It is also well known that similar group names and similar attire are used by *bosozoku* groups in many parts of the country. In other words, the *bosozoku* subculture is a nationwide subcultural style which amounts to a kind of mannerism.[9] We should also note that during the heyday of *bosozoku* activity the subculture had been affected by continuous changes in fads and fashions. It needs hardly be added that group names, insignia, and dress are used in the context of gang activities, in order to emphasize collective participation. These considerations seem enough to refute the psychological and reductionistic assumptions implicit in the pathological interpretations of *bosozoku* artifacts. They also suggest that the significance of the outrageous and "unnatural" symbols can be meaningfully interpreted and understood within the framework of sociological studies treating fashion and style as mediums of communication. Such studies also point out that fashion and style serve as mechanisms for social and personal control amid social change.[10] Blumer maintains that "Fashion is a very adept mechanism for enabling people to adjust in an orderly way to a moving and changing world which is potentially full of anarchic possibilities."[11]

On the other hand, ethnographic or theoretical studies of some of the more spectacular youth subcultures and rebellious styles in Britain, such as punk, skinheads, rockers,[12] and ethnographic works on expressive styles in American slums[13] have shown that subcultural styles quite often are embedded in the interactional processes of specific groups.[14] That is, subcultural styles are not merely adopted by willful individuals but must be somehow congruent with sociocultural situations of a specific group and the "focal concerns" and interaction among its members. The "definitions of the situation" implicit in the youthful styles are not necessarily definite "scripts" or schemes of action which youngsters must stick to. They often provide raw material which the youngsters fashion to fit their individual needs and the needs of the group.[15]

This chapter, on the basis of behavioral observations, interviews, and media analysis, will show that the *bosozoku* artifacts serve as important stage props by means of which the youths clarify and affirm the playlike, dramaturgical definitions of the situation evolving around the character image of *bosozoku* as heroic or picaresque speedsters. The definitions of the situation, embodied in the form of tangible things and consumer goods, enables the youths to create and share a meaningful and intelligible universe of discourse which gives them an enhanced sense of self. Many of the themes in the definitions are also found in Yankee style: e.g., valor, masculinity, defiance. Indeed, the "focal concerns" of Yankees or corner boys are represented in almost ideal manner in the three domains of *bosozoku* artifacts and symbols: vehicles, groups names, and costumes and insignia.

VEHICLES
Patterns of Modification

Motorcycles. For *bosozoku*, the factory product, which they call *nomaru* (normal), is nothing but raw material. They modify the "normal" vehicles into *kaizosha* (modified vehicles) of their own style. While Hell's Angels use motorcycles of formidable displacement (1,200 cc), most *bosozoku* use vehicles displacing 250–400 cc.[16] Under Japanese law motorcycles displacing more than 750 cc cannot be sold on the domestic market. It is very difficult under the current licensing system for civilians to obtain a permit for motorcycles over 400 cc. Thus both *bosozoku* youths and the general public regard bikes displacing 400 or 750 cc as "huge." Motorcycles are usually called by their nicknames. In most cases these are acronyms derived from the original manufacturer's names, e.g., *Pekejei* (Yamaha XJ400), *Efupeke* (Kawasaki FX400), *Jiesu* (Suzuki GS400), *Zettsu* (Kawasaki Z750F).

To outside observers, *bosozoku* motorcycles appear to be quite similar. Indeed, informants' answers to my questions about modification patterns were very similar. The following response was typical:

> Well, first of all I put on a *shugo* [custom header pipe]. Then, I painted the body and made the handlebars *shibori* [created the effect of squeezed handlebars]. You may want to put in a *sanren* [three-trumpet horn]. Some may use Beet's point cover and alphin cover. I also put on a *hotaru* [lightning bug].

Shugo is an exhaust system which consists of a multiple-tube header and a single collector pipe connected to one muffler. *Shugo* may increase horsepower and improve acceleration, even if the engine itself is not custom-made. But it is for greater sound rather than increased power that *bosozoku* youths install their own exhaust systems.

Shugo generates a high-pitched exhaust noise. While driving their motorcycles, *bosozoku* youths often race the engines twice or three times in rapid succession. When it is done twice, the exhaust noise sounds like *hon, hoon!* *Bosozoku* youths call this procedure *daburu akuseru* (double acceleration). When they do it three times, the sound is like *hon, hon, hoon!* It is then called *toripuru akuseru* (triple acceleration). Bike riders usually take the diffuser pipes and the fiberglass packing out of the mufflers in order to further "improve" the sound effects.

The horn also contributes to these sound effects. The names *sanren* (three-trumpet horn) or *yonren* (four-trumpet horn) are derived from the number of horns connected vertically to each other. The horns are of different lengths and make sounds of different pitch. They are fitted in combination with small air compressors on the backs of the bikes. *Bosozoku* youths call them "music horns" because they play specific melodies by relay. (In the United States such devices are called "musical air-blast horns" or "air horns.") The number of horns varies from one to ten. Bikes are usually equipped with three or four of them. Some automobiles are equipped with "music horns," one large horn which plays various melodies from a computer chip.

Some modifications are specifically aimed at visual appeal. Many *bosozoku* paint the bodies of their bikes in primary colors. In particular, they draw figures and words on the bike's gasoline tank. There are also many varieties of accessories (e.g., decorative mirrors, custom-made frame covers) of different shapes and colors. Extreme specialization exists in the market for accessories, especially for those which have definite visual appeal, such as fenders, side (frame) covers, and point (distributor) covers. "Beet" in the above-mentioned account by an informant is one of the most prestigious brand names for accessories of this sort. Other well-known brands include Napoleon, Moriwaki, Yoshimura, and Select. Brand names are often clearly shown in raised relief or as emblems on parts.

At night, lights are important for visual attraction. There are many varieties of headlights and turn-signals, of different shapes and colors. The turn-signals are connected with "high flashers," relays which regulate flickering of the lights. *Hotaru* (lightning bug) is a tiny blue lamp which can be fitted to the back of a bike. It is used for its visual appeal and is purely ornamental: it does not serve as a tail lamp.

There are some modifications that affect drivability. *Shibori* is a set of handlebars which are bent almost double. They are illegal and used almost exclusively by *bosozoku,* while other motorcyclists use less extreme, though custom-made, handlebars. Some motorbikes are also power-jumped by increasing the size of the bore and the length of stroke. This modification is called *boa appu* (bore up). Harder suspension coils and shock absorbers, tires with special tread patterns, and racer seats also enhance the sensation of driving: that is, they communicate the motion of the vehicle more directly to the rider.

Each accessory costs a considerable sum of money. For many *bosozoku,* the total cost of modification often exceeds the original purchase price of the motorcycle. It was not easy to estimate average expenses for modification because many informants had acquired already modified bikes from senior gang members or friends. In addition, they exchange used parts for cash on an ad hoc basis. Nonetheless, in most cases the sums cited were not less than ¥100,000

TABLE 2.1 Examples of Modification: Motorcycles

Parts	Informant M		Informant N	
	Brand*	Price** (Yen)	Brand*	Price** (Yen)
(Body)	Honda CBX400	420,000 ($1,680)	Kawasaki FX400	150,000 ($600)
Headlight			CBA	6,000
Light stay				3,000
Turn signal			European	4,800
Relay for light		2,500		
High flasher		3,800		
Brake flasher		3,800		
Mirror	Napoleon	3,000	Napoleon	1,500
Alphin cover	Beet	18,000	Beet	15,000
Point cover	Beet	5,000	Beet	3,000
Generator cover	Beet	7,000		
Chain cover	Hurricane	2,000		
Tire		25,000	Pirelli	50,000
Stabilizer	Beet	12,000		
Shock absorber			Koni	28,000
Trail air scoops	Beet	22,000	ZII	5,600
Fender	Select	8,000	Beet	8,000
Seat		5,000		
Seat rail	Hurricane	3,500		2,000
Double disc brake			(Customized)	60,000
Custom header pipe	Yoshimura	46,000	Moriwaki	46,000
Power lever	Kitako	1,500		1,500
Handle grip		1,000		
Breather pipe		2,000		
Painting		10,000		10,000
Total cost of modifications		181,000 ($724)		248,000 ($992)

*Only those brand names which the informants could recollect correctly were listed.
**Prices include labor charges.

($400).[17] Table 2.1 shows in detail the modifications two informants made on their motorcycles. (M and N are the initials of their last names.)

Automobiles. According to popular stereotypes, *bosozoku* are youths on motorcycles. But the nationwide censuses taken by the police show that 54 to 67 percent of *bosozoku* vehicles have been automobiles.[18] Although sports cars have long been the favored type of automobile, a trend during the research period was the use of sedans with large bodies and large cylinder-displacement, such as Toyota Crown, and

Nissan Cedric. *Bosozoku* usually have nicknames for automobiles, such as *Suka G* (Nissan Skyline GT), *Gokiburi* (roach) or *Zetto* (Nissan 280Z), *Koro G* (Toyota Corona GT).

As with motorcycles, *bosozoku* cars are also modified in recognizable ways. The single most salient characteristic of *bosozoku* cars is *shakotan,* a "low rider" modification of the suspension system. *Shakotan* literally means lowering the body (ground clearance) of the automobile.[19] *Bosozoku* youths achieve this effect by shortening the coil springs in the suspension. Some even remove the coil springs altogether. This modification is called *abunomi* (absorber only), because only the shock absorbers are left in the car's suspension system. Again, the aim is to experience the unmediated "feel of the road."

The use of wide tires in conjunction with *shakotan* creates the appearance of a race car. Oversized fenders are used to complete this impression. A recent fad is the use of thin tires set on wide wheels, which then resemble racing wheels except that these wheels are extremely decorative. "Designer wheels" constitute one of the most profitable portions of the market for automobile parts in Japan. Numerous brands of wheels are manufactured in Japan or imported from European countries, especially Italy. A steering wheel that is small in diameter and custom bucket-seats also create the impression of a racing car and are suitable for abrupt turns.

Increased engine bore and stroke, taken with combined intake and exhaust systems, as in racers, not only increase horsepower but amplify vibrations, which combine dull and low sounds from the air intake and the exhaust. As when buying wheels, *bosozoku* youths usually choose intake manifolds, carburetors, exhaust manifolds, and mufflers with specific brand names.

Other accessories include "music horns," headlights and turn-signals of specific shapes and colors, spoilers and side-steps and other "aeroparts" so decorated that the usual aerodynamic effects are reversed, chandelier-shaped interior lights, carpets of primary colors that cover the dashboard and the rear-seat shelf as well as the floor, and expensive car stereos illuminated in primary colors.

The total modification cost for automobiles generally exceeds those for motorcycles. An informant estimated that the minimum modification costs for *bosozoku* cars was around ¥500,000 ($2,000). While *bosozoku* youths can modify motorbikes by themselves, automobile modification requires techniques so specialized that most of the work is left to mechanics. Therefore labor costs add to the expense of automobile modification. Table 2.2 shows an example of car modification.

TABLE 2.2 Examples of Modification: Automobiles

Parts	Brand*	Prices** (Yen)
(Body)	Toyota Camry 2000GT	1,870,000 ($7,480)
Fender		40,000
Suspension coil	Tokiko	12,000
Shock absorber	Nayaba	30,000
Tire	Advan	200,000
Wheel	Techno Racing	
Exhaust manifold		35,000
Straight muffler	(custom-made)	38,000
Yellow plug wires		7,000
Music horn	Mitsuba	20,000
Air-blast horn		24,000
High flasher		3,000
Headlight	Marshall	30,000
Steering wheel		25,000
Bucket seat	Recaro (driver's seat)	60,000
Bucket seat	(passenger's seat)	35,000
Painting		130,000
Car stereo	Pioneer	200,000
Total cost of modifications		924,000 ($3,696)

* **See notes for table 2.1.

Meanings of Modification

Modification and Group Boundary. As Hell's Angels draw a clear distinction between "garbage wagons" (standard Harley 74s) and their own "chopped hogs," *bosozoku* distinguish sharply the differences between "normal" vehicles and their *kaizosha* (modified vehicles). They are also sensitive to the "appropriateness" of styles of vehicle modifications for corresponding social groups.

In their weekly meetings, several members of Ukyo Rengo (the motorcycle gang confederation I studied) would often squat down by the roadside and look at passing vehicles. Among them I sometimes heard comments such as "Gee! Doesn't the guy on the *pettan* [low-rider-style car] have straight hair?" and "Hey, look! A surfer's driving such a low-cut [Nissan] Cedric!" To the *bosozoku* youths, who usually have permanent waves, it appears quite incongruous for a low-rider-style car to be driven by someone with "straight hair" (conventional youth) or a "surfer" (tame social type). As Angels cannot wear the "colors" while

PLATE 3. MODIFIED MOTORCYCLE. Huge sound from *shugo,* a multiple-tube header and a single collector pipe connected with a muffler, engrosses motorcycle gangs in the frame of *boso* driving. Various decorative parts are sold by manufacturers: e.g., frame covers, custom-made mirrors.

riding on "garbage wagons," those who drive low-slung cars should be *bosozoku* or Yankees, youths with permanent waves and deviant lifestyles.

Gang members share a prototypical image of "*bosozoku*-style" modification. This image is prescriptive as well as descriptive, and sets a boundary between *bosozoku* and other youths.[20] Much of the conversation at gatherings and weekly meetings deals with "the" pattern of modification. Senior gang members give junior members advice about "proper" or "nice-looking" modifications. *Bosozoku* youths also observe and discuss the different modified vehicles that pass before them on the roadside. The prototypical image also has proscriptive aspects. Those who deviate from the gang image usually are the object of verbal ridicule. Occasionally those who use "normal" cars are excluded from a *boso* drive.

The vehicle is also the focal point for sociability among *bosozoku* youths. Much of their conversation centers around vehicles and includes gossip and rumors about vehicles other gang members have purchased, comparison of new models by different manufacturers, and locations of garages that perform illegal modifications. Each group hangout is also a marketplace for vehicles and accessories. In order to

PLATE 4. MODIFIED AUTOMOBILE. Many *Bosozoku* cars imitate the style of racing cars. Yet modifications are often so decorative that the usual effects are reversed: e.g., oversized "aeroparts," too-thin tires.

become an accepted participant in such gatherings, one must know technological jargon and have specific knowledge of garages, parts shops, and local dealers.

Language, however, is only one form of communication concerning vehicles. Modified vehicles are, above all, props by means of which youngsters create and share the carnival atmosphere of *boso* driving, which consists of several types of sensations. The strong visual appeal of the vehicles, achieved by the drawings on the bodies, lights of various colors, oversized fenders, and various "aeroparts," is further amplified by the spectacular massed presence of a great number of vehicles. Custom header pipes on motorbikes, racer intake and exhaust systems on cars, "music horns," and car stereos create overwhelming auditory impressions, engrossing *bosozoku* members in the "frame" of *boso* driving.

Some vehicle modifications create a more direct sense of participation, and thus make it easy for *bosozoku* members to "get tuned into" the rhythm of *boso* driving. An automobile with a power-jumped engine, as well as modified exhaust and intake systems, has increased acceleration and vibrates more vigorously through the chassis. Racing tires and shortened coil springs create a sensation of close, almost unmediated contact with the road; and steering wheels of small diameter facilitate frequent and abrupt turns. All of these modifications generate bodily movements and sensations characteristic of a *boso* drive. Even an olfactory channel comes into play from the scorching smell of racing tires and the smells of exhaust and burning motor oil. In *boso* driving, all of these channels of communications are integrated into an intoxicating and quasi-mystical experience of "group flow."[21] Some informants emphatically maintained that, without direct experience, others cannot understand the euphoria produced by *boso* driving.

> After all, . . . I think only those who've experienced a *boso* drive can share the feeling. . . . Same as amphetamines. Only those who have taken them know the feeling. Yeah, the same [applies to the experience of *boso* driving]. Ya know, I mean, those people who never experienced it cannot understand it.

> I think you can never understand it [the experience of *boso* driving]. If you don't do it [participate in a *boso* drive], you cannot write a good book about it. After all, you cannot understand it, unless you experience it yourself.

Vehicles are the medium which enables *bosozoku* youths to share this esoteric experience. By sharing the experience, the youths can view themselves a comrades who have secrecy in common and are somehow superior to others.[22]

The Vehicle and the Self. While modified vehicles, as symbols of collective identity, serve to distinguish *bosozoku* from other youths, they also provide *bosozoku* with a number of relatively coherent personal identities. Or, it is more appropriate to say that the *bosozoku* is one of the possible identities that Yankee/corner boys form through vehicles.

The vehicle is a focal point of social and personal life of Yankees, and constitutes an important element of their social identity among their peers. Without vehicles, it is, indeed, quite difficult for Yankees to maintain their action-oriented life-style among their peers.[23] On vehicles they can easily go to such places as Kawaramachi, the parks, and video arcades—"where the action is." Motorbikes and cars also provide common topics of conversation for youths who may otherwise have little in common. The Yankee youth cares about fellow members' evaluations of his car above everything else, and regards it as an evaluation of himself. Other Yankees also often identify him with his car. As literary critics can identify novelists by the style of a short paragraph, Yankee youths can identify others' cars from minute differences in appearance or exhaust noise.

The vehicle, then, often becomes an important mnemonic cue for *bosozoku* in recalling events in their life histories. I often heard informants referring to the make and color of their cars (instead of dates) when they tried to recollect certain events—e.g., "Did it happen when you were driving the *Zetto* [Nissan 280Z]?" "Was it when your [Toyota] Camry was blue that we were arrested?" When informants wanted to remind others of someone not generally known to the group, reference to his car was one of the most effective ways. Even if this person was not known by sight, gang members could identify him by his car.

> I.: K.?
> F.: Don't you remember K.? The guy who lives in Kameoka and drives a black [Honda] City with spoilers?
> I.: Oh, yeah! I know him!

There is an interdependent, almost symbiotic, relationship between the car and the Yankee youth's self-image. He invests most of his discretionary money into his car and its modifications. He plays with his car all the time. He keeps its shining by waxing and polishing. He meticulously cleans the interior with a portable vacuum cleaner. The interior is completely carpeted and heavily decorated with mascots, chandeliers, illuminations, and stickers of parts makers.[24] Most informants kept pictures of their cars in their photograph albums. In many cases, no people were shown in the pictures. Several informants carried pictures of their cars in their wallets. Some of them insisted on my putting the pictures in my book. They said they would not mind my excluding their names or pictures of their faces if I agreed to use pictures of their vehicles. Similarly, some of my informants said that they could be seen (*medatsu*) in their cars, in spite of the fact that all of the windows had been opaqued with dark film.

By employing the vehicle, which has this symbiotic relation with one's social identity as well as self-image, the Yankee expresses not only who he is but also what he *can be* or *might be*. *Bosozoku* is, of course, one of the most important dramatized self-images projected by the modified vehicle, with its fierce and intimidating appearance providing an aura of ultramasculinity and valor. An informant said, "*Bosozoku* minus cars equal *gurentai* [hoodlums]." While the "Yankee" has an ambivalent image inherent in the character of "hoodlum," the *bosozoku*, with its strong implications of dramaturgical character, is relatively free from such ambivalence. By driving an "excessively" decorated vehicle and participating in the carnival-like *boso* driving, a

youth can play the role of ferocious beast and masculine hero and enact an idealized image of "action-seeker."[25]

Yankee boys can also present themselves as powerful and discerning
consumers through the modified vehicle. They not only invest a considerable sum of money in vehicles and their modifications, but also
try to use famous and prestigious brands of parts.[26] They can identify
parts at a glance, and can discern fine differences among them, such as
the diameters of wheels and steering wheels, and the material used in
tires. Brand names have a tremendous symbolic significance for informants. To them, the brands of parts are often far more important than
design and performance. They therefore prefer parts which show
brand names clearly in raised relief or on emblems. Quite often the
brand names are important as symbols in their own right. Numerous
stickers, sunshields, and emblems featuring brand names are sold sep-
arately. Some informants put them on other parts and display them on
their front windows or dashboards. Most informants purchase cars
through loans lasting over three or four years and some of them allocate more than half of their income to the loans. Still, they can present
themselves as powerful consumers if they own and use the expensive
vehicles equipped with famous-brand parts.

A self-image as a powerful consumer is closely related to the enjoyment of *medatsu,* or self-display. While the *bosozoku* youth is expected
to conform to the prototypical prescriptions and proscriptions affecting
his vehicle, he can in some measure display his individual innovative
capacities and creativity. The highly developed Japanese market for vehicles and parts makes it possible for him to show his individuality by
purchasing a new model and attaching novel parts to it, although he
may purchase it through a loan, even before another loan for an older
car has been paid off.[27] An informant who changed his car six times
during a couple of years said,

> *Medatsu* is like being a star. . . . When I bought a [Nissan] Laurel,
> very few *bosozoku* owned a Laurel. Of course, I made it low, terri-
> bly low. Then I sped down to Kawaramachi [Avenue] driving
> that car. Everybody looked at [the car and me]. Oh, ya know,
> what a feeling! I got gooseflesh all over me. Everybody looked at
> my car and said, "Look! That's a Laurel!"

Informants despise blind adherence to the prototypical image of a
bosozoku-style vehicle at the same time that they praise innovative
modifications. Being content with the prototypical image is like being
proud of wearing outmoded clothes. Fashion, according to Blumer, is
"a means of rediscovering the self through novel yet sanctioned depar-

tures from prevailing social norms."[28] By adopting an innovative modification, the *bosozoku* youth can make himself conspicuous even among other *bosozoku* fellows, and thus somehow evade subcultural norms and reaffirm himself. By doing so, he may regain personal autonomy and thereby achieve feelings of competence and control.

Another possible identity the vehicle confers upon the Yankee/*bosozoku* youth is that of a dilettante of modern technology. Informants enthusiastically discuss technological advancements in automobiles, such as innovative suspension systems, computer gauges, and improvements in turbo mechanisms. Those who first heard of particularly striking innovations proudly presented them to their fellows as though they had invented them. The automobile is the medium which brings Yankee youths into the universe of discourse of high technology.

Advertisements and articles in car magazines condense technological details and transform them into catchphrases which are far more readily grasped. Paradoxically, at the same time advertisements mystify the technology. Very few people understand the principles and details of "DOHC," "EFI," "V8," and "Turbo," which originally were taken from technological jargon among professionals. Yet the words themselves are quite appealing and impressive to laymen. They have an element of magic which brings those who repeat them quasi-mystical powers. Such terms make it possible for drivers to feel that somehow they can understand the forces behind tremendous horsepower and impressive acceleration.

Bosozoku youths have some advantages over outright laymen who are content with the "half-intelligibility"[29] the advertisements offer. Gang members have a more immediate grasp of technological jargon. This vocabulary, including numerous loan words from English, and *bosozoku* youths' wide knowledge of accessories and modifications constitute an esoteric universe of discourse. Even *bosozoku* youths who have only a slight knowledge of automobile technology and leave the modifications to mechanics have the pride of a dilettante in their technical learning. Their cars are the embodiment of that pride.

Metamorphosis and Graduation. Through the association with vehicles so closely related to the youth's sense of self, a metamorphosis seems to take place in which the Yankee/corner boy becomes a powerful and discerning consumer, a dilettante of car technology, and, above all, a masculine and heroic *bosozoku*. A vehicle stimulates the *bosozoku* youth by the action it implies—rapid acceleration, high-speed driving, acrobatic driving, and the aura of ultramasculinity, defiance, and challenge. Modification clarifies and crystallizes the scheme of action implicit in the vehicle. From this it is only a short step to participation in *boso* driving.

Many informants mentioned their first purchase of a bike (rather than any frustration or inferiority complex) as *the* proximate cause of their participation in *boso* driving. Many also had experienced *boso* driving as passengers on older member's vehicles before they obtained vehicles of their own. If countervailing social or psychological factors did not restrain the lure of vehicles and the enjoyment of *boso* driving, such youths would certainly start careers as *bosozoku* and continue them for relatively long periods.

Several factors, however, do impose restraints on the further development of deviant careers. The most general is the so-called "age norm," which, in this case, involves the age hierarchy of *bosozoku* groups. Gang members are expected to graduate from motorcycles at the age of eighteen, whether they have earned a driver's license by that time or not. (In Japan, eighteen is the legal age at which one may apply for a driver's license for automobiles.) Those who drive bikes after eighteen are openly ridiculed by their seniors and peers. Younger members talk about them behind their backs. For those above the age of eighteen, motorcycles are considered "kid stuff"; they are expected to drive automobiles, which are more "sophisticated" than motorcycles.[30]

After graduating from bikes to cars, the style of modification sets a further age norm. Gang members are expected to graduate from *pettan* (low-slung cars) to "normal" cars when they become twenty years old. By the age of twenty or twenty-one many gradually, or in some cases abruptly, disengage themselves from *bosozoku* activities, and more generally from life on the street. This process of disengagement is partly based on the age norm applied to "OB" (Old Boys) by active members. More important, *sotsugyo* (graduation) from *bosozoku* activities corresponds to other significant changes in the youths' social relationships. Youths consider more seriously the judgments of their girlfriends (or "steadies") and work associates than they do the opinions of their peers and juniors from the gang.[31]

A "normal" car is a visible symbol of the change of status from "youths" to "young adults." In contrast, those who use a *pettan* (low-slung car) after twenty, quite a few in number, symbolize an inability to make the transition. An informant stared in wonder at an older associate, who was twenty-two, driving a low-slung car, and said scornfully, "That old guy! How can he be so silly as to drive a [Toyota] Camry, the low-slung one [*pettan*]. He is already twenty-two!"

GROUP NAMES: THE MODIFICATION OF LINGUISTIC SYMBOLS

Since the mid-1970s motorcycle gangs have adopted "grotesque" and "shocking" group names in an "absurd" nomenclature.[32] Both scholars and journalists who have discussed *bosozoku* have sought perverse designs "behind" bizarre group names and have not analyzed the semantic structure of such designations. Preliminary interviews and tentative analyses of group names suggested that *bosozoku* share common images about such names. Only certain words were regarded by informants as appropriate for use as group names. Those who actually named their groups (leaders or executive members) said that they had consulted works of journalists on names suitable for *bosozoku* groups. In other words, informants assumed that there existed a "*bosozoku* style" for group names. Indeed, examination of the notational style and semantic structure of *bosozoku* names (for the technique used, see appendix A) shows that definite rules affect the choice of names. The names, which appear to be gibberish and nonsense to outside observers, convey information or images that are meaningful to *bosozoku* youths.

Language and Characters

Words of different linguistic derivations are found in the names of *bosozoku* groups, and different writing systems are represented, i.e., *hiragana* (the cursive form of *kana*), *katakana* (the square form of *kana*), as well as Chinese characters and the Latin alphabet. Among *bosozoku* names, the single most salient characteristic is the wide use of Chinese characters as phonetic symbols. Chinese characters constituting a name are frequently pronounced in irregular ways by *bosozoku*, and each character has its own discrete meaning. In themselves, the individual meanings often differ widely from the sense conveyed by the word as a whole. For example, the Chinese characters 怒 and 帝 are usually pronounced /do/ and /tei/ respectively. But in the group name "怒鬼砲帝" *Donkihote* (Don Quixote), 怒 is pronounced /don/, and 帝 is pronounced /te/. The four characters mean anger (怒), devil (鬼), cannon (砲), and emperor (帝). In its entirety, the name comprises five distinctive images, that is, the image of Don Quixote and those of the other four words.

The use of Chinese characters that have many strokes and are rarely used in Japanese is another salient characteristic of *bosozoku* nomenclature—e.g., 塵, 鏃 (Holocaust), 盥 (Washtub, which also means "gang rape" in delinquent jargon in the Kansai region). Older and more complex Chinese characters are preferred to their modern and simplified counterparts, as in 聯 instead of 連 (association), and 龍 instead of 竜 (dragon). Novel characters are even invented—e.g., 虜 (*Mushi no Iki*= Faint Breath), and 蚜 (*Mushi Kiba* =Decayed Tooth).

It is not uncommon for group names to be written in several notational styles. For example, "Black Emperor" is also written 黒い皇帝 (*Kuroi Kootei*, a translation of "Black Emperor"), ブラックエンペラー and, 武羅悪区　江無屁羅 . (The last two are pronounced /burakku empera/ [Black Emperor].) Foreign words are frequently used, but they often include misspellings such as "Sunaiper" (Sniper), "Alley Cat's" (Alley Cats), "Piero" (Pierrot), and "Ladys" (Ladies). In some cases, however, unusual orthography is not the result of misspelling but is intended to imply double or triple meanings. For example, "綺羅" (Twinkling Star), from one of the *bosozoku* groups I studied, is pronounced /kira/. In the Latin alphabet it is spelled "Killa," a corruption of "Killer."

Examination of "themes" found in *bosozoku* names shows that there are inseparable relations between notation and the connotations of group names. This form of communication, indeed, is an integral part of its content in *bosozoku* group names.

Themes

"Theme" in this section refers to the connotations of specific components of words. We can distinguish five themes in names, or words which collectively constitute names, for *bosozoku* groups: strength, evil, the grotesque, nobility and beauty, and separation and liquidity.

Strength. It should not surprise us that names of *bosozoku* groups, which constitute a subtype of the adolescent gang, include many words which imply strength and power. This is a major theme of adolescent gangs in Western nations as well, e.g., West Side Dragons, Egyptian Kings, Magnificent Gallants.[33] This theme is quite explicitly expressed in names of huge, fierce animals, or poisonous or grotesque creatures— 猛虎 (Fierce Tigers), 鮫 (Sharks), 蜘蛛 (Spiders), スコルピオ (Scorpions), and 虎武羅 (Cobras). (Hereafter Chinese characters are underscored to indicate where they are used as phonetic symbols.) In the name 虎武羅 (Cobras), "虎" signifies a tiger, and thus the name as a whole implies two fierce animals, the cobra and the tiger. Similarly, 毒蛇美 as a whole signifies *Hottuynia cordata*. In this word the Japanese prefix 毒 refers to poison, even though the herb is an antidote, as the characters following indicate. This name can be divided into 毒蛇 (poisonous snake) and 美 (beauty), and thus includes the names of a plant and a poisonous animal.

Names of legendary, fictitious, and historical characters also impart the theme of strength—Medusa, Genghis Khan, Dracula, Godfather, and Amazon.

Among Chinese characters frequently used as phonetic symbols or for meanings, the following suggest power and strength within the context of Japanese culture:

> Primary colors: 黒 (Black), 紫 (purple),
> 赤 (red), 緋 (scarlet)
> Black Emperor, Red Scorpions
> 紫悪 (Sharks), 緋竜 (Scarlet Dragons)

極 (extreme): 極悪 (Extremely Wicked)
鬼 (devil): 鬼夜珠流 (Castle), 鬼輪会 (Devil Wheels)
神 (god): 龍神会 (God of Dragons), 雷神 (God of Thunder)
威 (might): 魔風威夜 (Mafia), 流羅威 (Vagabonds)

Other names that suggest strength include those taken from right-wing or *yakuza* organizations and their slogans (e.g., 敬神愛国 [Love for God and Nation], 大日本国士団 [Great Japan Patriots]) and those names that stress territorial control and hegemony (e.g., 日本狂走連盟 [Japan Violent Racing Club], 関西連合 [Kansai Racing Club]). The name of the *bosozoku* confederation I studied was 全日本京都狂走連盟. The leader of the confederation translated this name into English as "All Japan Kyoto Racing Club," and had it sewn onto the members' newly ordered jackets in the Latin alphabet. This was a quite literal translation of the Japanese name, except that the word "Violent" should have been added between "Kyoto" and "Racing"—"All Japan Kyoto Violent Racing Club." Neither the Japanese name nor the translation make sense if we derive meaning only from the characters. But they are more meaningful if we consider the theme of strength implied in the emphasis on (imaginary) territory. The name includes the message, "Although our territory is currently Kyoto, we will conquer all of Japan in the future."

Evil. In many cases, the theme of evil is joined with that of strength because evil beings are supposed to have "the power of the forbidden."[34] Among the phrases mentioned above, the names of grotesque or poisonous animals and plants, those of right-wing and *yakuza* organizations, and the words, "black," "red," 鬼 (devil), and 極 (extreme) exemplify both themes.

On the other hand, the following words mainly emphasize the theme of evil:

悪 (evil): 悪盗 (Villains), 狂悪連合 (Felons)
地獄 (hell): 地獄族 (Hell Tribe), Hell's Angels
魔 (devil): 魔鬼死夢 (Maxim), 魔血呼 (Machiko, name of a girl)
獄 (prison): 獄死 (Death in Prison)

Bosozoku groups also use the names of particularly infamous villains (e.g., Dracula, Hitler, Bluebeard), and words signifying social outcasts (e.g., 無期懲役 [Imprisonment for Life], 外道 [Outlaws], 非国民 [Traitors], 守銭奴 [Niggards]).

The Grotesque. The theme of evil is closely related to that of the grotesque, which presents weird and ominous images. Many group names include Chinese characters signifying grotesque qualities, such as 闇 (darkness), 夜 (night), 死 (death), 影 (shadow), 呪 (spell), 魔 (devil), 墓 (grave), 血 (blood), and 妖 (weird).

Some group names refer to grotesque things or beings—轆轤首 (Long-Necked Monsters), 髑髏 (Skulls), Vampires, 蛞蝓 (Slugs), and 蝙蝠 (Bats). The grotesque is also expressed in themes of abnormality and social marginality—夜狂 (Midnight Crazies), Mad Special, 国賊 (Traitors), 無羅蜂武 (Ostracized), and Nazi.

Chinese characters may be distinguished in general on a calligraphic basis. In his study of wordplay in Japanese and Chinese, Tsukamoto argues that

> One of the charms of Chinese characters is that they visualize the meanings of words, even in the case of Chinese characters which are not pictographic in origin. Even abstract words such as "窈窕" (graceful), "鬱蒼" (luxuriant) . . . produce illusions which are appropriate to the meanings of the adjective. It is no wonder that [such words as] "薔薇" (rose) and "麒麟" (giraffe) . . . produce the images of colors and ecology [of the plants and animals]. Ominous characters and characters which signify disgrace or sin can threaten us by evoking negative images through their figurative images. In this sense, Chinese poetry (both in the periods of Han and Tang) is nothing but calligraphy in the broader sense. The same is said of Buddhist scriptures written in Chinese characters. There are some fables about evil spirits which cannot possess a person and are exorcised because a Buddhist scripture is written on his skin. This type of fable gives support to my argument.[35]

This calligraphic function of Chinese characters is important for every theme discussed here. But it applies more readily to the theme of the grotesque than to others, because for Japanese speakers unusual combinations of characters resemble incantations or scriptures. For example, in the group name 巫暗忌諱暴威洲 (*Fanki Boizu*=Funky Boys) grotesque images are conjured up both by three ominous characters (巫 [sorcery], 暗 [darkness], and 忌 [taboo]) and by the unusual combination of Chinese characters. Chinese characters of many strokes tend to have more visual appeal than those with few strokes. It is probably for this reason that *bosozoku* group names are frequently formed from Chinese characters of many strokes.

Nobility and Beauty. In terms of cosmic, social, and bodily topography the themes of evil and the grotesque form downward vectors.[36] In marked contrast, many group names contain words which imply clean, beautiful, noble, and bright images, which occupy upward vectors. This may be considered the "nobility and beauty" theme.

Names emphasizing this theme suggest noble status— 貴公子 (Young Noblemen), 貴族 (Aristocrats), Black Queen, 姫 (Princesses), Hell's Princess, 桃色男爵 (Pink Barons), and 薔薇子爵 (Viscounts of Rose). Names of beautiful animals and plants also invoke this theme— 蛍 (firefly), papillon, 蘭 (orchid), and rose.

A similar theme is found in the names of gangs in Western nations as well—e.g., Hell's Angels, Conservative Vice Lords, Junior Princess, Roman Dukes. Some theorists, especially those who assume that a delinquent subculture can almost compel complete conformity of its members,[37] may argue that the nobility and beauty theme manifests gang members' attempt to create an alternative status system where they can attain a substantial (i.e., not merely imaginative) social mobility, from a low-life delinquent to a respected gangster. They may also insist that deviant values of delinquent subcultures which "turn [norms of the larger culture] upside down"[38] underlie the theme emphasizing nobility and beauty of motorcycle gangs. Examination of the fifth theme—separation and liquidity—and of the interrelationship between the five themes, however, shows that the theme of nobility and beauty presupposes a detachment from, rather than blind conformity to, a fixed set of values.

Separation and Liquidity. While the themes of "evil," "the grotesque," and "nobility and beauty" have specific schematic reference points, the theme of "separation and liquidity" does not and signifies instead emancipation from or transcendence of general social norms. The word 流 (flow, current, stream) represents this quality. This Chinese character is frequently used in many group names as a phonetic symbol or to convey additional meanings, as in 流 (Flow), 水流 (Stream), 流羅威 (Wandering), 流犯 (Lepin; name of a thief in a French novel), 流紫亜 (Lucian). The theme of separation and liquidity is frequently expressed in names of flying creatures or phrases implying continuous movement, such as 渡鳥 (Migratory Birds), 蛍 (Fireflies), 蝶 (Butterflies), 旋風 (Whirlwind), and 浮浪 (Vagabonds). This theme is undoubtedly inseparably related to the image of mobility and movement characteristic of motorcycle-gang activity. But other names that can be included in this thematic group convey the image of separation and liquidity at another semantic level. They are names of tricksters and foreign women—Chaplin, Pierrot, Mickey Mouse, 聖紫涙 (Cecile), and 聖楽 (Ceila). A trickster transcends moral and cognitive categories of human beings and mediates culture, nature, and the supernatural. In Japan, foreign women (especially Western) are considered exotic and romantic, existing apart from the drabness of everyday life.

As is obvious, there is considerable overlap among these five themes. The category to which a certain group name may be assigned depends on which aspect of the name we consider. For example, although 貴族 (Aristocrats) suggests the theme of nobility and beauty, this group name also implies strength, because the word "aristocrat" connotes the authority and power of noble status. This name also may be considered under the separation and liquidity theme because it implies transcendence of middle-class mediocrity and banality. On the other hand, this group name apparently has no connotations of evil or the grotesque. The group name "Tarantula" suggests the themes of strength, evil, and the grotesque. It also implies separation and liquidity because the poisonous spider eludes moral and cognitive categories, as is suggested in the use of animal figures in primitive rituals. But "Tarantula" clearly does not suggest nobility and beauty.

In this way, examination of adjoining areas among five themes shows that the separation and liquidity theme is a common denominator with respect to the other four themes. These four categories, indeed, share a transcendence of, or antipathy toward, fixed, routine, and mediocre elements that are neither weak nor strong, neither evil nor good, and neither beautiful nor ugly. This aspect of group names of *bosozoku* seems to subvert the very self-defining function of names and to include the most essential message encoded in group names and in other subcultural symbols.

The Polysemy of Group Names

Magic powers often are attributed to nomenclature, such as execration or cure through the utterance of names, use of names in inscriptions, or changes of names. It is also widely believed that certain names have transmutational powers. There is a self-labeling process involved in which one using a certain name believes that "if I behave as the label says (under coercion or voluntarily), and my primary others react to me as such, then 'I must be it'—'I am what the name says'."[39] The same seems to hold for group names or those supplying collective identity. When a name is applied to a group, its members expect and often actually do act as the name suggests: "We are what the name of our group says." As a modified car implies certain actions for *bosozoku*, there is a self-fulfilling process by which *bosozoku* members try to emulate the names of their groups. Some themes seem pertinent to this interpretation. The themes of strength, evil, and the grotesque seem not only to reflect but also to affirm and reaffirm the association of *bosozoku* members with a violent and criminal gang. Similarly, the theme of separation and liquidity appears to reflect and affirm the marginality of group activities, and exemplifies rebellion, challenge, and defiance toward the wider society.

This interpretation, however, is difficult to apply to the other theme, that of nobility and beauty. Moreover, the theme of nobility and beauty is frequently juxtaposed with other, contradictory images. The difficulty with this interpretation is mainly derived from an overly literal search for "what the name of our group says." In the previous section it was shown that the juxtaposition of various themes, rather than emphasis on any single image, is a salient characteristic of *bosozoku* group names. I also suggested that the theme of separation and liquidity is closely related to the juxtaposition of various themes. We must, therefore, read "what the group names say" more carefully to determine the meaning derived from this juxtaposition.

As is shown in figure 2.1, we can conceive of a semantic space where all five themes, except that of separation and liquidity, are located. The three axes defining this semantic space are "good-evil" (X), "strong-weak" (Y), and "beautiful-ugly" (Z).

Many of the *bosozoku* group names can be located at some distance from the coordinate "O," which suggests entities that are neither weak nor strong, neither good nor evil, and neither beautiful nor ugly, that is, groups that are fixed, routine, and mediocre. The theme of separation and liquidity corresponds to the coordinate vectors of the point where a certain group name is located. The direction of the vector is, of course, away from "O."

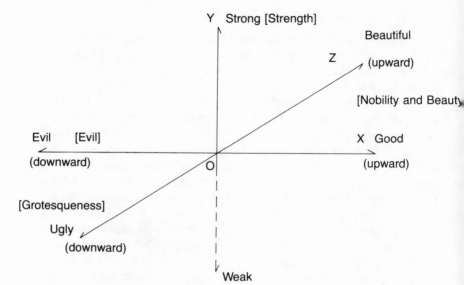

Fig. 2.1. Semantic Space of Five Themes in Group Names. (Reprinted, by permission, from I. Sato, *An Ethnography of* Bosozoku [Tokyo: Shin'yosha, 1984], 121.)

Some group names cannot be located at fixed points in this semantic space because they include so many themes. In such cases, the theme of separation and liquidity corresponds to incessant movement induced by the juxtaposition of various themes. For example, as is shown in figure 2.2, while the English name "Tarantula" does not suggest nobility or beauty, the Japanese characters 多蘭蝶羅 (pronounced "Tarantula") convey all five themes to the point of redundancy. The three Chinese characters 多 (*ta*, abundance), 蘭 (*ran*, orchid), and 蝶 (*cho*, although the pronunciation is /chu/ in this context; butterfly) each signify their respective themes. The character 羅 (*ra*) has no specific meaning in this context and is used as a phonetic symbol. But even this character contributes to the visual appeal of the group name by the many strokes it includes. The visual appeal of the name as a whole augments the effects of juxtaposed themes and images in movement.

This extreme emphasis on the theme of separation and liquidity, and the juxtaposition of contradictory themes, suggest that *bosozoku* group names deliberately subvert self-defining functions. That is to say, the message encoded in group names is not just "We are what the name of

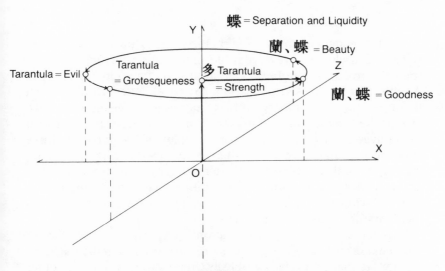

蝶 = Separation and Liquidity

蘭、蝶 = Beauty

蘭、蝶 = Goodness

Tarantula = Evil

Tarantula = Grotesqueness

多 Tarantula = Strength

Fɪɢ. 2.2. Multiple Meanings in 多蘭蝶羅 (Tarantula). (Reprinted, by permission, from I. Sato, *An Ethnography of* Bosozoku [Tokyo: Shin'yosha, 1984], 121.)

our group says" but, at another level, includes the message "We are *not* what the name says." When two different levels of meaning are considered, the names of *bosozoku* groups presuppose the Batesonian frame of "This is play"[40] and are a kind of self-parody. To use the previous example, 多蘭蝶羅 (Tarantula) on the one hand depicts this *bosozoku* gang as strong, evil, and grotesque characters, like poisonous spiders. On the other hand, the juxtaposed themes of nobility and beauty (orchid, butterfly) and separation and liquidity imply that the gang's image is a disguise or staged self-presentation.

In general, *bosozoku* youths recognize clearly that they play quasi-theatrical roles, using dramatized self-images that are viable only during adolescence. Most of my informants admitted that *bosozoku* indulge in *gaki no asobi* (literally "children's play," "kid stuff").

Bosozoku youths adopt "grotesque" and "shocking" group names in "absurd" orthography to suggest chimerical creatures, and thus they take on quasi-theatrical roles. These parts are quite alien to the routine and banal social roles they must play in everyday life. In part they do so by using Chinese characters which have great potential for "polysemy" (multiple meanings), even if they are used as phonetic symbols constituting a single word.[41]

Secret Societies

The frequent use of Chinese characters made up of many strokes, which are rarely used in everyday life, reflects another crucial aspect of the collective identity of *bosozoku* groups. As fraternity members at American colleges use the less familiar Greek letters to distinguish themselves from "ordinary" others, members of Japanese *bosozoku* groups use complex and unfamiliar Chinese characters to distinguish themselves from *ippanjin* (ordinary people). The complex Chinese characters separate "us" from others, from "them," who use simpler and more familiar Chinese characters in conventional ways.[42] The group names made up of complex Chinese characters are, indeed, "Greek" (gibberish) to most Japanese. Names of this sort therefore depict *bosozoku* as a subtype of secret societies.

It should be noted, however, that ordinary people are supposed to see (*medatsu*) the activities of the "secret" society, just as the fraternity attempts to make especially visible its Greek acronym. Whereas other secret societies may make every effort to conceal their identities or existence, *bosozoku* activity is aimed at displaying a group "secret." It is paradoxical that one of the most effective ways of attracting attention is to make some aspect of one's identity available but especially difficult to decipher.

As many fraternities put Greek acronyms above the entrances to their houses, *bosozoku* youths frequently and willingly disclose their secrets to the general public. My informants were delighted when I expressed curiosity about the names of their groups, and they eagerly taught me how to write them in Chinese characters. An informant taught me the "authentic" way of pronouncing "極" (Extreme), the name of a *bosozoku* group in Kyoto. He said that although many phonate it /kiwami/ (the ordinary form of pronunciation of this Chinese character), it should be pronounced /kiwame/ because the leader of the group had so determined. Informants were also delighted that the names of their groups appeared in the popular press. Many of them kept such newspaper clippings in their photograph albums.

The use of complex Chinese characters to attract attention among the general public suggests that such unusual signs are not intended to make a fundamental distinction between "us" and "them." Unlike members of some countercultures who attempt to create an exclusive or totally alien "counterreality" by systematically using an alternative language,[43] *bosozoku* do not strive to separate themselves completely from the dominant society. To them, the complex Chinese characters are just an effective means of making themselves mysterious. They do not employ the characters as a metaphor for a life-style alternative that is totally opposed to the dominant Japanese culture.

Just as few fraternity members are acquainted with classical Greek language, literature, or philosophy, few *bosozoku* members are interested in classical Chinese culture or language. They simply consult Chinese-Japanese lexicons for the sole purpose of finding exotic and bizarre characters for group names. They know clearly and consciously that their alternative reality is largely limited to adolescence and that *bosozoku* activities are performed weekly at specific intervals. This "separation and liquidity," then is to a considerable extent confined to the bracketed contexts. This emphasis on the bracketed nature of *bosozoku* activities is also found in various *bosozoku* paraphernalia and is related to the most important theme in *bosozoku* symbolism.

COSTUMES AND OTHER ARTIFACTS

Two salient characteristics of *bosozoku* costumes and other artifacts are their extreme expressiveness and apparent affinity with nationalist symbols. As in the case of "excessively" decorated vehicles and "gibberish" group names, these characteristics of *bosozoku* artifacts led people to attribute pathological dispositions to gang members. The public also assumed and feared close relationships between *bosozoku* groups and right-wing organizations. Yet, if one observes how gang members use these artifacts, he will soon notice that such interpretations are groundless.

Bosozoku Artifacts

Tokkofuku. While the almost "classical" and "orthodox" combination of leather jacket and jeans has been prevalent throughout the history of Japanese motorcycle gangs,[44] *tokkofuku* came into wide use during the *bosozoku* period. *Tokkofuku* literally means the costume of the kamikaze party. The *tokkofuku* of *bosozoku*, however, are working clothes, chiefly dark blue or black jackets and pants, whereas the original suicidal military groups wore other overalls, the ordinary uniform for pilots on fighter-bombers. *Bosozoku* youths even use pink, white, or red *tokkofuku*.

A group name is usually sewn with gold or silver thread on the backs of *tokkofuku* jackets. It may also be stitched into the upper sleeve or onto the upper left pocket. Other symbols which are used on *tokkofuku* include the rising sun, the Imperial chrysanthemum crest, and words or phrases suggesting nationalism, such as 憂国烈士 (patriot), or 愛国尊皇 (Protection of the Nation and Respect for His Majesty). Military ranks (e.g., Captain of the Kamikaze Party, Maximum Leader) or personal names are also used.

Prices for *tokkofuku* range from about ¥7,000 ($28) to ¥20,000 ($80). The price of such attire is higher if it is made to order. Although *bosozoku* prefer *tokkofuku* jackets with long hems, when they do not have enough money for custom-made outfits they wear ordinary work clothes. Additional embroidery on the *tokkofuku* costs another ¥5,000 to ¥10,000 ($20 to $40).

Dokajan. This term is an abbreviation of "*dokata* jumper," a dark blue or black jumper often worn by *dokata* (a slightly pejorative term for construction laborers) during the autumn and winter. The *dokajan* is made of nylon or cotton and has a thick lining, with a large collar of relatively long pile. This jumper is quite suitable for motorcycle riding in winter. Some wear *dokajan* over leather jackets during the dead of winter. Ordinary *dokajan* cost about ¥5,000 ($20). As with *tokkofuku*, *bosozoku* members often put gang names or emblems on *dokajan*.

Sentofuku. The term literally means "combat uniform." That worn by *bosozoku* is a dark blue overall made of cotton. Originally this jacket was standard dress for right-wing organizations. As in the cases of *tokkofuku* and *dokajan*, group names and nationalist symbols are sewn into *sentofuku*. Leather lace-up boots are frequently worn with *sentofuku*. (I failed to check the prices for this clothing and some other articles.)

Aloha, Jimbei, Chaina. During a *boso* drive in summer many *bosozoku* wear aloha shirts, or *jimbei*, although they are not necessarily regarded as uniforms. The *jimbei* consists of a jacket and short pants of thin cotton, which is used for *yukata*. Both aloha shirts and *jimbei* have been worn by Yankees and racketeers. Some *bosozoku* youths also wear *chaina*, which is satin from nylon and resembles a Chinese dress. *Chaina* is usually pink, yellow, or purple in color.

Hachimaki and Flu Mask. *Hachimaki* (headband) and flu masks are often used in combination with any of the outfits mentioned above. The rising sun or the Imperial chrysanthemum crest is usually printed or embroidered in the middle of the *hachimaki*. Group names or nationalist slogans may also be featured alongside these symbols.

Similar symbols are written on flu masks with marker pens. Flu masks are often used for protecting the nose and throat from cold winds and are useful for concealment from the police.

Group Flag. For *bosozoku* youths, a group flag is the most important sign of collective identity during a *boso* drive. It is usually held by a
hatamochi (flag holder) on the pillion seat of a motorcycle. Sometimes
it is hung from the window of a car. The group name and/or the group
emblem are displayed on the flag. *Bosozoku* youths may use common
national flags taken from others' homes; often they have group flags
made to order. Those custom-made often show the rising sun or the
Imperial chrysanthemum crest. Group names are often written across
the symbol of the rising sun, the most sacred part of the national flag.

Group flags have strong visual appeal, and thus works about
bosozoku by journalists often have pictures of gang members showing
their flags. During intergang fights, *bosozoku* often steal and tear up
their opponents' flags.[45] Sometimes flags are turned over to the police
when groups are dissolved.

Stickers. Group emblems and names in calligraphy are also
printed on stickers, which then are put on the bodies or window of
vehicles. The usual size of such stickers is about 20 cm by 9 cm. Such
stickers often are made to resemble the national flag, with the symbol
of the rising sun in the middle. Other stickers, however, show the national flag in small insets in the middle.

The leaders and executive members of gangs decide on the content
and design of stickers. Often a new sticker is chosen when a new leader
is elected or a new gang confederation is organized.

Matchbox, Lighter, Name Card. Small articles such as matchboxes,
lighters, and name cards also bear agreed-upon gang symbols. While
name cards are used almost exclusively by executive members, often
matchboxes and lighters are sold to nonmembers. Even stickers are
sold to outsiders at a premium. The average price for stickers is about
¥2,500 ($10). When they are resold at a premium, stickers may bring
more than ¥5,000 ($20).

Significance of Nationalist Symbols

The apparent affinity between *bosozoku* and nationalist symbolism
suggests that there are close relationships between gang activities and
the work of right-wing organizations. There have been, in fact, some
contacts between such groups. Some *bosozoku* organizations asked
right-wing organizations for protection after new traffic laws were
passed in 1978. To avoid police sanctions, the *bosozoku* groups disseminated political propaganda during *boso* driving. The right-wing
organizations also believed they could recruit members from *bosozoku*

gangs,[46] and some *bosozoku* leaders have become card-carrying members of such organizations.

These instances, however, are special cases and do not represent a general pattern. Although they use political symbols, the fact that these apolitical motorcycle groups almost always have no affiliation with right-wing organizations casts doubt on the idea that nationalist themes establish an underlying relationship between the two kinds of groups. Moreover, motorcycle gangs adopted nationalist symbols well *before* right-wing organizations established contact with them.

At the organizational level, there had been no cooperation between the *bosozoku* confederation I studied and right-wing groups. On the contrary, when there was conflict between two *bosozoku* groups, a right-wing organization intervened in an attempt to exploit the differences between the two. In general, my informants' attitudes toward right-wing organizations were negative. A female informant, who was once asked to become a member of the right-wing *uyoku* organization, declared, "*Uyoku?* I don't care. Ha-ha! I don't mind if there're such people [as *uyoku*]." Some informants explicitly hated *uyoku*. An informant said, "I hate *uyoku* more than *yakuza*. . . . I hate *uyoku* because they support the establishment." Many informants found little difference between *uyoku* and *yakuza*. To them, the only seeming distinction was the "pretense" of a political stance.

My informants were also indifferent to nationalist ideology. To them, the Emperor Hirohito was no more than a "person who can enjoy an easy-going life without working." They paid little respect even to the sacred qualities of the national flag. Group names were written across the symbol of the rising sun, often in English! The flags themselves, in many cases, were stolen from the residences of ordinary citizens.

The following answer is typical of responses to questions about the use of the national flag. It offers insight into the meaning of nationalist symbols for *bosozoku*. "No specific meaning. It is used just because it is the most conspicuous [*medatsu*]."

Bosozoku can gain attention and shock people by using nationalist symbols, which are associated with right-wing militants and imply fanaticism and violence. The symbols serve to set a boundary between *bosozoku* and *ippanjin* (ordinary people). The image of "discipline and order" implicit in nationalist symbols also appeals to them. These images contribute to the theatrical atmosphere in which *bosozoku* youths take on the roles of devotees of groups with ironclad discipline.

Gang members may also use the image of "discipline and order" to underscore a component in the character image of *bosozoku* as *koha* (hard-type) or stoic and chivalric heroes. The heroic image of *bosozoku* is frequently found in narratives in youth-oriented media[47] and makes it possible for the youths to detach themselves from a negative image inherent in "Yankees," i.e., *nanpa* (soft-type) or hedonistic and degenerate hoodlums. Nationalist symbols, therefore, are convenient, ready-made devices by which *bosozoku* members enhance their own sense of participation, present themselves as chivalric heroes, and gain the public's attention for purposes of private parody and public outrage.

The drama, however, is to a considerable extent bracketed in time and space. It is mostly staged in the specific contexts of weekly *bosozoku* meetings and *boso* driving. *Bosozoku* are not like Hell's Angels, who "play the role seven days a week; they wear their colors at home, on the street, and sometimes even to work; they ride their bikes to the neighborhood grocery for a quart of milk."[48] None of my informants went to their work places wearing their *tokkofuku*. Only one informant went to his work place wearing a *dokajan*. The only way someone wearing a *dokajan* could be identified as a *bosozoku* was by a series of English words sewn into the upper right sleeve of his jacket. The letters were so small that few observers would have noticed them. Nonetheless, his fellows were impressed by his "bravery."

After all, the costume and other artifacts of *bosozoku* are stage props for "part-time outlaws."[49] The extreme expressiveness of the artifacts subverts the meanings of nationalist symbols and suggests make-believe. In this sense, the artifacts seem to maintain, alternately, "We are what our costume (flag, sticker) says," and "We are *not* what our costume (flag, sticker) says."

Upon graduation, many of the outfits are given to junior gang members. Stickers are taken off vehicle bodies and put in photograph albums. The police may be given the group flags.

CONCLUSION: COLLAGE OF "UNNATURAL" SYMBOLS

Playlike Transformations

Outrageous Modifications. In the *bosozoku* subculture, "normal" cars are modified into low-rider custom cars, or *shakotan*. Complex characters which usually appear only in Chinese works are used for the names of gangs. Working clothes suitable for hard and tedious labor are transformed into *tokkofuku*, stage costumes for leisure activity. And the Japanese flag, which is (or should be) a symbol of national unity, is employed as a kind of parody of solidarity within a youth gang, thus ironically separating the gang from the rest of the nation.

The *bosozoku* subculture as a whole, then, is a collage of miscellaneous and heterogeneous symbols and artifacts, each of which has another "authentic" use or meaning. The artifacts and symbols are taken from their original contexts and made to serve *bosozoku* symbolism and activities. This is possible because symbols and props are taken from many contexts, none of which are represented to the extent that they would engulf or specify the *bosozoku* image. For example, technological jargon is used without specific expertise in automobile mechanics, and nationalist symbols are displayed without ideological commitment.

Small children construct an imaginary adult society from bits and pieces of the larger world; this is make-believe play. Similarly, *bosozoku* youths construct a theatrical "frame" featuring *bosozoku* as heroic characters by assembling miscellaneous fragments and artifacts of various symbolic systems. But they are not as innocent as small children. Nor are they content to create only a play world in which *they* provide the audience. They attempt in their drama to capture the general public as an audience. "Unnaturalness" is a keynote of *bosozoku* props, and this reflects their concern for public attention. To startle and offend people with grotesque and shocking images is, indeed, one of the most effective ways to obtain their attention. It is because these items transgress linguistic and sartorial codes which define what is "natural" (i.e., culturally normal) that they appear "unnatural."[50]

The outrageous "modifications" characteristic of *bosozoku* artifacts and symbols are a process in which clear-cut playlike and dramaturgical definitions of the situations are created and clarified through playlike transformations. The conventional (and "natural") definitions of the situation provide the ground against which the playlike *bosozoku* schemes appears as a figure with clear contours. The definitions of the situations are affirmed, reaffirmed, and in some cases further modified according to the needs of specific groups and individuals through the use of tangible things.[51]

Esotericism and Intelligibility—Modification of Identity. The *bosozoku* subculture appears to be unnatural and irrational because gang members also collude to conceal, disguise, or mystify some of their subcultural features. They attempt to create an aura of mystery through cryptic group names and nationalist symbols. This intentional unintelligibility impedes communication between *bosozoku* youths and the general public, and thus creates the impression of unnaturalness and irrationality. This unintelligibility, however, is by design, and aims to stimulate the general public's curiosity and to create a special universe of discourse in which one's identity is established.

While many elements of the *bosozoku* subculture are unintelligible and unnatural to the general public, these elements are intelligible and seem quite natural to *bosozoku* youths. Gang members are aware of this difference and hope that the subculture is fully intelligible only among themselves. It should be an esoteric universe of discourse, in order to establish clear distinctions between "us" and "them," and to strengthen the youths' sense of self within a collective identity. At least within the context of *bosozoku* activity, youths may become accepted participants in a subculture or "secret society" open only to the "select." In a way they are like Boorstin's "celebrity"; a person who is known because he is known. And like rock stars and other "image makers" they must present themselves at the boundaries of intelligibility.

It should be noted that the *bosozoku* youth's specialized universe of discourse is composed of a number of specific items which emphasize participation in the group more than a general subcultural image. As those in a fraternity demonstrate their membership through badges, gestures, rule books, and initiation rites, membership in *bosozoku* groups is shown through items associated specifically with the gang. Artifacts such as stickers, matchboxes, and lighters bear, as it were, the original "brand" of their creators.

The specialized universe of discourse is quite accessible to members of the group not only because it consists of tangible "things" and symbols which are readily understood and manipulated, but also because the artifacts and symbols are closely related to their collective life and activities. While they may be faceless unskilled laborers or not very promising high school students in their everyday lives, they can become "somebody" with a definite status through their universe of discourse. A boy named Taro no longer would be just another adolescent but a member of the group, "All Japan Kyoto Racing Club, Ukyo Association, Killa, Taro."[52] The group version of *bosozoku* subculture is, so to speak, a life-sized universe of discourse within which members can have a feeling of competence, whereas they may be bored or feel worried in another context of life.[53]

We also need to consider the significance of *bosozoku* artifacts in relation to the distinctive style of the population out of which *bosozoku* members are most likely to be recruited: Yankees. As will be shown later in detail,[54] several themes or "focal concerns" characteristic of *bosozoku* are also found in Yankee style: ultramasculinity, bravado, defiance, and an emphasis on violence. *Bosozoku* artifacts serve in dramatic and romantic ways in the acting out of these focal concerns. Although the themes are also represented in Yankee artifacts and are dramatized in street-corner narratives, in those cases they largely remain a fragmentary collection of occasional performances. In contrast, *bosozoku* artifacts are material enactments or props of a narrative about *bosozoku* which has a relatively coherent story line and is shared by a large segment of the youth population. In other words, the *bosozoku* image gives Yankees a "lasting, romance-glazed image of themselves, a coherent reflection that only a very few had been able to find in a mirror," as Thompson characterizes the significance of the Hollywood representation of Hell's Angels to American "outlaw bikers."[55]

From Symbolism to Action

The collective and personal identity that *bosozoku* youths project through subcultural items usually presupposes certain behavior. In other words, the assumption that "We are what the name of our group (vehicle, costume etc.) says" postulates another assumption, "We will behave as the name of our group (vehicle, costume etc.) suggests." The use of subcultural artifacts as a means to achieve a certain identity seems a two-way process. That is, in some cases the artifacts may "use" us to enact schemes of action implicit in them. As Wagner points out, we can say that "tools 'use' human beings, toys 'play with' children, weapons lure us into battle."[56]

The definition of the self implicit in subcultural artifacts, however, also includes many cues for redefinition. While the artifacts are utilized to construct a meaningful self-identity, their extreme expressiveness redefines the self on the stage of presentation. The "age norm" defining the age limit for the use of "excessively" decorated vehicles, the separation and liquidity characteristic of "gibberish" gang names, and the extreme expressiveness of costumes defining *bosozoku* as "part-time outlaws" all contribute to redefine the action-prone identity of *bosozoku* as a temporary and situation-specific identity. Thus the self-identity includes a Batesonian, metacommunicative "frame" of "this is play." On the active level, the playlike frame can be paraphrased in two similar statements: "We will behave in real earnest as the name of our group (vehicle, costume) says," and "As in a stage performance, we will behave as the name (vehicle, costume) of our group says."

It should be noted that this "bracketed"[57] nature of the self-labeling function of *bosozoku* artifacts is not always stable and does not guarantee the youths' relatively detached stance. The stability of the bracket largely depends on the factors surrounding specific *bosozoku* groups and activities. On the one hand, there are groups called *hashiranai bosozoku* (*bosozoku* who don't drive) that proliferated since new traffic legislation was enacted in 1981 and whose members are content to use *bosozoku* artifacts and just talk about vehicles and other active *bosozoku*.

On the other hand, there are those core members who have to behave, almost literally, in the way "our group name (vehicle, costume) says" when gang fights break out or conflicts with the police intensify. In such a case, "fantasy," "make-believe" or in some cases a "nightmare" comes true, and group activities become much more serious undertakings. They are no longer bracketed leisure activities from which members can easily detach themselves.[58]

I will discuss this aspect of the tricky relation between "fiction" and "reality" in gang activities in Part II. Before that, I have to examine the last component of the dramaturgical system of *bosozoku* play: the script. As compared to the first component (performance—*boso* driving) and the second (props—*bosozoku* artifacts), the definitions of the situation found in narratives or "myths" featuring *bosozoku* include many verbal cues, though nonverbal cues also play an important role in this genre of *bosozoku* play.

3   Drama and Dramatization: *Bosozoku*, the Saturday-Night Hero

> The press becomes increasingly harsh in its treatment of *bosozoku*.
> On the other hand, know-it-all scholars appear [in the mass me-
> dia] and solemnly comment that "They are a sign of the times, an
> evil produced by society. They themselves are not responsible for
> the evil." The more fuss the media make about us, and the more
> they repeat police statements, the more violent our fights become.
> We say, "Hey! They say we are an 'evil produced by society'! Then,
> shouldn't we try to look more evil?" [The connotation of] "Evil"
> [*aku*] sounds terribly nice [*kakkoii*] to us.
> —Yoshiharu Urita, *Only Saturday Is Left for Us*

"I want to write a book about your kind of people." Field
researchers sometimes make this type of statement to gain access to
informants. Publication of a book about them, however, had a special
meaning for my informants. During the first few months, I had to respond to certain kinds of questions almost every time I met a new
informant, because my contact with them aroused their interest in the
publication of a book. Such questions included, "Are you a reporter
from Daisan Shokan?" "Are you working to publish the *Boso Retto* [
Bosozoku Archipelago]?" "Is *Boso Retto 1983* going to be published?"
Daisan Shokan is a publisher which was established in 1979 with its
publication of books on *bosozoku*. The publisher attained a considerable commercial success by a series of books entitled *Boso Retto*, which
presented profiles and pictures of *bosozoku* groups throughout Japan.

Media presentation is an integral part of *bosozoku* activity. *Bosozoku*
youths throughout Japan send numerous photographs and statements
about their own groups to Daisan Shokan and other publishers. *Boso*

driving itself is often carried out at the request of journalists or in the hope that it will receive news coverage. Some even notify the news agencies before carrying out a *boso* drive, knowing that this might lead to easy arrest.

This close, almost inseparable, relationship between the mass media and *bosozoku* activity may give one the impression that the activity is fabricated to a considerable extent by the mass media to exploit the desire of youths in motorcycle gangs for self-display. One may also consider that motorcycle gangs are merely imitating the schemes of action suggested in the media reports. Indeed, the outrageous *bosozoku* paraphernalia and defiant poses for pictures shown in *Bosozoku Archipelago* and other publications look quite similar and almost standardized.

WHY ARE *BOSOZOKU* SO PREOCCUPIED WITH MEDIA PRESENTATION?
The Pathological Answer

As compared to the interpretations concerning motives for *boso* driving and meanings of motorcycle-gang paraphernalia, academic interpretations about the relationship between *bosozoku* activity and the mass media are quite few. Most of them interpret the relation in pathological terms. Kaneto treats the exploitation by the mass media of *bosozoku* activity as a manifestation of social pathology.[1] Kikuchi regards the mass media treatment as satisfying a "perverse [or "peculiar"] desire for showing-off" by *bosozoku* youths.[2] There is virtually no academic study which regards media presentation as a type of play. Journalists, who make profits from the youngsters' interests in media presentation, just comment on their "desire for showing-off" or describe their enthusiasm for media presentation.[3]

Neither these (semi-)academic studies nor journalistic reports attempt to analyze the content and form of media presentation in detail. Nor do they present gang youths' own statements about the media presentation. In other words, while the scholars and journalists acknowledge the considerable influence of the media upon *bosozoku* activity, they do not try to elucidate which aspects of media presentation specifically appeal to *bosozoku* youths. In their reports, then, it is not clear what types of images *bosozoku* youths attempt to project and in what form.

Deviance, the Media, and Social Drama

Pathological interpretations of motives "behind" *boso* driving, outrageous paraphernalia, and preoccupation with media presentation are widely disseminated through the mass media, including newspapers, TV, and radio. These pathological interpretations are often coupled with characterizations of the *bosozoku* either as a cruel and abominable devil or as a pathetic victim suffering from chronic frustration and anxiety.[4] Each characterization is also often combined with advocacy, in impassioned tones, of the coercive or rehabilitative measures to be taken against or for *bosozoku*. On the other hand, youth-oriented media often glorify the *bosozoku* as a heroic figure who rebels against the oppressive establishment. Each of these characterizations, then, transforms complex reality into a coherent set of plots and themes and encourages a certain line of action by mobilizing the emotions of people.

These characteristics of media reports on *bosozoku* suggest that the reports can be meaningfully analyzed as a type of drama presented at the societal level, or as a "public drama."[5] A number of sociological studies on deviance and social control point out that the mass media often play a crucial role in creating public definitions of deviance and, as a consequence, in mobilizing social-control agencies.[6] These studies also point out that a public presentation of the deviant sometimes leads to unwitting consequences by presenting a novel style of deviance to the public and by allowing divergent interpretations by a heterogeneous audience. The ostensible intent of the original public drama as morality play may be modified or even distorted for the purpose of sensational news reports, entertainment, popular reading, or for the sale and use of certain goods, such as clothing, auto parts, and thematic paraphernalia.

This chapter, on the basis of media analysis, field observation, and interviews, will show that even though mere appearance in the mass media and resultant "notoriety" as well as "fame" appeal to *bosozoku* youths, they favor certain character images and try to project them through the youth-oriented media: i.e., the picaro and the chivalric hero. Therefore, although Boorstin's concept of "pseudo-event"[7] is useful in clarifying the inseparable relation between motorcycle-gang activity and the mass-media reports, the *bosozoku* youth is not a mere dupe or copycat who is totally manipulated by the media. Through self-presentation in the mass media, the *bosozoku* youth makes sense of his marginality or "liminality," which is supposed ultimately to be resolved with the attainment of adulthood. The media portrayal of the *bosozoku* is, in other words, a reflexive commentary on the youth's temporary status and its eventual end.[8]

THE MEDIA AND HEROIC DRAMA

The major news industry, which usually depicts the *bosozoku* as a diabolical or pathetic figure,[9] sometimes leans toward fascination and amusement rather than dread, outrage, or pity when it reports on *bosozoku* activity and paraphernalia.[10] The *bosozoku* subculture, after all, is "spectacular." It stimulates public curiosity, and thus it has great news value. In particular, "grotesque" and flashy outfits and scenes of *boso* driving frequently are shown on television. While the producers of such programs contend that they are "digging into" the *bosozoku* problem or the problem of delinquency in general, they sometimes go further and ask groups to perform *boso* driving for their cameras.[11]

A certain segment of the news industry is more explicit than others, and goes to some length in exploiting commercial gains and romanticizing the *bosozoku* as a heroic figure. Most of the publications listed at the end of this chapter appeared between 1979 and 1982, a peak period of *bosozoku* activity, and they provided *bosozoku* youths with an ideal stage for self-dramatization.

There are three categories for these publications, according to their content and format:

1. Picture books: publications which consist mainly of photographs of *bosozoku* youths, their paraphernalia, modified vehicles, and scenes of *boso* driving and weekly meetings (nos. 9, 10, 14, 15, 20 in the list; prices generally range from ¥1,200 to ¥1,700, or about $4.80 to $6.80).
2. Catalogues: publications which list the *bosozoku* groups active in Japan, and provide photographs and profiles of their membership (nos. 2, 3, 4, 16, 17, 18, 19, and 21; prices are from ¥1,500 to ¥2,000 or about $6.00 to $8.00).
3. Reportage: compilations about one or several *bosozoku* groups, based largely upon interview records or memoirs by *bosozoku* youths (nos. 1, 5, 6, 7, 8, 11, 12, which generally cost between ¥690 and ¥1,500, or $2.80 to $6.00).

While Kadokawa and Shinko Gakufu are the major publishing firms of those mentioned in the list, Futami, Rippu, and Tairiku are firms of medium size, and Taiyo Shobo and Daisan Shokan are relatively obscure enterprises.[12] Daisan Shokan brought out ten books on *bosozoku* and among gang members was identified as the leading publisher of such works.[13] This publisher began in 1979 with its publication of books on *bosozoku;* the firm consists of four editors and frequently changes its address. Group Full Throttle represents a number of journalists who temporarily collaborated to produce works on *bosozoku* for Daisan Shokan.

Only three publishers replied to any of my inquiries concerning the sale of their publications. I estimated the sale of other books chiefly on the basis of the answers from the three publishers and the numbers of editions of the books.[14] Because of the limited information available, my estimates about the sale of the other books are also imprecise, but it appears that at least one million copies of books dealing with *bosozoku* life-styles had been printed in Japan by the summer of 1984.

Many of the journalists who composed or edited the publications about *bosozoku* also wrote for youth-oriented weekly magazines (e.g., *Weekly Playboy, Takarajima*). Several motor-vehicle magazines, such as *Young Auto* and *Car Road*, frequently featured techniques of vehicle modifications, memoirs of *bosozoku* members, and profiles of groups from the heyday of *bosozoku* activity. The circulations of major youth-oriented weekly magazines vary from some 450,000 to one million. Those of major motor-vehicle magazines (most of which are biweekly) range from about 160,000 to 460,000.[15]

Bosozoku were also sometimes romanticized in weekly comic magazines which are read by a wide range of adolescents, from those in primary school to college students. In 1979 the total circulation of the five major weekly comic magazines (*Jump, Sunday, Magazine, Champion,* and *King*) was estimated at about 12 million; *Jump,* the leader, sold approximately 2.9 million copies.[16]

The most salient characteristic of the publications listed at the end of this chapter is the use of visual or pictorial presentations. Except for three of the seven works classified under "Reportage" (nos. 1, 8, 11), there is at least one photograph for each two pages of text in books from the second and third categories. "Picture books" are relatively large (8¼ by 10¼ inches) and consist almost exclusively of photographs of *bosozoku* youths, their paraphernalia, and scenes from *boso* driving. In many cases, the youths either take intimidating, seemingly frozen poses, or use joyous gestures and facial expressions. Such poses constitute an important element in the *bosozoku*'s self-presentation, and figure prominently in stereotypical images of *bosozoku* youths. Pictorial presentation of *bosozoku* style is also a salient characteristic of the articles in the youth-oriented weekly magazines and motor-vehicle magazines. The latter frequently featured pictures of modified motorbikes and cars during the heyday of *bosozoku*. Fictive characters appearing in comic magazines seek *bosozoku*-related "action," driving such vehicles, wearing flashy costumes, and assuming menacing poses.

In the books categorized as "Catalogues" or "Reportage," the verbal statements of *bosozoku* youths, or of journalists accompanying them, tend to be flamboyant. The youths exaggerate the size and organization of their groups, use emotionally charged—and often onomatopoetic—expressions to describe *boso* driving and gang fights, and discuss the police with rough and vulgar terms of defiance and challenge. The statements of the *bosozoku* youths and journalists in these books and magazine articles often include numerous grammatical and idiomatic errors.

Most of these pictorial and verbal presentations, considered in themselves, are fragmentary and certainly not a coherent dramatic scenario written by a single author. At a deeper level, however, we can discern relatively coherent sets of plots and themes constituting a sort of narrative about the *bosozoku*. A review of the twenty-one publications about *bosozoku* shows that two dramaturgical characters can be found in the narratives: the picaro and the chivalric hero.

BOSOZOKU AS THE PICARO
The Picaro—Corrupted Hero

On 28 September 1983, the Australian movie *Mad Max* (an action film featuring violent confrontations between a ferocious motorcycle gang and a supercop named Max) was televised in Kyoto. That day was a Wednesday, the day on which the Ukyo Rengo held its weekly meeting. That night those who assembled at the parking lot of a fast-food store discussed the movie in vehement terms. One attempted, with his motorcycle engine running, to brake his front wheel and, with its as a pivot, to draw the rear wheel around in a circle; he was unsuccessful in replicating the circle of burned rubber one of the characters in the film drew. In *bosozoku* jargon, this technique is called *maddo makkusu* (Mad Max) or *kompasu* (compasses). Members of the Ukyo Rengo were most fascinated by the character of the motorcycle gangs and their paraphernalia, rather than by the personality of Max, the hero of the movie. They talked enthusiastically about the "nice-looking" (*shibui*) gang members and the fierce-looking Kawasaki 1000 (cc), vehicles they use in the movie.

For some audiences, rogues, villains, or rascals are fascinating as dramatic protagonists. If the role is successfully performed, an actor portraying a villain may win more applause than one cast as a hero. The weird and fearsome Darth Vader from the film *Star Wars*, is at least, or perhaps even more, popular and fascinating than major romantic characters. On the other hand, in the United States there is a continuing "perverse" veneration of villains such as Billie the Kid, Jesse

James, and Al Capone. Klapp calls this social type the "corrupted hero," who is "too good to be a villain, too bad to be a hero, too serious to be a mere clown, too interesting to forget."[17]

As Cohen points out, Klapp's major concern throughout his *Heroes, Villains, and Fools* is with the classification of various social types, particularly as manifestations of moral contours and confusion in American society.[18] Klapp regards corrupted heroes (the tough guy, the smart operator, the wolf, the bad-good character, the false good fellow) as symptomatic of moral confusion, and calls for more effective controls over the personality types presented in mass communication.[19] Thus he does not pay much attention to the origins of attractiveness in the "corrupted hero." He merely mentions the "tradition of the romantic outlaw" as the historic root of this confusing figure. He also refers to the "spiciness" or "piquancy" built into characters with some of the opposing qualities of hero and villain, which are exploited for entertainment.

Babcock's analysis of the "picaresque" literary genre suggests that our fascination with the "corrupted hero" has sources more profound than mere amusement, and that the character of the "picaro" (villain) presupposes a certain transformation:

> Historically, the picaresque dialectically develops and distinguishes itself as an inversion of the patterns of the chivalric romance and the pastoral. The base transformation of the romance is the substitution of a lowlife delinquent for a princely hero.[20]

The picaresque also perverts the status passage found in the chivalric romance. The romantic hero's career is characterized by an "exile-and-return pattern" in which the hero goes "beyond the margins of society and there undergo[es] a liminal experience to find his sense of self and thus realize[s] symbolic power through victory in his tasks."[21] Similarly, in the picaresque, the protagonist goes through a change of status akin to that found by Van Gennep and Turner in rites of passage.[22] This form, however, is a parody of the romance, and contains two sets of metacode messages: "this is a romance"; "this is a picaresque anti-romance." Instead of fighting against evil powers, as the romantic hero does, the picaro often plays at social conventions and rules in order to reveal the hypocrisy of conventional people. He also often does not return to society but remains on its margins, and continues to display a liminality which is "betwixt and between," and which is antithetical to the consensual model of society. Thus the picaresque shows us another aspect of society and human experience: the arbitrary quality of man-made rules, and our ability to mock and violate them in the effort to regain autonomy from social constraints.[23]

A review of the twenty-one popular publications about *bosozoku* shows that they have many, if not all, of the features of the picaresque. In such publications, we can discern an implicit plot involving the pilgrimage of the picaro. Although the descriptions are quite fragmentary even for books categorized as "Reportage," the dramatic presentation of the *bosozoku*'s adventures, and of his role as a sort of "trickster," serves to criticize hypocrisy and contradictions in conventional society, and thus presupposes the pattern of status passage similar to that found in rites of passage: separation—margin—reaggregation.[24]

Pilgrimage of the Picaro

Separation. In rites of passage, during the phase of separation, the initiate becomes detached from "either an earlier fixed point in the social structure or from an established set of cultural conditions."[25] The romance and the picaresque begin in similar ways, but they differ markedly in detail. The romantic hero begins his adventure by losing his patrimony because of external social factors. He is usually supposed to be born of a noble family. In contrast, the picaro's parentage is low and marginal. In some cases he is an orphan or begins his journey by disowning his parents.[26]

In many publications about *bosozoku*, separation from conventional society is explained in terms of adverse social conditions. He is, as it were, orphaned by society. Dysfunctions of the educational system and numerous other social maladies are mentioned by *bosozoku* youths themselves or by the editors of books about them.

> *Bosozoku* exist because teachers and parents do not take care of dropouts properly.[27]

> The [general] social environment, education, family life, the mass media, including TV, the press, etc. . . . Haven't the maladies in such areas and the problems of capitalist society [in general] produced *bosozoku?*[28]

> From the interviews I have done so far, I feel acutely that the *bosozoku* leaders who are usually called *"atama"* [heads], are the last hope for dropouts who feel lonely, alienated, and desperate in this so-called competitive society.[29]

The storm and stress of adolescence, or *seishun* (the springtime of life), are mentioned as frequently as adverse social conditions in accounting for the separation. These two themes constitute the major explanations for the origin of the marginality of *bosozoku*. While social

PLATE 5. MENACING POSES BY "LADIES." These are typical poses for a *satsueikai* (photo-shooting meeting). Only two of the *redisu* (ladies) or female *bosozoku* members, wearing red *tokkofuku* (kamikaze party uniform), can actually drive motorcycles.

conditions are external forces which influence specific groups of youths, the "storm and stress" are internal and leave many young people on the margin of society.

> Saturday is the only day in the week when we can really live. Unless we vent the pent-up feelings which fill every cell, our bodies will burst.[30]

> During the period of *seishun* (adolescence), we feel the urge for speed in *boso* driving, an urge which comes from within our bodies.[31]

> I just want speed. I bet my youthful energy on speeding.[32]

The Margin. In the "margin" phase, the initiate becomes "ambiguous, neither here nor there, betwixt and between all fixed points of classification; he passes through a symbolic domain that has few or none of the attributes of his past or coming state."[33] In the romance and the picaresque, this is the main part of adventure and training. While the romantic hero learns skills to achieve a great end, under the supervision of his mentor, the picaro learns the art of deceit and decep-

PLATE 6. IMAGE OF THE PICARO. "Killa" is a corruption of "Killer" and pronounced /kira/. The picaresque image is also accentuated by the skull and crossbones sewn onto the *tokkofuku* (kamikaze party uniform).

tion from one or more corrupted preceptors, and soon outwits those who taught him.[34]

There is no comparable plot of mentorship, whether noble or villainous, in the publications about *bosozoku*. Productions of this sort are not intended to be coherent literary pieces. They are, in essence, collections of fragmentary statements by *bosozoku* youths. Ironically, however, such pronouncements, which are fragmentary, exemplify the theme of liminality that they announce. In several ways, the *bosozoku* is depicted as a liminal being who transcends the "structural" principles of society and who is (or should be) beyond the conventional rules. He even reproaches the conventional, non-*bosozoku* world for its hypocrisy. This common theme of liminality is similar to the image of the picaro as a marginal man who "exploits and makes permanent the liminal state of being 'betwixt and between all fixed points in a status sequence'."[35]

The liminal character of *bosozoku* and their immunity from social rules are often associated with *seishun* or the "springtime of life," the word Japanese use when they idealize and romanticize adolescence.

> [*Bosozoku* activity is a manifestation of] youthful *seishun*. We can
> do everything we want to do [during adolescence]. You know,
> youthful *seishun*.[36]

> [*Bosozoku* activity is] a privilege of youthfulness, a proof of
> youthfulness. *Bosozoku* is youthfulness![37]

Once *bosozoku* activity is defined as a "natural" consequence of
youthful energy and urges, the external forces which attempt to sup-
press it can be criticized as "unnatural." In the liminality, oppressive
structural principles are contrasted with "nature," which such principles cannot discipline or tame. The contrast sometimes is indicated
by metaphors for the body. The *bosozoku* youth is depicted as an embodiment of candid, untamed nature, while the "ordinary citizen"
(*ippan shimin*) may be viewed as a hypocrite who is "castrated" (*kyosei
sareta*) or "emasculated" by social conventions; he attempts, with some
cunning, to gratify his impulses through legal but unnatural means.

> The Yami (Darkness) [are] unspoiled guys who bet their lives on
> speed amid a society filled with vanity.[38]

> He [the *bosozoku* boy] is different from those castrated stars who
> dance about in flashy clothes on television. He is a superstar with
> flesh and blood, who speeds while his body is smeared with
> blood, and goes ahead, ignoring all traffic signals.[39]

> Aren't those who appear to be serious, "ordinary citizens," who
> seek an outlet for their dirty lusts in Shinjuku [a ward in Tokyo
> which includes one of Japan's largest pleasure districts] filthy
> and obscene hypocrites? The police tolerate such hypocrites,
> while they violently assault those who deviate even a little bit
> [from conventional norms]. For the police, our existence must be
> terribly irritating. [They may call us] "social outcasts" or "out-
> rageous felons." It's OK. We called ourselves the "Gokuaku"
> [Felons] before they gave us the label. We have our own way of
> living. But we don't want to say that society or politics are re-
> sponsible for it. It's just because we cannot live as castrated
> [emasculated] Mr. Ordinary Citizen does. We cannot find the
> reason [for our rebellion] anywhere but in our own bodies.[40]

The "nature" emphasized here is not that which was contrasted
with "unnatural" *bosozoku* paraphernalia in chapter 2. The second
usage symbolizes the conventional moral and cognitive categories
which are taken for granted and "reified" in the ongoing social
order.[41] On the other hand, the first connotation represents the
human potential which can overturn the mutually reinforcing cultural
codes and social order. *Bosozoku* activity is depicted as the untamed

human potential to challenge the oppressive social order and its cultural codes, which human beings originally made but which became external until they resembled "nature."

Although it is never stated explicitly or articulately, this theme of "conflict between two natures" may be discerned in many passages from the publications about *bosozoku*. *Boso* driving on Saturday nights is often described as a climactic point where the untamed human potential of one's life (during *seishun*)—youthful energy held back on working days—is detonated in a moment.

> While playing video games, I wash away the scurf [in my mind] that accumulated from Monday to Friday. Now I can say goodbye to boring, lonely, disgusting weekdays. Our Saturday finally came![42]

> Saturday night! On this night, I tear off the iron chain that binds me and dash out [for *boso* driving].[43]

> The spark of heated youthfulness. Words cannot express the energy, which is like a tidal wave. All our emotions are compressed and amplified [only to explode]. Exploding *seishun*, that's *boso* driving![44]

The splendor of *boso* driving on the margins of society is also likened to a carnival. The publications frequently cite terms such as *kaanibaru* (carnival), *omatsuri* (festival), and other related expressions.[45]

> *Boso* driving is Saturday night fever for us, the Kaguyahime [the name of a legendary princess used as a group name]. The curtain of the splendid midnight parade now is raised.[46]

> We get together on Saturday night and make a really big noise. . . . How shall I say it? It's like an *omatsuri* [festival]. I can really feel, "This is Saturday!"[47]

> I will show you my life.
> Even if you don't want to see it.
> One-night party on the road.
> Though we say goodbye by dawn.
> We find our buddies in a one-night carnival![48]

The theme of "conflict between two natures" describes the *bosozoku* youth as a free, unbounded being. He is, as it were, an untamed beast who resists the oppressive *kanri shakai* (managed society).

Reaggregation. In the last phase of the rites of passage, "The passage is consummated and the ritual subject, the neophyte or initiand [initiate] reenters the social structure."[49] This "reaggregation" into society is the end of the pilgrimage for the romantic hero or the picaro. According to Babcock, there are three patterns of endings in the picaresque novel: "(1) the picaro reenters society, sometimes through marriage, and is apparently reintegrated into the social structure; (2) the picaro is killed or punished; and (3) the picaro's adventure is 'to be continued'."[50] All of these patterns may be found in the publications about *bosozoku*.

At the outset, the second alternative resembles the ending of the social drama featuring the *bosozoku* as a diabolical figure. In the drama of scapegoating and purification, which will be discussed in chapter 7, the diabolical *bosozoku* is ultimately to be "eliminated" or "exterminated." But in the drama created by the youths, the ending differs diametrically from the ordinary conclusion to a morality play, in which the news media and the police proudly announce the "elimination" of *bosozoku*. The publications on *bosozoku* include several descriptions of the funeral of group members who were killed in traffic accidents. They also repeat eulogies by fellow members.[51] Group members have also produced repentant reminiscences about their own careers.

> I could not get anything [meaningful out of *bosozoku* activity]. Though I appeared in books or magazines thirty or forty times, nothing was left for me.[52]

> I quit *bosozoku* activity because I was arrested by the police on 12 November 1979. . . . I made a resolution never to repeat any wrongdoing. The sentence was one year in prison, suspended for three years.[53]

If the picaresque is a parody or mockery of the heroic narrative, it should end with "to be continued," that is, with no conclusion—the inversion of the clear-cut (often "happy") ending used in romantic works. Without an ending, the picaresque perpetuates the sense of marginality, and thus accentuates its central theme. We can find several statements of this type in the publications about *bosozoku*.

> The tighter the cops regulate us, the more frequently we will speed. . . . *Bosozoku* are eternal![54]

> After all, *bosozoku* should continue to speed. Those who stop speeding often mention their ages. But that sounds just like a pretext to me. . . . The excitement of speeding has nothing to do with age, does it?[55]

In most cases, however, the narrative about the *bosozoku* is *not* "to be continued." In the publications about *bosozoku*, the ending most frequently found is the reincorporation of youths into society, generally with the coming of adulthood or through marriage. The two words *sotsugyo* (graduation) and *ochitsuku* (settling down) are widely used to refer to this pattern of disengagement from *bosozoku* activity. In Japan, adulthood for legal purposes begins at the age of twenty; coming-of-age ceremonies (*seijinshiki*) are held throughout the country. At about this time of life most group members end their careers.

> I was already twenty years old. Every time I met old friends on the streets of Shinjuku, they said to me in plain words, "Are you still doing such stuff [*bosozoku* activity]?" . . . "Graduation"— this word tripped off my tongue when I was watching junior members taking off [after *boso* driving] from Ohi Wharf, making great exhaust noises from motorbikes.[56]

> I went through the coming-of-age ceremony and will no longer be [treated as] "Bartender D" [a pseudonym I would be given in the press if arrested]. I have to graduate from the *bosozoku*.[57]

> I want to continue to be a *bosozoku* at twenty. After that, I will settle down and get married to make a home.[58]

Metaphors likening the termination of *bosozoku* careers to initiation ceremonies are found in references to "burning out." The *bosozoku* youth's *seishun* (adolescence) is burned out during gang activity, and he is supposed to be reborn as a *shakaijin* (a full-fledged member of society).

> Why do we continue to speed? We are burning up our *seishun* until it is exhausted.[59]

> I can now say that I bet my *seishun* and my life on *bosozoku* activity and have burned out.[60]

> Now I work at a delivery agency . . . from 7 A.M. to 8 P.M., without any leisure time. I went through the coming-of-age ceremony and became an adult this year. My dream about the future is to become the owner of a small store.[61]

In this theme of death and rebirth, the ending of this drama becomes the beginning of another story which may be less dramatic but is accompanied by far fewer risks. Thus the typical conclusion of the *bosozoku* narrative is quite different from the inconclusive ending which generally is found in picaresque works, where marginality is perpetuated. Again, as with the character of *bosozoku* as protagonist, the *bosozoku* narrative itself is incomplete as a picaresque drama. The same can be said of the other type of romanticization of the *bosozoku*, which resembles a chivalric romance.

BOSOZOKU AS THE KOHA
The *Koha*—A Hero *Not* Corrupted

While the dramatization of the *bosozoku* as the picaro presents a character who, albeit incompletely, mocks the existing morality and norms, another characterization of motorcycle gangs idealizes him as the *koha:* a hero with a strong sense of self-control and discipline. Different from the picaresque presentation, the heroic (self-)presentation of the *bosozoku* does not presuppose a specific plot concerning an "exile-and-return" pattern or its parody, but mostly consists of episodic accounts or poses.

Koha (硬派; the hard-type) is a traditional image of (adolescent) masculinity which combines violence, valor, and bravado with stoicism and chivalry. We can find many instances of concepts derived from this image, both in publications about *bosozoku* and in gestures favored by the youths. In Japan, the word has been often used in categorizing delinquents into two major types: *koha* (a young rough [or tough]) and *nanpa* (軟派; the soft type—a skirt-chaser or ladies' man).[62]

In the publications considered here, however, the term *koha* refers to a more ethical figure. *Koha* is often described as a "man of character" who maintains his equipoise in risky situations[63] and has a high degree of self-discipline and control. This *koha* image is contrasted with that of the *nanpa,* who is morally degraded and, apart from *bosozoku* activity, engages in various despicable deviant acts, such as glue sniffing, gang rape, and theft.

> The Black Emperors are *koha.* Anyone born as a male should be a *koha.* A *koha* boy has the *samurai* spirit.[64]

> Though many other *bosozoku* are *nanpa,* ours is a group consisting exclusively of those with guts and the real *koha* spirit.[65]

> We are warlike Zorro! The *koha* spirit is our policy. . . . I want to warn other groups, "Don't speed while sniffing glue!" Besides, they often take girls with them [in their cars or their motorbikes]. . . . They even commit gang rapes! If we allow girls to join a group, we will [easily] lose group discipline. I say it again. We are Zorro! We specialize in fights![66]

The image of *koha,* of self-control and discipline, is also expressed in group codes that proscribe the use of paint thinner, taking girls on *boso* drives, picking up girls, gang rape, and other "detestable" acts.

> We do not allow girls to join *bosozoku* drives. We do not pick up girls, don't sniff paint thinner.[67]

The group rules are
1. No theft
2. No gang rape
3. No drugs
We stake our lives on speeding and fights. The White Claw is the best *bosozoku!*[68]

Koha is also manifested in statements about the group hierarchy and strong leadership.

> Groups lacking discipline and team spirit look so shabby and lousy. In weekly meetings, our group always acts in unison and swiftly [*bitto ugoku*], according to the leader's orders. Other undisciplined groups always dawdle along.[69]

> A group cannot exist without a tight senior-junior relationship. We will let any half-hearted junior members leave our group. After all, we have strict rules about using respectful language [to senior members]. Only those juniors who have guts and strong character [*bitto shiteru*] can remain in our group.[70]

The phrase *bitto* (*shiteru*) in these quotations is an onomatopoetic expression which, as an adjective or adverb, refers to well-disciplined groups or persons. Such an individual also should have strong will power and character. *Bitto*, then, is often associated with the qualities of a *koha* hero. The sense of *koha* is also imparted by visual means. This, as we have already seen in chapter 2, is apparent in *bosozoku* paraphernalia with nationalist motifs. Symbols such as the *tokkofuku* (kamikaze party uniform), *sentofuku* (combat uniform), the Imperial chrysanthemum crest, and *hachimaki* (headband) with the rising sun, not only convey intimidation and esoteric membership, but also signify discipline and order.

> I hate the *uyoku* [right-wing organization]. . . . *Bosozoku* speed just because they want to speed. This has nothing to do with political things. . . . We call this uniform the *tokkofuku* [kamikaze party uniform]. We use the *tokkofuku* because *uyoku* people wear this costume. Only *koha bosozoku* use this type of costume.[71]

Nationalist emblems are not the only hallmarks of *koha*. The *bosozoku* appropriate symbols and rituals from various groups which have characteristics of what Etzioni generally calls "coercive organizations,"[72] and combine them into a "*bosozoku* style." On the whole, *bosozoku* use a collage of symbolic motifs from such organizations as college cheering groups, the armed forces, right-wing organizations, and *yakuza* (organized criminal group). Ranking members of *bosozoku*

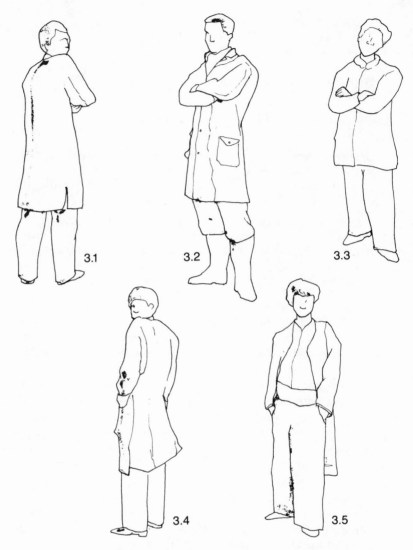

Fɪɢ. 3.1–3.12. Intimidating *Koha* Poses. (Reprinted, by permission, from I. Sato, *An Ethnography of* Bosozoku [Tokyo: Shin'yosha, 1984], 240–43.)

groups sometimes include the *tokko taicho* (kamikaze party leader), the *shin'ei taicho* (leader of the bodyguards), and *tosei taicho* (section leader charged with group discipline), although the group may not have such subsections. Many *bosozoku* groups also have institutional methods by which leaders or executive members give orders and the rank and file

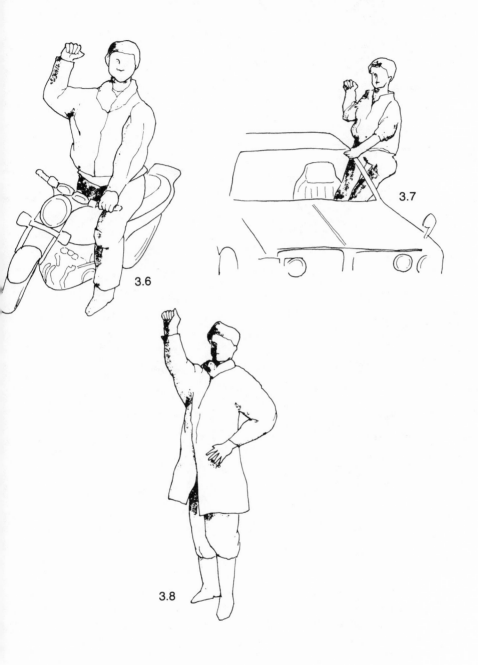

3.6

3.7

3.8

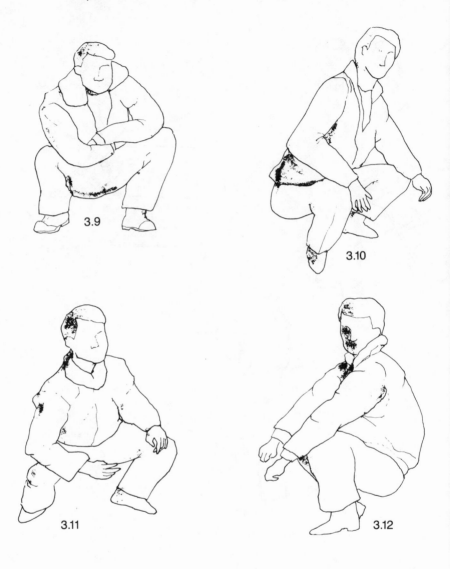

3.9

3.10

3.11

3.12

specifically respond. When the leader addresses them, the members line up and shout *Osu!* (Yes, sir!) to each of his directions. This pattern is taken from a similar ritual used by college cheering parties or by athletic clubs for combative sports, such as karate and judo. During the heyday of *bosozoku,* such sequences of order and response, and physical punishment of junior by executive members, were often shown on television or in films.

The most prevalent and popular presentation of the *koha* image is through gestures, particularly in the poses found in publications, notably in picture books. Figures 3.1 through 3.12 show the categories of poses that frequently appear in photographs. The almost universal signs of masculinity and intimidation are folded arms (figs. 3.1, 3.2, and 3.3), and hands in the pockets (figs. 3.6, 3.7, and 3.8). Figures 3.9 through 3.12 need some explanation. These poses are called the *unko suwari* (shit-squatting), after the Japanese manner of squatting above the toilet. *Bosozoku* youths, more generally "Yankees," often crouch this way to rest when they hang around outdoors. This stance is also called the "Yankee *suwari*" (Yankee-squatting) in Kyoto. When they fold their arms or crouch in an oblique stance, the shit-squatting or Yankee-squatting also signifies masculinity, intimidation, and menace. The poses shown in figures 3.1 through 3.12 are almost always performed impassively or with threatening facial expressions, such as knitted brows or a wry mouth.

If they are taken literally, the verbal and visual statements emphasizing the *koha* image will make *bosozoku* appear well-disciplined, self-controlled, or even quite moral. Other features, however, cast doubt on the credibility of such a romantic conception.

Paradox in *Koha* Poses

When I carried my Nikon or small Pentax autofocus camera to weekly meetings of the Ukyo Rengo or several hangouts of Yankees in Kyoto, the members often assumed *koha* poses, although I rarely asked them to do so. On such occasions some of them said, "Let's take the *unko suwari* [shit-squatting] pose!" The Informants and other Yankees learned the poses from publications they or their friends had bought or "swiped" from book stores. Similarly, when I trained my camera on my informants, they often assumed frozen, *koha* poses. After the shooting, they almost always gave sighs of relief, then looked at each other, and laughed somewhat from embarrassment. One youth broke into laughter before I released the shutter and teased the others, saying, "Hey! You! You really look like *bosozoku!*" Others also broke out laughing when he spoke.

For most of the Yankee boys, the romanticized image of *bosozoku,* especially that of *koha,* is fiction. They are not dupes who take literally media-created illusions or "pseudo-events" for reality. An informant, who posed in *koha* stance for *Bosozoku Archipelago '80,* said to me, "That's just a *pozu* [pose], just for taking pictures. We quickly become *nanpa* whenever pretty chicks pass in front of us." An informant gave me a personal snapshot in which he assumes a *koha* pose, and asked me to put it in my book. In an interview session, he said about the *koha* poses frequently found in the publications on *bosozoku,* "That's just a bluff. Just for the picture, you know. Everyone wants to put on airs for pictures." A female informant assumed *koha* poses wearing *tokkofuku* when I took her picture with other female members. She, however, was quite critical about the self-presentation as *koha* in journalistic publications: "It's ridiculous that they put 'Ardent Patriots' or some other words in the books. They are just like *yakuza.* I think that's just for taking pictures. Besides, they put bragging-like phrases under the pictures."[73]

There is, indeed, a fundamental paradox in the combination of "bragging-like phrases" and an essential characteristic of *koha.* The *koha* is a "man of few words," who manifests his will not through equivocal pronouncements but through physical action with a highly univocal and consequential message.[74] The *koha* is, therefore, contrasted with the *nanpa,* who tempts women with sweet talk and flattery. He is also contrasted with hypocritical "ordinary citizens" whose words (*tatemae*) are contradicted by their real intentions (*honne*).

While reticence and sincerity are taken to be characteristic of *koha,* these qualities are belied by the *bosozoku*'s self-serving assertions. In the publications about *bosozoku,* the youths are quite vocal in asserting that they are *koha.* They also criticize and dwell upon other *bosozoku*'s claims to be *koha,* and maintain that they are liars. While the *koha* should be stoic and reticent, the *bosozoku* youths narcissistically indulge in abundant self-assertion and in criticism of others. In other words, they eloquently depict themselves as those who do *not* speak eloquently. My informants were well aware of these self-contradictory *koha* images in the publications, and discredited them by saying, "That's really perverted," or "That's only a show-off. Only a pretense. *Bosozoku* are all *nanpa.*"

The same paradox is inherent in the *koha* image imparted in gestures for photographs. The *koha* poses represent intimidation and rejection of communication and verbal negotiation. The poses are usually accompanied by either expressionless faces or intimidating expressions. The poses and facial expressions say, as it were, "I am a *koha* who hardly speaks and who cannot be fooled around with." Here, again, he communicates his reticence. Although the communication is unspoken, the frozen and fabricated poses are eloquent enough to undermine the credibility of his message, "I am a *koha,*" or "I really mean it."

This conflict between the style of communication (how something is told) and the content (what is told) is not unlike the paradox inherent in the picaresque. Babcock points out that picaresque works usually are written as first-person autobiographical reminiscences. Thus the narrator (picaro) tells the reader to accept his tale as credible, and then portrays himself as a master of deception and deceit. This situation is comparable to Epimenides' "liar" paradox—"All Cretans are liars. I am a Cretan"—and is both a criticism of narrative statement in the picaresque itself, and an oblique criticism of absolute judgment or convention in general.[75] The paradox in *koha* poses and statements is less challenging to the principles of human judgment but equally has an element of play.

Indeed, the relationship between the media and *bosozoku* activity allows self-presentation which is antithetical to the image of *koha:* narcissism. The eagerness of *bosozoku* youths to obtain a media audience facilitates the collection of materials for publication. A member of the Group Full Throttle maintains that,

> *Bosozoku* all over Japan cooperate with our efforts to gather data. It's more than cooperation. They are almost aggressive. They phone the publisher night and day and demand to be interviewed. Some even come to the publisher's office driving motorbikes. . . . I am so overwhelmed by their *"medachitagari seishin"* [*medatsu* spirit; desire to show off] that I feel I am not gathering data but serving at their beck and call. I feel like a subcontractor who is working under orders for a magazine which might be called, say, *"Monthly Bosozoku."*[76]

Although this journalist may be exaggerating somewhat, and may understate his own "commercial exploitation" of the deviant,[77] the youths, rather than the journalists, actually are the playwrights in the drama featuring the *bosozoku* as a *koha* or a picaresque hero. This is most apparent in the publications from Daisan Shokan. While in some books material was collected by journalists (nos. 12, 13, 14 in the list at the end of this chapter), most statements, particularly in the other books, were sent in by *bosozoku* youths themselves. The publisher sent the short form of a questionnaire to *bosozoku* groups and solicited letters and pictures from them. Books that are "Catalogues" are, as it were, patchwork compilations of pictures and letters. The editors seem merely to have produced collages from materials originating in various prefectures. Books from other publishers also offer assorted statements and pictures without regard for credibility. Futami Shobo, the publisher which spearheaded the publication of *bosozoku*-related books by bringing out Urita's best-selling *Only Saturday Is Left for Us,* solicited information from the youths themselves in the preparation of Ueno's *Bosozoku Documentary* series.

In the heroic narrative of motorcycle gangs, then, distinctions among the "playwright," "actors," and "audience" are blurred. The *bosozoku* youth writes a romantic scenario, plays the hero's role, and cheers his own performance. The paradox of the *koha* is fundamentally based on this narcissistic nature of self-presentation through the media.

Bosozoku as Celebrity
Moral Neutrality of Celebrity

It is little wonder that the picaresque and heroic depictions of the *bosozoku* appeal to gang youths. The two images provide them with clear-cut dramaturgical identities which enable them to have, if only temporarily, a heightened sense of self. The images also enable them to overcome negative overtones of public stereotypes of the *bosozoku* by transcending conventions (picaro) or by presenting an alternative model of morality (*koha*). In other words, the romanticized images give Yankees and other street-corner boys in Japan a "romance-glazed image of themselves, a coherent reflection that only a very few had been able to find in a mirror,"[78] as the portrayal by Marlon Brando in the movie *The Wild One* once did for the self-image of Hell's Angels. A specifically picaresque or *koha* image, however, is not always indispensable to Yankees. However diabolically and detestably the media depict the *bosozoku*, the mere appearance in the media often appeals to motorcycle gangs. This aspect of the relationship between the media and *bosozoku* shows the third character of *bosozoku:* celebrity.

One of my informants considered the influence that news reports of other gangs had on his own *bosozoku* group, and commented:

> After all, if there is sensational press coverage of [*bosozoku* groups] in other prefectures, . . . we also hear about it [by word of mouth] and think, "Oh, we also have to make it!"

Two female informants talked about the "fame" surrounding them when newspaper reports dealt with their group, the Ukyo Rengo,

> E.: The press always makes mistakes, great mistakes. For example, they [sometimes] treat some other guy as "the leader." . . . But, well, how will I say it? If the press says, "The *bosozoku* . . . " or, for example, if they report, "Ukyo Rengo's So-and-So did . . . ," it's really exciting for us.
> A.: Yeah, it's really exciting. We can become famous.

My informants were also pleased when incidents involving them were reported in newspapers. Members of the Ukyo Rengo appeared in *Kyoto Shimbun* (the major Kyoto newspaper) at least twenty-one times between January 1978 and August 1984. Many of my informants kept clippings of these newspaper articles in their photograph albums, together with pictures of themselves and their vehicles. In Japan, news reports on crime committed by minors usually employ pseudonymous initials such as "A" and "B." When *bosozoku* outbreaks were reported in newspapers, some of my informants approached each other saying "Hey, Mr. A!"—"What, Mr. B.?" Several times I asked informants who were mentioned in newspapers why they were pleased with such reports. The typical answer was, "Of course, that's because we can become famous [*yumei ni naru*]!" While *medatsu* is used to refer to the enjoyment of self-presentation, notably in *boso* driving or through conspicuous paraphernalia, *yumei ni naru* (becoming famous, being widely known) is the common expression for the enjoyment of media publicity.

Bosozoku youths' preoccupation with self-presentation through the mass media is a nationwide phenomenon. Group members themselves sent in many of the materials used in journalists' works on *bosozoku;* indeed they also sent in newspaper clippings about *bosozoku* incidents. We can find boastful statements, such as the following in the publications.

> Our group was the first to appear in press reports about the incident of police shooting *bosozoku*.[79]

> We had the disbandment ceremony last November. Mickey Yasukawa [a television celebrity] and others interviewed us.[80]

Bosozoku often inform publishers, the press, and television stations of the times and places of their large-scale *boso* driving and ceremonies of disbandment.[81]

Bosozoku and the "Pseudo-Event"

These features suggest that motorcycle gangs involve collective behavior characteristic of a "pseudo-event," or one that is fabricated for mass consumption[82] (although the assumption of total passivity of the "mass" implicit in Boorstin's arguments should be qualified here). As Boorstin points out, an individual depicted in a pseudo-event is not a real hero but a "celebrity," someone who is known primarily for his "well-knownness."[83] Boorstin comments on the distinction between hero and celebrity:

The HERO was distinguished by his achievement; the celebrity by his image or trademark. The hero created himself; the celebrity is created by the media. The hero was a big man; the celebrity is a big name.[84]

The celebrity attracts attention because he is "well known" rather than for achievements which are morally evaluated. Before the camera or microphone, virtually any kind of person can be a celebrity or star.[85] The *bosozoku* youths' preoccupation with media presentation exemplifies this indiscriminate morality of celebrity. Almost any news reports, even those of a criminal assault on police stations, or of traffic accidents, can enhance a person's or group's status as a celebrity. For them, "fame" and "notoriety" are often synonymous with "publicity" (*yumei ni naru*). During *boso* driving, spectators and participants both create and are affected by self-presentation that leads to the enjoyment of *medatsu*. Similarly, the mass media become a "mirror" for the *bosozoku* youth's narcissistic self-presentation, from which he can derive the enjoyment of being well-known. Urita writes in his memoirs, *Only Saturday Is Left for Us,*

> Media appearance is our pride. The reports are so often groundless that we say, "What a mess they make when they write!" But we feel in our hearts, "We did it!" and feel as if we became heroes. . . . We go into ecstasies if our picture appears in weekly magazines. We buy several copies of the magazines and show them proudly, even to our parents, not to say to our friends.[86]

This almost symbiotic relationship between the *bosozoku* youths' preoccupation with media presentation and the media's curiosity about them even led to incidents in which *boso* driving was performed at the request of journalists.[87]

The temptation and danger of this type of incident were also inherent in my research. Several informants frequently made offers such as, "Hey! We will make a big *boso* drive, if you take our pictures." Some offers were less straightforward. An informant said to me, "We're gonna carry out a big *boso* drive in the near future. So why don't you come and shoot pictures?" I declined by saying that I had taken enough pictures in their hangouts; the *boso* drive was never carried out. In fact, reporters writing for Daisan Shokan, and free-lance journalists who had subcontracted with that publisher, visited Kyoto several times. On several occasions, *boso* driving was carried out for their *satsueikai* (photo-shooting meeting). In 1980 a free-lance journalist subcontracting with Daisan Shokan planned a *boso* drive, and some of my informants joined it. Several groups took part and went to Shiga prefecture (adjoining Kyoto), and several *bosozoku* were assaulted by *yakuza* members there. Some were injured and some had to return to Kyoto (hours away) on foot because they fled, leaving their vehicles behind. Only one small picture taken in the course of the *boso* driving appeared in one of the publications. For many participants, then, the *boso* drive for *satsueikai* was not worth the effort.

Among my informants, a few executive members noted that rumors of a "photo-shooting meeting" can mobilize unusual numbers of youths for group activities. An ex-*bosozoku* leader said that he even spread such rumors to secure enough participants for a *boso* drive. In fact, a few months after the first contacts with my informants, I noticed that members of different groups appeared in several pictures in journalistic works, though each picture was presented as showing members of a single group.

In this way, the media, whether they portray the *bosozoku* as a devil, the picaro, *koha*, or celebrity, played a crucial role in amplifying the size and magnitude of the youthful deviance by making it an item of mass consumption. There is, however, another element in the relationship among motorcycle-gang activity, the media, and the consumer market. Commercialization of a deviant style sometimes leads to unexpected effects of social control as well as to unexpected "deviation amplification."[88]

COMMERCIALIZATION, DIFFUSION, AND STYLIZATION

From the very beginning, *bosozoku* activity and subculture have been closely associated with certain commodities. Motorcycle gangs have employed vehicles, costumes, and other commodities in order to dramatize their group's and their own identity. The self-dramatization was soon incorporated into the mass consumer market. The commercialization of *bosozoku* style facilitated nationwide diffusion of *bosozoku* symbolism and mass participation in the subcultural style. On the other hand, it highlighted the fashionable or faddish features of *bosozoku*—aspects that eventually contributed to making the style obsolete. Although the commercialization is not a form of intentional social control, it has a similar effect on deviant styles in the long run.[89]

The publication of books on *bosozoku* is just one form of the commercial exploitation of *bosozoku* styles, and they delineate the *bosozoku* narratives most explicitly. The style has been also adopted in various sorts of consumer goods. Such goods, in some form or other, presuppose the plots and themes in the narratives about the *bosozoku*.

Some *bosozoku* paraphernalia, which were originally made by youths themselves, or by local manufacturers, were produced by larger concerns for a nationwide market. For example, at one time *bosozoku* youths made oversized fenders for their cars by cutting and bending steel plates. Nowadays, a wide variety of fenders and spoilers are available throughout Japan. Similarly, the headband, *tokkofuku* (kamikaze party uniform), and stickers can be bought from mail-order houses. Stickers with lettering and symbols that resemble those used by *bosozoku* are widely available in auto-parts stores.

The *bosozoku* style has also been taken up by the popular music industry. Several rock'n'roll groups adopted such fashions and achieved great commercial success. A rock group called Carol began the trend in 1972; they made their debut in leather jackets and ducktail haircuts, and were popular with many inside and outside of *bosozoku* groups. Eikichi Yazawa, the leader of this group, became a solo singer in 1975; he was considered a charismatic figure both for his songs and for his autobiography *Nariagari* (The Upstart) (1978). In the book he describes his childhood without parents, miserable and uncertain beginnings with obscure bands, and success with the group Carol and as a solo performer. This success story, with its main motif of youthful challenge and ambition had great appeal to adolescents, especially among *bosozoku*.

The Cools, another rock group, made their debut in 1978, also with leather jackets and ducktail haircuts. They explicitly described themselves as a *bosozoku* group,[90] and carried out promotional campaigns on chopper-type Harley Davidsons with the "colors" of Hell's Angels on their gas tanks. As a younger successor to Carol, the Cools gained considerable, though not as extensive, adolescent support.

The Yokohama Ginbae (Yokohama Silver Flies) made their debut in 1980 and adopted costumes resembling more recent *bosozoku* garb— leather jackets with wide collars, Afro hair styles, and baggy white pants. Many of their songs deal explicitly with *bosozoku* and juvenile delinquency, and use exhaust noises for sound effects. Although as music their performance was not on the same level as that of Carol or the Cools, they became a popular group among teenagers, who were attracted by their unique costumes and the overt themes of youthful defiance in their songs. They won popularity at a time when juvenile delinquency in general was a serious social issue, so much so that publicity-conscious Prime Minister Nakasone invited the group to a party in 1983.

A picture book entitled *Namennayo!* (Don't Mess Around with Me!)[91] and commercial goods modeled on those in the book are caricatures of *bosozoku* symbolism and display a crucial aspect of such symbols and the commercial exploitation of them. This work, which was published in 1981, and had a sales of about 335,000 copies by the summer of 1983, features a cat called Matakich. Throughout the book there are numerous pictures of cats who stand upright wearing human clothes. Miniature props (such as motorcycles, cars, and buildings) are also provided. The plot concerns Matakichi's youthful experimentation with several expressive styles including *bosozoku, takenoko-zoku* (bamboo-shoot tribe; a dancing tribe in Harajuku, Tokyo) and rock'n'rollers. The youthful experimentation eventually ends with Matakichi's attainment of adulthood, and the story about the feline character, as a whole, may be taken as a parody of the *bosozoku's* pilgrimage.

Not only did the picture book itself attain great commercial success, but *bosozoku*-style commodities bearing Matakichi's picture sold in large quantities. More than sixty separate articles were produced, including stickers, imitation driver's licenses, wallets, erasers, and celluloid sheets (which are placed under writing paper).[92] This feline incarnation of the *bosozoku* made possible more extensive marketing than was the case for commodities using human models.

The use of *bosozoku* motifs on commercially produced merchandise has diffused such fashions and the dramaturgical plots and themes concerning *bosozoku* among a wide group of adolescents. In the process, deviant style became more accessible to youngsters. Mass participation diminished the risks involved in the adoption of aberrant styles.[93] The paraphernalia was no longer the sign of a stigmatized minority but was displayed by the fashionable among their peers. Adolescents also mimicked characteristic *bosozoku* gestures. Many *shin'eitai* (an organization of male or female groupies) who followed pop music stars imitated the poses of defiance seen in *bosozoku* pictures and wore headbands as well when journalists took their pictures. Delinquent groups formed in junior and senior high schools were eager to buy stickers and posters showing major *bosozoku* groups and obtained them from mail-order houses that operated across the nation. At home, or even in classes at school, they also played aloud on cassette recorders the rock songs that were popular among *bosozoku*.

Among adolescents, some attempted more challenging imitations of the *bosozoku* style. Several groups of junior high school students organized "*charinko* [bicycle] *bosozoku*" groups instead of motorcycle gangs. They even wore *tokkofuku* bearing the name of neighborhood or nationally known *bosozoku* groups.[94] Occasionally they might participate as passengers in *boso* driving, and eventually form actual *bosozoku* groups.[95]

While the commercialization of *bosozoku* styles made such fashions accessible to many adolescents, and in this sense contributed to the diffusion of *bosozoku* activity, marketing techniques of this sort led to eventual obsolescence of such styles as well. The adoption of *bosozoku* fashions was made less risky because of commercialization and mass participation in the styles. But the styles of the *bosozoku* also began to seem less rebellious, less challenging, and less "exclusive." The character image of the *bosozoku* lost its "aura" when it was reproduced repeatedly in the mass media and in the form of merchandise for mass consumption.[96] As in the natural history of fashion, or of novel artistic styles, what began as innovation, rebellion, and a shock to the conventional styles later became part of the conventional, conformist, commonplace, and "natural," thus no longer serving to mark one's identity. *Bosozoku* styles were even used for "pet items," through the feline imagery added to many articles. Before the widespread commercial use of such fashions, it would have been unthinkable for the prime minister to meet with the *bosozoku*-style rock group, Yokohama Ginbae.

Commercialization and diffusion of the style also led to changes in the demographic distribution of the *bosozoku* population. Increasingly younger adolescents began to take part in *bosozoku* activities. Such groups and their styles came more and more to be regarded as "kid stuff," and "graduation" took place at earlier ages. Tame and commonplace styles were no longer effective in sustaining youths' sense of self, especially among the older ones. The less challenging and less rebellious styles no longer served the purpose of making oneself conspicuous (*medatsu*) and affirming one's distinct sense of self.[97]

While *bosozoku* style became less challenging, group activity became more and more risky because of strengthened police regulation, especially after 1981, with the enactment of the amended traffic laws. A considerable portion of the *bosozoku* population graduated from gang activity to far less risky activities, such as those of surfer, rock'n'roller (a dancing tribe imitating American youth styles in the 1950s), and *takenoko-zoku*, (a dancing tribe in Harajuku), which were then considered novel.[98]

The obsolescence of *bosozoku* style is also apparent in the publications about such groups. No journalistic book worthy of note has been published since the appearance of *Bosozoku Archipelago 1982*. While *Bosozoku Archipelago '80* reached its ninth printing within eight months, its counterpart for 1982 was still in its first printing by the summer of 1984. The publisher Daisan Shokan has shifted its attention from *bosozoku* to other youthful styles and published a picture book, *Our Hearts Are Those of Teddy Boys: A Picture Book of Japanese Rock 'n'*

Rollers, in 1983. While *bosozoku* styles still sometimes appear in popular comic strips and movies, most of these are purely fictional pieces and do not deal with any existing *bosozoku* groups.

In several respects, *bosozoku* styles are quite vulnerable to obsolescence. First, the style depends heavily upon tangible items, and upon gestures and activities that do not require complex learning. Symbolism of this sort can easily be reproduced on articles of mass consumption, and gestures and activities can be easily mimicked by a wide range of people.

Second, the style consists of bits and pieces of several preexisting symbols, notably nationalist motifs, *yakuza* images, and the paraphernalia of professional racers. The *bosozoku* style is a collage of such fragments that are easily understood. For example, one does not need detailed knowledge of nationalist thought to make an impression; one need merely wear an army uniform and a headband with the rising sun. Thus the *bosozoku* style was not only imitated literally but also became an object of various forms of parody and caricature such as feline *bosozoku* and bicycle *bosozoku*. In other words, the *bosozoku* style, which is itself a parody, lends itself to further comic twists. In the process, the original shock of the deviant style is diluted and even becomes an object of unqualified mockery.

Third, the underlying theme of the style is youthfulness. The plot of youthful rebellion and eventual maturation ("graduation") as a conventional adult is increasingly clarified and stylized while the style is codified into the heroic drama that I call "*Bosozoku*, the Saturday-Night Hero." This plot resolution, and changes in the demographic composition of the *bosozoku* population, reinforce each other and trivialize the style's meaning.

Bosozoku was a symbolic rebellion which was born and nurtured partly by the mass media and producers of consumer goods. The meaning of this symbolic rebellion was soon diluted and made obsolete by those very forces. I once asked the leader of the female subsection of Ukyo Rengo, "What do you think will be in vogue after *bosozoku*?" She answered rather indignantly, "We didn't do that because it was fashionable!" Several months later, and after she had graduated from *bosozoku*, she asked me, "Is our book [my monograph about *bosozoku*] really going to be published? I'm afraid that it might not, because *bosozoku* are not as fashionable as they used to be."

SUMMARY

The media appearance is an integral element of *bosozoku* activity. Motorcycle-gang youths make every effort to present themselves through the mass media. Youth-oriented media, including weekly news magazines, comic magazines, music records, and movies, have provided stages for their self-dramatization. Books dealing exclusively with *bosozoku* are published and attain a considerable commercial success.

Two dramaturgical characters can be discerned in the publications on *bosozoku:* the picaro and the *koha.* The picaresque representation presupposes a pilgrimage of the protagonist and depicts the *bosozoku* as a being transcending conventional norms. The presentation of the *bosozoku* as *koha* portrays him as a stoic and chivalric hero. Both of the picaresque and heroic representations provide Yankees with a romanticized definition of self. Mere appearance in the mass media also appeals to *bosozoku* youths insofar as it provides them with publicity as a "celebrity" and serves to enhance their sense of self.

The media presentation, however, soon lost its ego-supporting function. The diffusion of *bosozoku* styles through the mass media and mass production of *bosozoku* paraphernalia have led to the loss of "aura" in the image of the *bosozoku.* The *bosozoku* style, born with the systems of a highly developed mass media and consumer market, is made obsolescent by these very forces.

Playlike definitions of the situation of *bosozoku* are acted out in *boso* driving, embodied in the form of tangible commodities in paraphernalia, and delineated in the mass media.[99] By creating and elaborating playlike definitions of the situation in the three genres of *bosozoku* play, the *bosozoku* youth occasionally undergoes a flow experience, in which he has a heightened sense of self and feels in touch with a "reality" which he can rarely experience otherwise. The playlike world of *bosozoku,* then, provides numerous opportunities for enjoyment. In this chapter and the preceding two, I have used a dramaturgical metaphor in analyzing the structure of, and process in, the play world of *bosozoku.* The three genres of *bosozoku* play, indeed, roughly correspond to the three components of a theatrical play: performance, props, and script. As in the case of a theatrical play, *bosozoku* activity creates an alternative reality in a bracketed spatiotemporal context and includes an element of excitement and heightened experience. The *bosozoku* youth, like a stage actor, is more or less clearly aware of the fictive nature of the alternative reality, though he may be totally involved in the theatrical "frame" at the apex of his performance.

There are, however, a number of important differences between *bosozoku* play and a theatrical play—especially a conventional one— performed on stage. Although the differences do not always stand out, some of them are quite important in understanding the meanings of *bosozoku* activity for Yankees. The differences are also closely related to the issues to be taken up in the next part of this volume.

First, there is no clear distinction between playwright, actor, and audience in *bosozoku* play. As has been already discussed, this is related to the narcissism inherent in the *bosozoku*'s self-presentation. Second, there are crucial differences between the narratives in the mass media and the schemes of actual *bosozoku* activities in specific situations.[100] I will deal with this issue in chapter 5 when I describe the role played by street-corner narratives in the metamorphosis of Yankees into *bosozoku*. Third, there is a lack of consensus between *bosozoku* and a great portion of the Japanese public as to the interpretation of the dramatic (i.e., spectacular and emotion-arousing) acts of motorcycle gangs. The public may regard the acts as outrageous or pathological and characterize the *bosozoku* as diabolical or pathetic. In other words, while *bosozoku* youths define their own activities by the indicative "This is play," the general public and the major news industries cast doubt on the nature of gang activities with the interrogative "Is this play?"[101] Also, the public and the media often define the situations in terms of interdictions such as "This should not be play" or "You [*bosozoku* as devils] should be terminated." In chapter 7, I will deal with the social conflicts, or "social drama" in a Turnerian sense,[102] arising from these divergent and conflicting definitions of the situation.

Finally, acts performed in the play world of *bosozoku* often have critical consequences in real life and "become part of one's biography forever."[103] That play world is insulated from the reality of everyday life far less than is the world of a theatrical play: the acts in a *bosozoku*'s play world often are irreversible. Certain youths, more than others, are willing to assume the role of *bosozoku* in a play world, that involves great risks.

The *bosozoku* youth usually comes and goes between the primary reality of everyday life and the alternative reality of *bosozoku* play during a certain period of adolescence. His playlike activity, however, sometimes turns into a more serious undertaking than "mere play" and becomes, indeed, a reality. The chapters in Part II will deal with this delicate relationship between fiction and reality.

In short, while the first part of this volume has dealt with the "text" of motorcycle gang activities, the second part will deal with the problems associated with the "context" of the *bosozoku*'s social play.

APPENDIX; LIST OF *BOSOZOKU* BOOKS

1. Urita, Yoshiharu. 1975. *Oretachi Niwa Doyo Shika Nai* (Only Saturday Is Left for Us). Tokyo: Futami Shobo.

2. Ueno, Jiro. 1980. *Dokyumento Bosozoku I* (*Bosozoku* Documentary Part I). Tokyo: Futami Shobo.

3. ———. 1980. *Dokyumento Bosozoku II* (*Bosozoku* Documentary Part II). Tokyo: Futami Shobo.

4. ———. 1980. *Dokyumento Bosozoku III* (*Bosozoku* Documentary Part III). Tokyo: Futami Shobo.

5. Mita, Toru. 1981. *Boso Saizensen* (The Frontline of *Boso* Driving). Tokyo: Rippu Shobo.

6. Nakamura, Kiichiro. 1981. *Bosozoku Shonen* (The *Bosozoku* Boy). Tokyo: Tairiku Shobo.

7. Takemura, Jun, ed. 1980. *Bakuso! Rediisu* (Explosion! Ladies). Tokyo: Tairiku Shobo.

8. Toi, Jugatsu. 1980. *Shakotan Bugi* (Motorcycle Gang Boogies). Tokyo: Kadokawa Shoten.

9. Project Liberty Bell. 1980. *Sakebi: Urakaido No Seishun* (Cry: Adolescence on the Byroads). Tokyo: Taiyo Shobo.

10. Tsuda, Takeshi. 1981. *Namennayo!* (Don't Mess Around With Me!). Tokyo: Shinko Gakufu Shuppan.

11. Dojo, Takeshi. 1982. *Dokyumento Bosozoku* (*Bosozoku* Documentary). Kobe: Kobe Shimbun Shuppan Senta.

12. Nakabe, Hiroshi, ed. 1979. *Bosozoku Hyakunin No Shisso* (The *Boso* Driving of 100 *Bosozoku* Guys). Tokyo: Daisan Shokan.

13. Toi, Jugatsu, ed. 1979. *Tomerareruka Oretachio* (Nobody Can Stop Us). Tokyo: Daisan Shokan.

14. Inukai, Nagatoshi, ed. 1980. *Boso Kaido No Seishun* (Adolescence in *Boso* Driving). Tokyo: Daisan Shokan.

15. Inukai, Nagatoshi. 1981. *Shashinshu: Boso Saizensen* (Picture Book: The Frontline of *Boso* Driving). Tokyo: Daisan Shokan.

All of the following six books are edited by the Group Full Throttle and published by Daisan Shokan.

16. 1979. *Boso Retto '80* (*Bosozoku Archipelago '80*).

17. 1981. *Boso Retto '81* (*Bosozoku Archipelago '81*).

18. 1982. *Boso Retto 1982* (*Bosozoku Archipelago 1982*).

19. 1980. *Boa Appu Bosozoku* (*Bore Up! Bosozoku*).

20. 1980. *Za Bosozoku* (*The Bosozoku*).

21. 1981. *Rediisu* (*Ladies*).

II   *The Natural History*
      of Yankee Style

4   The Birth of the Yankee

Yankee guys spit on the ground.
Yankee guys shave their brows.
Yankee guys shave their hairline.
Yankee guys have a permanent wave.

Yankee guys wear cardigans.
Yankee guys wear sunglasses with slanted lenses.
Yankee guys stroll in groups.
Yankee guys walk bowlegged.

Yankee guys turn out in droves at festivals.
Yankee guys ride on Passols [motorbikes with small displacement]
    with their legs outspread.
Yankee guys do the "shit-squatting."
Yankee guys wear 22.5 cm women's sandals on their 26 cm feet.

"Who cares if we're Yankees!"
            —Tastuo Kamon, *A Song for Yankee Guys*

YANKEE AND *BOSOZOKU*
What Is Yankee Style?

Only questionable folk etymology is provided for the word
"Yankee" (pronounced /yankii/).[1] Some of my non-Yankee friends
who grew up in the Kansai region point to a general impression of vulgarity and gaudiness associated with Americans or American popular
culture as a possible reason for the application of this term to a deviant
sartorial style. The 1984 edition of *The Basic Knowledge of Contemporary
Words* mentions a theory that the term is a corruption of the word
yakuza.[2] But the editor does not supply any further references that
might support this "hunch." When I asked them about the possible
etymology of this word, my informants just laughed and said, "That
doesn't matter at all," or "Yankee is . . . , well, Yankee is Yankee."

In spite of the uncertain origins of the term itself, the referent is quite
clear. It usually refers to a distinctive style adopted by youths as indi-

viduals or as a group. It also means a youthful social type who is often associated with juvenile delinquency, including participation in *boso* driving. In the Kansai region, which includes Kyoto, Kobe, and Osaka, most *bosozoku* are "Yankees"; or as one informant put it, anyone who is considered a *bosozoku* member is also regarded as a "Yankee," although the converse is not always the case. In other regions, a certain number of students and working youths with no college education affect ways of life and sartorial styles similar to those of the Yankees. *Tsuppari* (flamboyant defiance) is the most popular name applied to such life and sartorial styles. *Tsuppari* youngsters, like Yankees, form the population out of which *bosozoku* are most likely to be recruited. There are, indeed, many similarities among the public stereotypes of the *bosozoku*, Yankee, and *tsuppari:* a common denominator of the images of the three social types is the figure of the *ochikobore* (the dropout), who suffers from a chronic inferiority complex.

"Academic Pedigree" and Inferiority Complex

Police records show that the majority of *bosozoku* members are either working youths or high school students. Technical studies on *bosozoku* have found that working youths either perform blue-collar labor or are employed as store clerks. The studies also demonstrate that such youths of high-school age are enrolled in technical schools or institutions of low rank and have no plans to enter college.[3] Tamura's estimate of the highest levels of education or *gakureki* (academic pedigree) reached by various male *bosozoku* members (table 4.1) is based on these findings and, it would appear, applies to those who are committed to gang activity. As we shall see later, these findings seem to extend to Yankees.

Academic writers as well as journalists often infer psychological strain, an "inferiority complex" or "frustration," from data showing the limited education of *bosozoku*, and regard this as *the* proximate cause of participation in gang activity. As we shall see in chapter 7, most arguments of this sort are either mere speculation or are based on dubious empirical foundations. On the other hand, *boso* driving is a subjective experience which creates intrinsic enjoyment, particularly from active social contact and the psychological "flow" experience of high-risk driving: psychological strain arising from limited academic advancement is not the obvious factor here.

The same can be said of the life on the street of Yankees (and *tsuppari*). During my field research, I was often overwhelmed by the colorfulness and vividness of the street life of my informants. Their life on the street corner, indeed, included many opportunities for excitement and enjoyment of "action." It seemed to me that "action-

TABLE 4.1 "Academic Pedigree" of Male *Bosozoku* Members

Academic Pedigree*	A Age Cohort of Adolescents	B *Bosozoku* Youths	B/A
Junior high school graduates	40,000	4,375	11/100
High school dropouts	40,000	6,125	15/100
High school students } High school graduates }	720,000	3,500 } 3,500 } 7,000	1/100
Total	800,000	17,500	2/100

Source: Masayuki Tamura, "Social Psychology of *Bosozoku*," *Seishin Igaku* 25 (1983): 1039.
*Includes current academic status.

seeker"[4] rather than *ochikobore* (dropout) is a more appropriate characterization of the Yankee.

It should be noted, however, that motivation or "attraction" cannot be the only explanation for participation in activities that are fraught with risks. Moreover, individual "motivation" should not be cited as the most important issue where participation in group activities is concerned. We need to explore the life-style of participants, the dynamics of collective behavior, and their "natural history"[5] to understand the contexts of gang activities and the youths' involvement in them.

It is widely acknowledged that *bosozoku* youths often form a "spontaneous youth group"[6] in a community.[7] My field research and case study of the Ukyo Rengo confederation show that *bosozoku* groups in Kyoto were formed on a regional basis. Data from interviews, participant observation, and questionnaires indicate that Yankees also form spontaneous youth groups and engage in very risky activities. As youthful members of a "leisure class," they seek "action" on the street that will contrast with the drabness of a mundane existence. *Bosozoku* activity and other forms of deviant behavior (such as gang rape and fighting) are events that in the short run provide a sense of excitement and direct experience in the otherwise boring life of youths in a urban area. The Yankee's sartorial style symbolizes the seductions and risks inherent in action on the street.

PRIDE AND AMBIVALENCE IN THE YANKEE STYLE
Yankee Fashion

The hallmarks of the Yankees are their characteristic clothes and hair styles. Most male Yankees have permanent waves. The actual patterns vary from the *afuro* (Afro), featuring relatively long hair, to the short, close-cropped look, called *niguro* (Negro) or *panchi* (punch).

Yankees comb their permed hair with brushes that have widely spaced, thick bristles and are called *gaikotsu burashi* (skeleton brushes). Some Yankees who dye or bleach their hair may also shave their temples, an action called *sorikomi* (shaving in). The onomatopoetic counterpart of this word is *pachiki*. Some of the Yankees have thin mustaches, but none of them grow beards.

For their clothes Yankees favor black, white, and primary colors such as red, green, and yellow. Thin cardigans in these colors, knit from synthetic fibers, are among their favorite clothes for spring and autumn wear. Yankees also combine trousers and synthetic shirts of primary colors. A narrow belt is worn with the trousers. As with *bosozoku*, characteristic attire for Yankees includes the *dokajan* (a jumper worn by construction workers), aloha shirts, and *jimbei* (jackets and short pants of thin cotton).[8] Some Yankees wear a *jimbei* with a dragon embroidered on it, or with a flower stitched in gold, silver, or red against a black or white background. On formal occasions, many Yankees wear three-piece lounge suits combined with shirts of primary colors and contrasting ties.

As *A Song for Yankee Guys* comically puts it, many Yankee males wear women's sandals with thin heels, called *pinhiiru* (pin heel) or *pinhii* (a corruption of *pinhiiru*). They make so much noise that Yankees may be heard approaching from a considerable distance, especially when they come in couples or groups. Another kind of footwear Yankees frequently use is enameled shoes, which are mostly black or white. Yankees also prefer sunglasses that are slanted at sharp angles; the lenses may be set at a 45-degree angle to the earpieces, and are called *yonjugodo* (45 degrees).

Female Yankees also have distinctive hair and sartorial styles and use particular kinds of makeup. They have curly hair which is bleached or dyed; the tints include brown, ocher, yellow, and gold. Brighter colors are considered more extreme and described by onomatopoetic terms, such as *kinkin* or *makkinkin* (terribly dyed). Yankee females generally wear heavy makeup, which makes their faces look stern. Such uses of cosmetics are also described by onomatopoetic terms. Seiko, the outspoken leader of the female subsection of the Ukyo Rengo, described her own makeup as follows:

> I had no eyebrows at all. . . . I drew my eyebrows very very sharply [*gingin ni guatto* (an onomatopoetic expression)]. I also used brown rouge for my cheeks, and black rouge for my lips.

The attire of female Yankees includes blouses heavily worked in lamé, knit cardigans of primary colors, and black net stockings; they may also wear tank tops and miniskirts. Like male Yankees, they wear "pin heels." The sandals they wear may have mesh patterns or silver figures stitched into the insteps.

Unnatural Character of the Yankee Style

When I showed several photographs of "Yankees" to Americans, the Americans had difficulty in distinguishing the Yankees from other young Japanese; but once I had explained stylistic differences, they could identify the Yankees readily enough. On the other hand, most of my Japanese friends could recognize Yankees quite easily from the photographs. Some said, "They look quite alike!" Ethnic homogeneity and strict social mores concerning dress highlight the peculiar features of the Yankee style.

In contrast to the United States, with its many ethnic groups and different forms of attire, there is a basic similarity in the appearance and dress of most Japanese. Even though colorful clothing has become popular in Japan, an essential resemblance among most people remains. The Yankee style seems quite obtrusive and conspicuous—*medatsu*—when set against this overall homogeneity of appearance, and this effect is quite intentional.

> NATSUKO: When I first adopted the Yankee style. . . . Well, . . . I think I wanted to attract people's attention [*medachitakatta*]. That was the major reason.
> MASAHIKO: After all, isn't it because we want to be conspicuous [*medachitai*] [that we adopt the Yankee style]?
> TOSHIO: I think it's because people. . . . What shall I say? It's because people will not mess around with those who adopt such styles that we become Yankees.

For male Yankees, obtrusiveness, intimidation, and conspicuousness are achieved by imitating the style of the *yakuza*, who are often called *gokudo* (mobster and "good-for-nothing") in the Kansai region. Several elements of the Yankee style, such as short, permed hair, shaved eyebrows and hairlines, clothing of primary colors, and narrow belts, are apparently borrowed from the *yakuza*. This appearance is especially typical of young *yakuza* on low-level assignments who try to appear menacing and dangerous.

The female version of the Yankee style is, in many cases, also obtrusive and intimidating. Although many Japanese women have their hair permed, it is quite rare for them to bleach or dye it as Yankee girls do. It is also rare for Japanese girls to draw their eyebrows "terribly sharply" or have black rouge on their lips. The Japanese also consider blouses heavily inlaid with lamé to be quite gaudy.

As with the *bosozoku* costume, "unnaturalness" is a keynote of the Yankee style, which in turn is inseparably related to the "unnatural" or aberrant characteristics of Yankee behavior. To most of my non-Yankee friends who had grown up in the Kansai region, the image of the Yankee was closely associated with delinquency or delinquents. The same was true of my informants' view of "Yankees." They frequently defined their own style from the standpoint of the general public. (Some even said they didn't like the word "Yankee," though their style was typical of this group).

> SEIKO: Those who commit delinquent acts. . . . Well, "Yankees" mean those who commit delinquent acts.
> TOSHIO: *Yakuza, uyoku* [members of right-wing organizations], and *bosozoku* . . . All of these groups are "Yankees" from the public viewpoint.

These statements indicate that Yankees have a viewpoint that is similar to that of the general public. Yankees differ, however, in that they have a sort of pride in their distinctive style of attire and way of life. Many of my informants lamented that the explicit message of defiance was somehow diluted recently, because many "ordinary" youths had adopted Yankee styles, and these were becoming a "mere fashion." They also ridiculed their friends who did not have permanent waves.

Permanent waves can be quite conspicuous in Japan where the majority of people have black, straight hair. Indeed, those with short, permed hair are regarded as Yankees, even when wearing other forms of attire, while the converse is seldom the case—those who dress as Yankees but do not have permed hair tend to be regarded as mere hangers-on.

Yankee Style and Group Boundary

Although my informants were relatively tolerant of variations in their friends' attire, they generally rejected those whose hair styles seemed "peculiar" from their standpoint. During the summer of 1983, there were eleven sixteen-year-old members in the Yakyo (Midnight Crazy) group (see table 4.2). Among them Keiichi, Nobuo, Naoyasu, and Tetsutaro were relatively new to the group and did not have perms, though they had committed delinquent acts during their junior high school days, and became acquainted with several senior members of the group. Their peers and senior members frequently ridiculed them for their hair styles. Older group members sometimes stroked their hair and said contemptuously, "Hey! Have your hair permed!" By the winter of 1983, Keiichi and Naoyasu had permed their hair, Nobuo had started combing his hair straight back from his forehead, and Tetsutaro had quit the group.

Such norms are often carried over even among "OB" (old boy) members who only occasionally meet each other. Whether in downtown Kyoto or at parties, those without permanent waves are objects of derision. Seventeen OB members attended a barbecue party held at the house of Shintaro, an ex-leader of the Ukyo Rengo. Among those present there were three, including myself, who did not have perms: Ichiro had a short haircut and Tetsuya wore his hair in the *nyuu ueibu* (new wave)—a long forelock with no tufts below his temples. Other OB's teased them about their "peculiar" hair styles. (I was not teased about my hair, probably because of my age and marginal status as field researcher.) Some of them mussed the hair of Tetsuya and Ichiro, saying, "Hey! What's this hair? It's weird." Ichiro was a few years younger than the others and was openly embarrassed; he could only reply, "Oh! Please, please stop it!" Tetsuya was among the oldest and brushed aside such treatment; he responded angrily, "You know, nowadays, 'Yankee' is a mere fashion. During the old days, delinquents [like us] were Yankees. . . . I still have the guts of a Yankee. Though my hair is like this now, I still have the guts of a Yankee." Then he began to talk about how Yankee styles had changed. When he had finished, Shintaro maintained "I will remain a Yankee even when I get old."

To the youths who acknowledge themselves as "authentic" Yankees, style is meant to symbolize their masculinity and pride of character, as well as a criterion that sets their group's boundary. They admit that their style is deviant and "unnatural," and in its most extreme versions may be regarded as "kid stuff" (*ichibiri*). Younger gang members who shaved their eyebrows and hairlines, or dyed their permed hair, were often teased by older members who considered such measures extreme by comparison with their own more "sophisticated" styles. The older members still had permanent waves but wore more expensive, often imported, clothes, which did not resemble typical Yankee attire. Even the younger Yankees felt they would eventually graduate from the extreme styles they affected at the time. I once asked a fifteen-year-old Yankee boy, "Will you shave your eyebrows and hairline when you are twenty years old?" He replied with some embarrassment, "Only *gokudo* [*yakuza* or mobster] would do such a thing."

Dual Perspective in Yankee Style

The Yankee style, then, is based on a dual standard which includes ambivalent evaluations of one's own appearance. In other words, the Yankee's self-esteem depends upon the equilibrium that is reached between subcultural and conventional standards. On the one hand, the extreme form of the style evokes valor, ultramasculinity, and youthfulness, themes which are borrowed from the *yakuza* image. On the other hand, conventional norms, which contrast with this conspicuous and obtrusive style, have been also internalized in the Yankee's mind. The relationship between conventional and subcultural standards may be compared with that between a figure and the background in a picture. This dual perspective is accentuated by the Yankee's frequent use of onomatopoetic expressions. This extremely vivid style seems to defy ordinary, conventional usage, which on a semantic level is too roundabout and indirect to describe the contrast between figure (Yankee style) and ground (conventional standard). Any consciousness of an "obtrusive" and "conspicuous" (*medatsu*) style, however, presupposes awareness of conventional standards, just as a figure exists against a background, and vice versa.

Comical, and in some ways grotesque, twists take place when *yakuza* themes are added to the Yankee style. They also attest to the dualism in Yankee's dandyism. For example, while many *yakuza* members wear very dark sunglasses, they do not use the comical *yonjugodo* (45 degrees) kind. Nor do they wear women's sandals, though some of them favor *setta,* straw sandals, which make sounds similar to *pinhiiru* (pin heels). Yankees, then, perform a sort of parody of the *yakuza* style, and convey two contradictory messages: "I am not a *yakuza*" and "I am a *yakuza.*" The "Yankee," then, has an ambivalent image, which falls somewhere between the style of outright deviants like the *yakuza* and the norms of the "square" or "ordinary citizen" (*ippan shimin*).

In some ways these performances, which begin as parody, become parodies of themselves; Yankees are irritated at some of them but find some enjoyable. Yankees in Kyoto particularly dislike the style of those from Shiga prefecture, whom they call the *shigasaku* (rustic Shiga bums). As their own area has relatively little night life, this group often comes to Kyoto to seek action and to pick up girls. Often they affect outmoded Yankee fashions. This is regarded as a twofold intrusion, from Shiga onto the territory of the Kyoto Yankees, and as an affront to "authentic" styles. Yankees in Kyoto feel that the *shigasaku* style reflects in exaggerated forms the negative aspects of their own style. In other words, the "rustic Shiga bum" acts as a mirror in which the Yankees of Kyoto find a grotesquely parodied self-image.

> TOSHIO: Country bumpkins. . . . They [rustic Shiga bums] have no taste at all. . . . Fashion, fashion is different. After all, everything is outmoded over there [in Shiga prefecture].

SHIN'ICHIRO: [The guys in] Shiga prefecture are, you know, they are certainly so-called "Yankees."
TAKETOSHI: They're so rustic!
SATO: You mean outmoded?
SHIN'ICHIRO: That's right! I really want to tell them, "Never come to Kyoto again!"

In contrast to such an irritating version of their way of life, some parodies of Yankee style are seen as highly attractive. One is the comic image portrayed in the popular song, *A Song for Yankee Guys*. It achieved great commercial success in Japan, particularly in the Kansai region during the summer of 1983. None of my informants were indignant or angry about the song but rather smiled at its comical portrait of themselves. Informants were also amused by the Yankee styles children in primary schools adopted. Some of them were brothers of their friends and others were boys they saw on the street. When they saw them, my informants said, "They're so cute."

The difference between my informants' attitude toward *shigasaku* and toward *A Song for Yankee Guys* and primary-school Yankees seems to be based on the distance between obvious parody and imitations. *Shigasaku* are too close to my informants' own self-concept to be an enjoyable parody. By contrast, the other two forms keep an "aesthetic distance" from this self-image and thus can be a source of amusement.[9] As the king may amuse himself by watching a clown imitate him, Yankees enjoy popular songs or primary-school variations of their style, because the ambivalence in their own style is presented in an abstract manner.[10]

Ambivalent features of the Yankees' tastes are not simply based on their affinity with the *yakuza* style. They are also closely related to the natural history of the Yankees' way of life. This action-oriented lifestyle begins in junior high school and in many cases continues into adulthood. Yankees are well aware of the temporal limits within which their fashions and activities are developed, and they also have a clear view of their eventual "graduation" from the deviant styles.

THE BIRTH OF THE YANKEE: INITIATION
INTO A DEVIANT LIFE-STYLE
The Onset: Junior High School Days

Most informants agreed that their careers as Yankees began in junior high school and that their development as delinquents followed a gradual process as they interacted with companions of the same age.

SEIKO: It's out of curiosity. At first . . . , in our case, at first we smoked cigarettes [at home], and then smoked in school, . . . dyed our hair, and then had perms.

KEIICHI: We began with cigarettes, and then wore modified school uniforms. After we got accustomed to such stuff, we began having perms.

The order varies because of several factors, including relations between older and younger delinquent cliques in junior high school, and acquaintance with older delinquents through friends or older brothers and sisters. A new and "more serious" step is often taken as a result of imitating the actions of a clique of older Yankees. My informants generally described the sequence of deviant acts as follows:

Smoking at home
Smoking in school
Coming late to school frequently
Wearing modified school uniforms
Dying hair
Having perms
Truancy, staying up late, sleeping over at friends' houses
Inhaling paint thinner or glue
Joining *boso* driving
Using (meth)amphetamine

In many cases, junior high school delinquents experiment and move from less serious to more serious acts (though most of the acts may sound like "kid stuff" for many Americans). A person identifies himself as a "Yankee" and is acknowledged as such when he wears a modified school uniform or has a permanent wave, both of which are prohibited in most junior high schools. The most common school uniforms in Japan include, for male students, a black jacket with a stand-up collar, and black trousers; the females generally wear a dark blue middy blouse and a skirt. The Japanese term for school uniform is usually *gakuseifuku* or *seifuku*. A modified school uniform is called a *gakuran*, from *gaku* for student and *ran*, a vernacular term used by racketeers, and meaning "cloth."[11] For boys the jacket of *gakuran* has longer hems than the ordinary school uniform; various forms have separate names according to the lengths of the hems. They range in size from *churan*, with a medium hem, through *choran*, which is longer, to *yoran*, a *gakuran* with the longest hem. On *gakuran* the stand-up collar generally increases in length with the hem, and the sleeves then have additional gold buttons. While conventional school uniforms have plain black cloth linings, with no pattern, linings of modified uniforms are often red or scarlet, with dragons, flowers, or other figures embroidered on them. School regulations usually require white shirts under the uniform, but Yankees wear colored shifts or T-shirts. Baggy pants with high waists may be combined with the modified uniform. Yankee boys may wear belts of bright colors, sometimes of snake skin or imitations of it.

When they begin to wear modified school uniforms, many Yankee boys also adopt hair styles that are proscribed by school regulations. Such styles include ducktail haircuts, *ooru bakku* (all-back; hair combed straight back from forehead), and permanent waves. Some begin with less conspicuous, relatively long permanent waves curled with tongs, and then experiment with shorter perms. Some may also bleach or dye their hair.

In junior high school many male Yankees apparently borrow elements of style from college cheering groups, which consist entirely of men. Valor, prowess, rigorous discipline, and "guts" are central themes of such groups. Although they favor close-cropped haircuts or permanent waves, they wear school uniforms with long hems, stand-up collars, and many buttons on the sleeves.

The style of college cheering groups is widely imitated by Japanese delinquents in junior high schools, and to a lesser extent by those in high school who engage in school violence and other misconduct. This style is generally called *tsuppari* (flamboyant defiance).[12] Yankees in junior high school affect a version of the *tsuppari* style, which includes valor, prowess, and ultramasculinity as its main themes. The modified school uniforms are then mass-produced and can be easily purchased from retailers.

It is widely assumed that Yankees adopting more radical styles (such as shorter perms and uniforms with longer hems) tend to commit more serious or risky delinquent acts than those who take up less extreme styles. Although only a limited number of junior high school students join in *boso* driving or use amphetamines, their experiments with other activities may go as far as paint-thinner inhaling. Many also become involved in violent outbreaks at school, both against each other and against their teachers.[13]

Yankees also engage in truancy and gather at hangouts (*tamariba*) where they talk, gossip, smoke, and inhale paint thinner or glue. In the absence of parental surveillance, group members use private rooms as hangouts and gather there with their peers. Other groups patronize shops whose owners seek to attract them. There are some Yankees in junior high schools who associate with older groups, on street corners or in *bosozoku* groups, and subsequently go on to *boso* driving or commence amphetamine abuse. But it is after graduation that their deviant acts become more serious as they acquire independent hangouts.

PLATE 7. JUNIOR HIGH SCHOOL YANKEES. In many cases, the career as Yankee begins in junior high school. Modified school uniforms, leather jackets, and *tokkofuku* are worn to express their defiance and bravado. Permed hair, shaved eyebrows, and sunglasses also accentuate their stylistic deviation.

A Turning Point: Entering High School or Getting a Job

Most informants recalled that they began thinking seriously about careers during the third, or last, year of junior high school. By autumn of that year career guidance takes a definite form as parents and teachers inquire more frequently about the choices open to students. Although for a time their action-oriented life-style precludes such considerations, Yankees do become aware of critical turning points so far as careers are concerned. Some disengage themselves entirely from gathering at hangouts and begin to prepare for high school work; informants call them *korotto majime ni naru yatsu* ("old friends who abruptly became straight"). By winter, other Yankees also consult with teachers, to determine whether they should find a job or, on the basis of their academic record, apply for admission to high school.

Graduation from junior high school is also a critical turning point for the patterning of social groups among Yankees. "Old friends who abruptly became straight," and many others who enter high school, leave the cliques; such groups then may dissolve. Those who remain may join the remaining members of other cliques to form a new group.

PLATE 8. YANKEE HANGOUT. Fast-food stores, because they do business until late at night and have big parking lots, are often used as hangouts by Yankees and *bosozoku*. They include those of American origin: e.g., Kentucky Fried Chicken, McDonald's, Mr. Donut. Some Japanese scholars mention this as more evidence of American influence on the Japanese delinquent scene.

In some of these groups or gangs, which are drawn from various cliques, different schools may be represented. Since Japanese school districts are drawn from existing neighborhoods, gangs formed before and after graduation tend to be organized on a regional basis.

Among those who affect the same life-style and join the newly formed gangs are high school students who are not very much dedicated to their studies. Some take part in gang activities after school or during days of truancy. Many of them quit or are expelled from high school, and then become further involved with gangs. In contrast to junior high school, deviant acts in high school often lead to expulsion and arrest. Most Yankees, however, do not plan to enter college and do not regard their high school education as leading to possible job advancement. For example, when their delinquency was reported to their high schools, Michio and Saburo were expelled. Because of his delinquency, Kazuro was suspended from school in the summer of 1983 and was expelled during the winter. Keiichi enrolled in a high school but was sometimes absent. He said that he had no interest in academic work and wanted to get a job; he left school by March 1984.

A number of my informants went to high school at night on a part-time basis; some of them chose this form of education because they failed, or did not take, the entrance examinations for full-time schools. Others said that they wanted to work during the day to earn spending money. Most of these students had little real commitment to academic work. They found night school boring, and it deprived them of night life. Since four years are required to complete night school, as against three years for full-time high schools, some of those who entered part-time studies eventually left the school.

A considerable number of Yankees who get jobs after graduating from junior high school continue their action-oriented life-style. In many cases, they are concerned as much with their leisure pursuits as with job advancement, and for periods of time they frequently choose what may be called "voluntary unemployment." Most of them live with their parents and most of their income may be used for discretionary purposes. Those with their own apartments let them serve as gang hangouts, where Yankees are free from parental surveillance and can engage in illicit pursuit or sleep over. Gang members often hide bottles or cans of paint thinner in such apartments.

Most Yankees at this stage are either blue-collar workers or store clerks. They may also be factory workers, construction workers, bartenders, or waiters. As unskilled workers, they frequently change jobs. Often they leave their work at a time when they wish to join other gang members in group activities.

Among the fifty-six male respondents to the questionnaire, forty-three had jobs when the survey was conducted. Twelve were store clerks (such as gas station attendants, or waiters), ten were factory workers, seven worked in forwarding agencies, six were construction workers or carpenters, and eight listed miscellaneous occupations, such as cooks and delivery men. Their average monthly income was some ¥122,000 ($488). Among the forty-three respondents, twenty expected to change jobs in the future. Of the twenty-two who answered that they would continue at their jobs, at least six had changed employment by the spring of 1984, which was six months after the administration of the questionnaire.

My informants' accounts of job changes fell into two categories. One was "to search for a more profitable and/or suitable job through trial and error," and indeed they actually did so when they were about to "graduate" from the life-style of Yankee. Although some informants also claimed to be seeking work in this way, their actual behavior was of the second sort, "too busy playing to continue on the job." Since social gathering among the Yankees takes place at night, and often lasts until dawn, it was difficult for them to maintain their employment, especially when the group became more active during the summer. Even during periods of diminished activity, jobless members urged those who worked to remain with them at night, and scorned protestations by working members that they had to get up for work in the morning.

In some cases, Yankees got jobs only to support their leisure activities or to purchase expensive goods. Some of my informants had worked as bartenders or waiters at midnight tearooms when they needed to buy vehicles. Although these jobs are quite remunerative, they have a drawback—it is not possible to hang around with other Yankees at night. Often they gave up their nocturnal employment after they had earned the desired sums of money. A Yankee's employment is also often interrupted by police interrogations or incarceration; indeed, excesses in their action-oriented life-style often subject them to police sanctions.

"ACTION" AND THE YANKEE: STREET LIFE OF THE FULL-BLOWN YANKEE
Gathering and Talking (*Tamaru*)

A number of informants characterized the *tamariba* (hangout) as a place "where someone is always there." Yankees rarely gather at hangouts for any specific purpose or according to any plan. Several times I asked Yankees who gathered on street corners in Kyoto, *Nani shiten noya (minna)*? (What are you guys doing here?) The typical answer was, *Nanimo shitehen. Tamatteru dakeya.* (Nothing. We are just gathering).

There are many outdoor places in Kyoto where Yankees can gather at night, including parking lots, fast-food stores, and video arcades.[14] They can purchase canned drinks, iced coffee, and cigarettes and alcoholic beverages from outdoor vending machines.[15] They can also use pay phones to call their friends if necessary. If hungry, they may go to convenience stores or all-night fast-food establishments.

At their hangouts, Yankees stop to talk beside parked motorcycles or cars. They often assume the "shit-squatting" (*unko suwari*) position, which has now come to be known as the "Yankee-squatting" (*yankii suwari*) position. Some of them may drive around near the hangout, but for the most part they only talk and smoke.

Because Yankees are of the same age and from the same neighborhoods, they have common topics of conversation. As graduates of the same junior high schools they gather together nearly every night. It is thus possible for others in the group to join conversations at any juncture; regulars who came later than usual or were absent for a day might be asked, "Hey! Why are you late?" or "Why didn't you come last night?"

An uneasy pause may ensue when suitable topics for conversation are exhausted. At such points, a member may propose to go "somewhere," notably to a video arcade, a park on the hill, Kawaramachi Avenue, Biwako Lake in Shiga Prefecture, or to a seaside area of Fukui Prefecture. To take such excursions on bikes or cars is more thrilling than mere conversation, and furthermore, something exciting may happen in such places. But it may take one or two hours for some or all of the Yankees to agree and actually leave the hangout. Some may object to the proposal and mention other places. Some may object that they must be back at work in the morning. In many cases, some will not explicitly reject such plans, but will demur and say that the weather is too cold, they are too tired, or they don't feel like going. Unless the member who proposed the plan insists, his motion may be suspended unless he takes up the suggestion later. Meanwhile conversation goes on, and the one who proposed an excursion may well forget about it himself.

Even if some or all of the members present agree to the plan, it may take another hour or two for it actually to be carried out. Some boys may not have vehicles and will call friends to borrow theirs. Others may not have money to buy gasoline and will ask friends for a loan; or they may have to go back home for money. In some cases they may use a vinyl tube, or a small manual siphon, which ordinarily is used with a kerosene heater, to "swipe" (*pakuru*) gasoline from others' vehicles.

In hangouts, events usually follow this course—not according to prearranged plans, but from ideas or impulses that originate with one member. Otherwise, Yankees just gather and talk. Because a group usually consists of a number of boys of the same age, there is no clear leader or other distinction of roles. Although Yankees claim to feel at home and like to relax in such social settings, the pervasive tone of their gatherings is boredom and the vague anticipation of something that may happen.[16] *Tamaru* (to gather) in *tamariba* (a hangout) is an intransitive verb with the connotation of stagnation, as with standing water or puddles by the roadside. In this context it seems particularly apt, as it refers to inactive gatherings without clear-cut plans and little differentiation of positions within the group. Most of the topics of conversation also seem trivial and monotonous. Yankees exchange rumors and gossip, talk about friends and girls, discuss vehicles and their modifications, and concern themselves with recent fashions. Anyone who accompanies them, however, still notices that after sever-

al nights the conversation will turn to story-telling and vivid reminiscences, generally of something exciting the Yankees encountered
somewhere in their search for action. Fights and instances of picking
up girls are outstanding examples of this genre, and command the attention of Yankees gathered in their hangouts.

Beating Up (*Shibaku*)

At hangouts, in video arcades, or on the street, groups of Yankees
sometimes stare at each other with knitted eyebrows and wry expressions. A number of my informants said that they often "felt"
others looking at them when they passed Yankees they did not know.
Menchi kiru (staring at each other) is an expression referring to this
preliminary confrontation. Clothing and hair styles have important
roles in inciting fights among Yankees. Short permanent waves seem
to signify, "I will take up the gauntlet at any time," especially when
combined with certain styles of clothing.

> EIKICHI: The permanent wave is the sign of fighting. No surfers
> dare fight. If two Yankees, if two men who have perms, en-
> counter each other, that means they are ready to fight.
> TOSHIO: Those who have perms have pride, a pride [which can be
> stated as] "I don't want to be seen as a sissy."

According to my informants, utterances before fights include "Who
do you think you're looking at!" "What are you staring at!" (or
"Whachulookingat!")[17] (*Nani menchi kittennen!*) and "Hey! You putting on a [bold] front!" (*Nani ikitten noya!*) Eye contact and aggressive
words do not necessarily lead to fighting, in which the Yankees "beat
up" (*shibaku*) each other. The provocative words and gestures are
often followed by such inquiries as "How old are you?" "Where are
you from?" "Which grade are you in?" and "Which junior high do
you attend?" or "Which junior high did you graduate from?" If it turns
out that both parties have the same acquaintances they may not fight
each other. Fights can also be avoided when there is an age difference
between the two parties.

Age is the most important consideration that precludes actual fights
among Yankees. It is generally assumed that older gang members
should not challenge younger ones, and vice versa. When fights occur,
they should involve Yankees of the same age, or, more precisely, of the
same junior high school grade. The series of Yankee cliques in junior
high schools embody an age hierarchy, from older members, to those
of the same age, to younger ones. This is also the case with cliques
where members are from different schools. Many times Yankees be-

come friends with one or more Yankees of the same grade but from other junior high schools. This criterion indicates the relative social positions of Yankees even after graduation.

In hangouts, extravagant descriptions of gang fights almost invariably lead to inquiries about the opponent's age (e.g., "How old was he?") or grade (e.g., "Wasn't he one grade younger than you?") particularly for opponents who are not well known. Those who have knowingly defeated younger opponents are often ridiculed, especially if they lost such fights. One who boasts of having defeated the younger opponent is regarded as overvaluing an easy fight. Although it may seem unusual, many informants claimed it was hardly possible to lose fights with junior members; they seemed to believe that there was an exact correlation between age and fighting ability.

In spite of such ingrained beliefs, sometimes fights do take place between Yankees of different ages. In some cases, the offenses are so great that age differences are disregarded; the fight then is kept secret, even by the victors, from other members. In other cases, incitement occurs so rapidly that age differences cannot be assessed. After a drinking party on Kawaramachi, a fight broke out in which I was involved along with Shintaro, Eikichi, and Matsuichiro. A sarcastic comment from someone in an opposing group set off the conflict in a moment. Even then, the combatants took close cognizance of age differences. Matsuichiro attempted to settle matters, together with me, and he said to the opponents, who looked eighteen or nineteen years old, "What do you think you are doing to those older than you are?" On the next day, when we were drinking and chatting about the fight, Shintaro said, "I beat 'em up because I thought it was humiliating to be battered by younger guys."

Fights among the Yankee guys sometimes, though not always, realign cliques, especially when members of the same age are involved. Often groups restructured in this way develop quite intimate bonds.[18]

> SABURO: First, we stare at each other, eye to eye, and then a fight begins. We say, "Hey! What do you want?" After the fight, we will say, "Where are you from? Oh, yeah? Are you a friend of that guy? I know him, too." There is a network of buddies [of the same age] all over Kyoto. We become buddies through fights.

Such a friendship network can be formed only among the Yankees. It is regarded as somewhat dishonorable to assault surfers, or other youthful types, such as punks or rock'n'rollers, who are supposed to be effeminate (*hetare*) and inferior to the Yankees in fighting ability.

Nonetheless, Yankees sometimes fight them because of some slight difference, or merely for fun. On such occasions, the Yankees do not clearly identify themselves, and generally leave before police can be called in.

When Yankees fight each other, there is little likelihood that the matter will be reported to the police, even if someone is seriously injured or a vehicle is severely damaged. It is regarded as a disgrace for Yankees to report such matters to the police. Yankees also avoid calling for police intervention because they are known to the authorities themselves for their own deviant behavior.[19]

> KAZUYA: If the opponent is also a Yankee, it is humiliating for us to complain to the police. It's a disgrace.
> SATO: Do you mean it's a disgrace to say, "I lost the fight?"
> KAZUYA: Yeah, to say, "I lost the fight."
> TOSHIO: We have to endure such a disadvantage if we are Yankees. . . . It's no good for those who have perms to lodge a complaint with the police.
> KAZUYA: Well, if you place complaints before the police, you will be regarded as a sissy [*hetare*] from that moment.

Thus, while the Yankee style sets off violence in some cases, it also limits the possible number of victims within the category of youths, and serves to prevent fights with other youths. Although the selective mechanism does not always work effectively, it certainly serves to circumscribe the range of deviant behavior. A similar mechanism can be found in Yankee youths' effort at sexual exploitation.

Picking Up (*Hikkakeru*)

By 10:30 P.M., the shutters have been put up on most stores facing Kawaramachi Avenue. At the arcades above the sidewalks of the shopping district most fluorescent lights have been turned off, and only street-lamps and signboards on stores cast light onto the streets. Although the side streets are still crowded with customers from the numerous bars and taverns in the area, there are fewer people on Kawaramachi Avenue than earlier in the day.

At about this time of night, Yankee boys gather on the avenue and, in smaller numbers, on Shijo Street between Kawaramachi and Higashioji Avenues. Usually there are no more than five Yankees in a group. Most of them stand or crouch around one or two automobiles. Some of them may sit sideways in their driver's seats, with the door open and their feet on the pavement; they listen to music from car stereos. Many of them remain around the cars and just chat and smoke.

They also idly watch the automobiles passing before them. When girls with curly, dyed hair pass by, most of them turn toward them. Some of the guys follow them and exchange a few comments; they may offer the girls rides or tea. In many cases, their overtures fail. But occasionally the girls are picked up and get into the cars, particularly if the automobiles seem "neat" and luxurious. The girls rarely walk alone, and those who are picked up generally are in pairs.

As the Yankee's permed haircut is the sign of a fighting spirit, dyed or bleached curly hair indicates one who is willing to be "picked up" (*nanpa sareru* or *hikkakerareru*). Other visual signs that are important in such encounters are fashions associated with female Yankees, heavy makeup, and a pair of girls.

Michio, Mako (his fiancée), and Ichiro describe the typical sequence of "picking up."

> MICHIO: Just come and see Kawaramachi Avenue. If girls walk at midnight or even two o'clock, that's the sign [stating], "Ok, please pick me up."
>
> MAKO: Yeah, they usually have heavy makeup.
>
> MICHIO: From midnight until two or three o'clock, you know, if the girls walk in couples . . . though they must not have anything specific to do there. . . . When the guys talk to the chicks, the chicks often say, "Eh?" [Here Michio imitated the strained facial expression by which the girls show astonishment].
>
> ICHIRO: Right. They say, "Eh?" A number of girls of that sort must be walking right now.
>
> MAKO: That's right.
>
> MICHIO: If we say, "Why don't you drive somewhere with us?" the pretty one asks the other, "Well, what shall we do?" One of the two is sure to be an ugly cow.
>
> ICHIRO: Yeah, and it's the ugly one who shows reluctance.
>
> MICHIO: The ugly cow must be reluctant . . . because, you know, she knows she will be ignored by the guys!

Kawaramachi Avenue is a stage or "scene"[20] for sexual adventures by Yankee boys and girls. In an anonymous urban setting, the Yankee style indicates a potential partner for a night. Yankee guys rarely try to pick up "ordinary girls" (*futsu no ko*), or those who look like college girls. Yankee boys think it quite difficult to pick up such girls because they have little in common with them. Being turned down by such girls is also embarrassing and damaging to their sense of masculinity.

> KEIJI: It's so easy to pick up Yankee girls.
>
> KENTARO: They are loose. Besides, Yankee girls are willing to ride in *shakotan* [low-slung] cars. They actually do. [On the other

hand] college girls will say, "What!" [with a contemptuous tone]. That's why we don't try to pick 'em up.

EIKICHI: It's easy to pick up girls. Well, it may depend on the girls. . . . There must be many college girls who are loose. . . . But Yankee girls share many topics of conversation with us. It's easier to pick 'em up.

Yankee girls seem to have similar conceptions of different kinds of boys. Seiko and Naoko had this to say about college boys.

SATO: What do you think about college students, I mean, college boys.

SEIKO: College boys. . . . Oh, they are weird.

SATO: "Weird"? Why?

NAOKO: They are weird. They look gloomy somehow.

SATO: You mean "dismal"?

NAOKO: I can't even guess what's going on inside their heads. I may commit suicide, ha-ha! I would be so depressed if I went steady with a college boy. I might become depressed and commit suicide! I don't like square boys.

SEIKO: Yeah, I can't even guess what's going on inside square boys' heads.

For a number of Yankee guys, more immediate rapport and the high probability of success are not the only reasons to pick up Yankee girls; they are also chosen because Yankee girls are not as likely to file charges of rape. *Gombo* in Yankee jargon means rape or gang rape. Among my informants, vivid reactions from other members were elicited when stories of *gombo* were brought up. Usually such recollections were called forth when someone teased another group member about his cowardly or comical behavior during a gang rape. Others would mock someone's effort, after the rape, to calm the girl or persuade her not to go to the police. Such stories generally would be concluded with loud laughter, and someone would observe, "I would have been arrested several times, if they'd been ordinary girls." Tales of sexual exploitation seem to affirm a sense of masculinity while strengthening group bonds through feelings of common complicity. Comic accounts of such incidents also seem to neutralize any feelings of remorse or guilt that perpetrators of the rape may have. My informants seemed embarrassed when rumors circulated about the marriage of girls they had raped. Similarly, while the behavior of group members might be the object of mockery, the victims generally are not held up to ridicule.

Although informants categorically regarded Yankee girls as loose, it was not uncommon for them to go steady with these girls. The boys

PLATE 9. GATHERING AND TALKING. Yankees often make excursions to Kawaramachi Avenue, the main street of Kyoto. Gathering and talking there, they wait for something to happen.

seemed to regard the girls they went with as exceptions. A girl who would go steady with a group member was regarded as "his girl"; she could not be approached by others and was seldom a subject of malicious gossip. There are, however, a number of girls who are known as especially loose. They are called *panpan* (prostitute) or *zubozubo* (public toilet). They became the objects of cursory love affairs or frank sexual exploitation.

Tamaru (Gathering and Talking) vs. *Iwasu* (Action)

Humdrum gathering at their hangouts leads to an urge for action on the part of Yankee boys. *Iwasu* is a transitive verb and in a generic sense designates "action" of many sorts.

> SHIN'ICHIRO: We use *"iwasu"* to describe everything, don't we? For example, "Let's pick up and rape [*iwasu*] a girl," "Let's beat [*iwasu*] that guy," "Let's make a big noise [*iwasu*] on Kawaramachi [Avenue] with our bikes," or "Let's swipe [*iwasu*] a motorcycle."

While *tamaru* (gathering and talking), an intransitive verb, refers to inactive and passive forms of existence, *iwasu* involves active and ag-

PLATE 10. LOOKING FOR PICKUPS. One of the reasons why Yankee boys often go to Kawaramachi Avenue is that they may find "chicks" there. Dyed or bleached curly hair, a typical Yankee style for girls, indicates a girl who is ready to be "picked up," or at least is so regarded by Yankee boys.

gressive undertakings. Although it is often accompanied by considerable risks, it provides Yankee guys with exciting and thrilling experiences. One may become an agent of action rather than a passive interlocutor in group conversations; and one may make "something" happen by oneself.[21] Subsequently, one's masculinity and prestige as an "action-seeker" are enhanced or reaffirmed when the story is told to others, and the presentation is further dramatized with gestures and onomatopoetic expressions.[22] Such oral narratives reduce both the accompanying fears and the sense of remorse.

Fighting and sexual exploitation are the most usual forms of "action." The anonymity of an urban milieu encourages deviant acts on the part of youths with relatively little stake in conformity. Aberrant behavior also arises from assumptions inherent in the deviant style. But the youths' search for action is not free from any kind of rules. The excessive risks of deviant acts are accepted because of several subcultural assumptions. The age hierarchy limits the scope of possible fights. Violence and sexual exploitation are mostly meant to affect only other Yankees. Spatial and temporal distinctions, especially those setting youths apart from others, also circumscribe the range of victimization:[23] few people other than Yankees visit their hangouts or Kawaramachi Avenue at midnight. In *boso* driving—"action" on a massive scale—these informal control mechanisms do not always work; youths may lose control of the action and the number of victims may mount.

5   From Yankee to *Bosozoku*

SABURO: In the old days, say, ten years ago, college students may have been special people. But now, everybody can be a college student. Right? About half of the kids in high school go to college. So, there's no prestige in being a college student any more.

—Personal interview

KENTARO: It's better not to go to college, if it is a third-rate one. The most important thing is to know the world; the younger the better. What's really important is interpersonal relationships. . . . You've got to know how to get along with other people. . . . Compare a guy who's really bright and graduated from Tokyo University with another guy who graduates from a junior high school and becomes a *sushi* chef. . . . Suppose the guy who graduated from junior high has his own restaurant. Well, he might not be able to earn as much as the college businessman for the first few years. But some of the college graduates, even the ones from Tokyo University, stay office workers for their whole life, if they can't get along with other people, if they're disliked.

—Personal interview

Not all of the Yankees in a hangout are "into action." Some go to gatherings only occasionally. Some leave to go home or to be at work the next day. Some may not have access to vehicles. It is also quite difficult to pick up girls if there are a large number of guys gathered in a group on Kawaramachi Avenue. In most cases action-type activities by Yankees involve a few people of the same age and are mostly episodic, spasmodic events in their lives. Weekly meetings and *boso* driving are exceptional in that they involve a great number of youths of different ages and that they are carried out on a relatively regular basis. Through these gang activities, Yankees are able to make something happen on a massive scale.

Boso driving, a grand-scale action, is also peculiar in its clear contrast to "gathering and talking." In contrast to the inactive social interaction among Yankees in their hangouts, the interaction in *boso* driving is ordered and organized. During *boso* driving, roles are differentiated, the flow of time is synchronized, and resources are structured for the sake of a single, simple, and clear-cut purpose.

Bosozoku activities, then, provide Yankee youths with exceptional types of excitement and enjoyment. The attraction of gang activities itself is, however, only one of the factors which transform Yankees into *bosozoku*. Several features of Yankee life-style (rather than any "inferiority complex" or resentment) are conducive to the metamorphosis of Yankees, more than other youths, into *bosozoku*. It should be noted that the metamorphosis also depends upon the coherence of the "frame" of *bosozoku* play, which in turn depends largely upon the articulateness of the group process. When, and only when, specific *bosozoku* groups can mobilize a considerable number of participants into *boso* driving and weekly meetings on a regular basis, can Yankees sustain coherent playlike definitions of the situations and transform themselves into masculine and daredevil *bosozoku*.

RESOURCES FOR MAKE-BELIEVE PLAY

Garvey's classification of the resources used for "make-believe play" or "pretend play" offers a framework in which we can categorize several conditions underlying the metamorphosis from Yankee to *bosozoku*. Garvey defines pretending as a "voluntary transformation of the Here and Now, the You and Me, and the This or That, along with any potential for action that these components of a situation may have." She maintains that there are three resources for such pretending or "make-believe play": (1) roles or identities, (2) plans for action or story lines, and (3) objects and settings.[1] Her analysis is mainly limited to communicative aspects of make-believe play by small children.[2] Different motivations for make-believe and "real" play must be taken into account when one applies her scheme to an analysis of the transformation of Yankees into *bosozoku*, which involves a greater number of participants and far more risks than the pretend play of preadolescent children.

Roles/Identities

Small children take on the identities of various toy animals, people, and imaginary beings when they are involved in pretend play.[3] A number of adolescents and adults also often engage in "fantasy role-playing games," where they are transformed into various real and imaginary creatures.[4] Although there is, of course, a much greater latitude in choices of imaginative roles in a make-believe world than in the choice of "social roles" in the mundane world, the role choice in pretend play is not a random process. Nor is it totally determined by situational factors specific to the play world. It may depend on such factors as the stage of cognitive and social development[5] or individual predispositions and skills.[6] In many cases, there are certain correlations between one's roles or identities in the mundane world and his transformed roles or identities within a play world.

Bosozoku as "Action-Seeker." One of the reasons why Yankees, more than other youths, take on the *bosozoku* role is that the *bosozoku* provides them with an idealized self-image which is not totally alien to their self-concept and life-style as Yankees. The *bosozoku* provides the youths with an alternative self-concept that is more attractive than that of the Yankee.

The "Yankee" has an ambivalent image, which falls somewhere between the image of outright deviants like *yakuza,* and that of the "square" or "ordinary citizen" (*ippan shimin*). The negative aspect of the Yankee image is most typically expressed by the word *gurentai* (hoodlum), which informants often applied to themselves in self-deprecation. Toshio, who tended to take the position of a cynical observer, held that "*Bosozoku* minus cars equals *gurentai.*" The extremely theatrical and dramatic quality of the *bosozoku* allows youths to overcome the ambivalent *gurentai* features of the Yankee image.

> TORAO: Of course, *bosozoku* are better-looking [than *gurentai*]. What shall I say? *Gurentai* sounds like those who only perform wrongdoing. There are some *bosozoku* who also do good things.
> KEIICHI: "*Bosozoku*" are those who actually speed. . . . *Gurentai* sounds very bad.
> HACHIRO: I will get angry if someone says that our group is a *gurentai*. Because, you know, we really speed.

Although *bosozoku* youths are clearly aware that their role is bracketed within a limited time and space, in this new role they can divest themselves of the negative images of Yankees or *gurentai*. By transforming themselves into *bosozoku,* the heroic or picaresque character associated with the images of the *koha* and the picaro, Yankees can express their focal concerns which evolve around "action" (e.g., valor, prowess, masculinity, resourcefulness) in an almost ideal manner. Yankees can act out the almost idealized image of "action-seeker" by assuming the role of *bosozoku*.

Bosozoku and "Delinquent." Yankees who are subjected to police sanctions and resent the designation "delinquent" may also find *bosozoku* activity an outlet for their resentment and vindictive inclinations. Masahiko was an ex-leader of the Ukyo Rengo and was incarcerated in training schools twice. He discussed the *bosozoku* and the first impressions he formed after seeing a *boso* drive in Kyoto:

> My heart throbbed at that time. After all, delinquents [*furyo*] are connected with the *bosozoku*. . . . Most delinquents eventually become *bosozoku*. . . . When I saw it [a *boso* drive] . . . How can I say it? I felt that they [the *bosozoku*] were similar to me. My heart beat, beat so fast. . . . I cried in my heart, "I want to be like that!"

Junko, the founder of the female subsection of the Ukyo Rengo, was more explicit. She was incarcerated in a Juvenile Classification Home once.

> We are hated by the public. . . . I wanted to say to them, "We are *bosozoku!*" I wanted to show them our youthfulness. . . . I wanted to make people understand what was in our minds. People may hate us. They do hate us. But I wanted to say to them, "Our minds are similar to yours!"

Bosozoku activities also provide the Yankees with the opportunity to challenge outright the police and other social control agencies. While the police are overwhelming and unchallenged in everyday life, they can be beaten and mocked within the bracketed context of *boso* driving. The usual role relationship between the police and Yankees is temporarily inverted in the make-believe world. In 1980, during the heyday of *bosozoku* activity, some informants crashed their vehicles into police squad cars. They also went to the street outside the Juvenile Classification Home in Kyoto, to create an uproar and cheer fellow members who were detained there.[7]

Bosozoku and "Dropout." It should be noted that my informants' resentment, when in *bosozoku* activity, did not seem to be related to an "inferiority complex," or "frustration" arising from lack of academic advancement. Their resentment, when shown, was more specifically derived from conflicts with the police or with other *bosozoku* groups. The fictive identity of the *bosozoku*, then, does not seem to constitute an identity alternative to the negative identity as *ochikobore* (dropout) for most Yankees.

The academic achievement of my informants is quite low as compared to the general pattern in Japan. Among the sixty-six respondents to my questionnaire, only five (7.6 percent) were then enrolled in full-

time high school and seven (10.6 percent) in part-time high school.
The majority of them, thirty-eight (57.6 percent), were junior high
school graduates.[8] In the last decade, in Japan as a whole, over 94 percent of the junior high school graduates have gone on to high school,
and more than 30 percent of the high school students have gone on to
college. Only about 6 percent of an age cohort eventually become high
school dropouts.[9]

My informants are clearly aware that they are in a minority with regard to "academic pedigree," or *gakureki,* and did have an inferiority
complex about their failure to attain the common level of schooling.
But it is quite unlikely that they were overwhelmingly preoccupied by
the problem of their poor academic pedigree. In formal interviews or
casual conversations, none of my informants, on their own initiative,
mentioned psychological stress or academic limitations as the basic
motive for participation in *boso* driving. Only when I asked them, "Do
you think such an inferiority complex has something to do with your
gang activity?" some said, "That may be possible," or "That may be a
reason." But others said, "That's nonsense." For many of my informants, enjoyment of gang activity was a proximate, sufficient
motive.[10] At a hangout for the Police, a subgroup of the Ukyo Rengo, I
overheard Toshihiko and two other members talking about this issue.
Toshihiko had just been released from the Kyoto Juvenile Classification Home.

> TOSHIHIKO: Why do we speed on *boso* drives? I don't know the
> reason very well. People often say it must be because we want
> to forget pent-up feelings. But I don't think it's true.
> HACHIRO: It's somehow addictive. . . .
> TOSHIHIKO: When I was asked by an investigator of the Family
> Court about that, I said, "I think it's because we want to attract
> people's attention [*medachitai kara*]. . . . After all, isn't it be-
> cause we want to be seen by people and we want to intimidate
> them by the exhaust noises of our bikes? [Hachiro and another
> boy nodded to Toshihiko.]

Kyozaburo, a high school dropout, was one of the most enthusiastic
participants in the *boso* driving. When I asked him and two other informants whether they thought there was a relationship between *boso*
driving and an inferiority complex regarding academic pedigree, he responded with,

> No way! It's the ones who work hard but can't do well at school
> who have the "complex." We just don't like school work. What
> we do has no relation to any inferiority complex.

While *bosozoku* youths may have an inferiority complex about their failure to attain an ordinary level of schooling or to earn the symbolic title of "high school graduate," they are quite skeptical of the practical and economic utility of higher education. They say that even a person who graduates from high school or college is likely to become a mere "salary man" (salaried worker; office worker) who is dependent on his firm. They also believe that they can earn as much or even more than those with a higher education, if they have "learned a trade" and can make their own way in the world.[11]

Although many of my informants were somewhat jealous of college students, whom they characterized as "playing around and living at ease and comfort at the expense of their parents," they did not regard themselves, finally, as losers. Nor did they strike me as being "traumatized and having a sense of defeat"[12] or having a serious "sense of defeatism in comparing themselves with students of high achievement, and with the social elite."[13] A considerable number of them, in fact, seemed to have richer lives (in all senses of the word) than white-collar workers with college degrees who are likely to be transferred to branches in outlying regions several times during their careers.[14]

Since Yankees regard the economic benefits of higher education as meager, they tend to be less committed to academic work in high schools. Among the seven high school students, none had college plans or thought that a high school diploma was a crucial qualification for a better job.

Nobuo and Keiichi, fringe members of the Ukyo Rengo, were high school students who attended high schools where, they say, "anybody can get in." They went to these schools partly because of their parents' wishes and partly because "everybody goes to high school now." But, they said, they didn't have much interest in school and frequently stayed out until midnight or even later with Naoyasu and Tetsutaro, other members of the Ukyo Rengo.

> NOBUO: The ones who start working right after junior high school change jobs one after the other. Right? They change their jobs [frequently]. And in the end, they find better jobs.
> KEIICHI: In the end, they find better jobs. A teacher in my junior high told us that there's no difference in jobs, whether you're a junior or senior high school graduate. It doesn't matter at all if we get jobs after high school. If you're a junior high graduate, you'll work for three years and get promoted. But if you start work after getting out of high school, you have to start at the bottom. So, there's no difference at all.

For high school students who feel imprisoned in classrooms for long tedious hours, the seemingly carefree lives of their *bosozoku* friends who play around with the money they get from occasional work look very attractive. The tidy sum of money their friends have is also a great incentive for the students, who have to rely on allowances given by their parents. In an interview, Keiichi explained, "I'd rather quit school. . . . If I [worked and] had money, I'd be able to do whatever I want. I could buy a motorbike and other things." He actually did drop out of high school by February 1984, although it took him a few months after that to decide to get a job. In the meantime, he spent his time "hanging out" with peers and was even injured in a fight.

My informants were also quite optimistic about the availability of jobs. They were able to get jobs in the large complex of food markets in Kyoto almost any time they wanted. There were also several factories located in the western part of the city where they could always apply for work. Occasionally small firms or stores run by parents or relatives of members of the Ukyo Rengo needed part- or full-time employees. Although in many cases my informants had to change jobs several times until they found suitable and profitable employment, they were able to sustain their relatively affluent consumer life-style with these jobs.

The Yankees' low academic achievement and their transformation into *bosozoku*, then, seem to be related to each other not by psychological strain but by little "stake in conformity." Yankees generally have relatively little commitment to academic advancement or jobs. Most of them do not plan to enter college, and the stigma of *bosozoku* membership does not greatly threaten their employment. Many Yankees have already encountered legal sanctions of some sort during their junior high school days; moreover, whatever punishment is administered to minors in Japan is relatively lenient.

Bosozoku as Working-Class. Two anonymous reviewers of an earlier version of this volume were perplexed with my treatment of the class origins of the Yankee/*bosozoku*. Indeed, it may seem to Western readers that I am presenting an incoherent picture of the *bosozoku*. The motorcycle gang may look middle-class in earlier parts of this volume and disproportionately working-class afterwards. Similarly, to those who are accustomed to a class theory of delinquency, the image of affluent and well-groomed Yankee/corner boys may look too middle-class and not sufficiently working-class. The Western literature on crime and delinquency is often heavily colored by class themes: e.g., structural or psychological strain arising from a lower class position, resistance to dominant middle-class values, attempts to reclaim community and reassert traditional working-class values.

What is remarkable about academic as well as popular conceptions of *bosozoku* in Japan is the lack of such class themes. As I will show in chapter 7, even though the mass media and academic literature frequently depict deviant styles of *bosozoku* as exemplifying resistance against meritocracy, the subordinate position of *bosozoku* in the meritocratic society is rarely attributed to their handicaps arising from ascribed class position. On the contrary, the Japanese public and scholars have indicated perplexity with the data showing that the majority of the *bosozoku* are from middle-class families.

Themes related to class antagonism are also absent in the public self-presentation by motorcycle gang members, as we have seen in chapter 3. Nor do *bosozoku* youths attempt to achieve symbolic status-mobility through their performances. They rather play at self-parody of the self- or media-created images of the *boso* as the picaro or hero. While they, like the general public and the media, sometimes mention frustration arising from inferior educational background, "class-conscious" statements are lacking both in their self-glorification and self-justification.

The same applies to my informants. Although I could not collect detailed information about socioeconomic status of their parents, most of their families are not poor and some are well-to-do.[15] I never heard them make class-conscious statements as explanations of their deviant behavior, although some of them commented enviously on the luxurious life or promising prospects of their *bosozoku* fellows from affluent families.

It seems to me that *bosozoku* activity is a matter of taste and a stake in conformity rather than of class origin. Taste differentiation among Japanese youths is more closely related to locality, academic attainment, and parents' or youths' own occupation than to socioeconomic status, race, or opportunity structure. Although the focal concerns found in the taste of Japanese corner boys (e.g., deliberate vulgarity, rough and tough masculinity) have much in common with those in lower- or working-class cultures in Western nations, I do not think similar characterization in class terms is readily applicable to Japan.

In short, while many motorcycle gangs may be categorized as working-class or blue-collar in terms of their occupations and tastes, class-consciousness or psychological strain play little, if any, part in forming their deviant behavior.

Plans

According to Garvey, a plan or "action plan" in a pretend play consists of "a sequence of events or actions performed or experienced by a cast of functional roles."[16] She mainly refers to improvisational performances by small children during a relatively short span of time. A more complex causal chain must be taken into account when we examine the schemes of action underlying a Yankee's metamorphosis into a *bosozoku*.

Ready-made Plans. Garvey suspects that children "have a repertoire of action sequences that can be indicated quite economically and then played out with little discussion of what to do next."[17] Such action sequences implicit in a certain plan also presuppose characteristic settings and props. The mass media provide Yankees with a set of action plans which can be subsumed under a general action plan, "Playing *Bosozoku*."[18] The action plans or "subplans" constituting the general plan include such activities as a session of *boso* driving, acrobatic performances during a *boso* drive, roll call in the weekly meeting, posing in "photo-shooting meetings." Each of these subplans is combined with characteristic props and gestures. Each subplan also includes a vocabulary of words referring to the stage props, gestures, and subjective experiences during a performance. The action plans form a nationwide mannerism and constitute, so to speak, a set of ready-made plans. Yankees learn the ready-made plans from journalists' publications that stress the romance and glamor of *bosozoku* activities.

The Ukyo Rengo appeared six times in journalists' publications. The following excerpt from Eikichi's statement in *Bore Up! Bosozoku* is one of them. The bravado and defiance in this excerpt illustrate the role the mass media play in providing ready-made action plans.

UKYO RENGO KILLA—KYOTO
Glory on Saturday Night from Fights and *Boso* Driving

> Motorcycles—50
> Cars—60
> Ladies [Female *Bosozoku*]—30
> Turf—Kyoto as a whole
> A [Pride in our Group]—Guts! We had a big fight with a *bosozoku* group from Osaka. They had 14 guys, and there were 7 of us. We cracked their heads with iron pipes. Fifteen members were arrested and sent to a Juvenile Classification Home. Shortly after leaving the Home, we crashed 60 cars [of other *bosozoku* groups] and became the strongest TEAM [*sic*] in Kyoto.

к [about the police]—We are ready to exterminate those policemen who are dependent on the establishment.[19]

If there are *bosozoku* groups in one's neighborhood, their activities
present action plans of "Playing *Bosozoku*" in more concrete and personified forms than the ones presented in the media. Some Yankees
may also participate as passengers in *boso* driving by senior Yankees
and learn the action plans through actual experience.

The ready-made action plans offered by the media and presented by
the neighborhood gangs constitute a common stock of knowledge and
schemes of action for younger Yankees. By referring to the knowledge
and action schemes, younger Yankees can easily create a make-believe
world of their own with little discussion about what to do next and
who shall take which functional roles.

Street Corner Narratives. Yankees, however, often talk about and
elaborate on the action plans before they translate them into behavior.
They also narrate actions as reminiscences after they take place. In
many cases the discussions and story-telling arouse a considerable degree of excitement. While ready-made plans suggest general lines of
action, the story-telling personifies them by adding details of specific
actions by specific members and relating them to their personal histories. In other words, the street-corner narratives impart communal
and esoteric significance to the actions.[20] Talk about *bosozoku*-related
actions constitutes one of the most notable genres of Yankees' narratives on the street. Other notable genres include fights, women and
sexual exploitation, cars, and rumors and gossip about the underworld
of the *yakuza*. The otherwise inactive gathering among Yankees is ani-
mated when the conversation turns to story-telling and vivid
reminiscences about one's own or others' "action." The street-corner
narrative is one of the most crucial elements in sociability among
Yankees. As narrators or listeners, Yankee youths have in *bosozoku*
activity one of the most splendid topics of conversation available to
them.

By reconstructing experiences in *bosozoku* activities in dramatic
forms through story-telling together with one's fellows, the Yankee can
impose certain meanings on his acts and disregard other, negative implications (e.g., fear, anxiety) that might be involved in the acts. Just as
a novice marijuana user may learn to get high on "pot" through symbolic interaction with trained users, a novice Yankee will learn to "get
tuned into the rhythm" of *boso* driving by participating in the story-
telling as audience, and may eventually become a narrator himself.[21]

The accounts, through the recognition of common complicity, also serve to neutralize the negative moral implications of deviant acts and attenuate the fear of extreme abnormality or insanity.[22] By imposing certain definitions of the situations on the actions, then, the narratives, or "'off-the-street' accounts of 'on-the-street' activities," not only chronicle past actions but also influence future behavior which will inspire still more narratives.[23] The street-corner narratives and actions, in this way, form an endless loop.

Although the Yankee may act out the clear-cut role of the picaro or *koha* during an ongoing performance of *boso* driving or in self-presentation through the mass media, he rarely emerges as a clear-cut villain or *koha*-type hero in street-corner narratives. The vivid exchange of harsh and aggressive commentaries on each other's behavior, which includes a lot of onomatopoetic expressions, assumes the character of "dozens," "signifying," or "sounding."[24] The word-games and duels, carried out in the mood of conversation "backstage,"[25] often discount any self-glorification or mystification. In addition, someone's failure is a favorite topic of story-telling and incites loud laughter. The Yankee emerges, then, as a trickster—"uncertainty personified, a creature fluctuating between competence and incompetence, success and failure, good and evil"[26]—rather than as a pure hero or villain in the narrative on the street.

My field notes include only fragmentary records of the narratives because I noticed the significance of this storytelling relatively late in my research. Yet, the following conversation between me and two informants conveys the atmosphere of typical street-corner narrative among Yankees.

> MICHIO: Everybody's nice-looking in *boso* driving. Even in a shabby car.
> SATO: Really?
> ICHIRO: Even *I* look nice.
> SATO: Ha-ha! Yeah, you look nice.
> MICHIO: But it's a shame to fall down when all the others are watching.
> ICHIRO: Yeah, like Kentaro. Ha-ha!
> SATO: Really? Did he fall down?
> MICHIO: It was a nice show, you know. There was a chick, you know. When we were all taking a rest after a *boso* drive. We were drinking. Shintaro and us were watching, and only Kentaro was riding on a motorbike, racing the engine like *hohohohooon!* (onomatopoetic expression of exhaust noise]. He said to the chick, "Come on baby, I'll give you a ride." The

chick rode on his bike. And then, *ronronpahn! pa* [onomatopo-
etic expression of exhaust noise and its sudden stop]. They fell
down!
[All of us broke into laughter.]
SATO: It sounds like a scene in a comic strip!
ICHIRO: Into a telegraph pole. . . .
MICHIO: Yeah, he crashed his bike into a telegraph pole and tum-
bled down. When we helped him to get up, he said,
"Everything is alright, alright. . . . Whoops, is something
wrong?"

Objects and Settings

In pretend play, it is not only the identities of participants that are
transformed. Objects and settings are also transformed into props and
stages in an imaginative world. Such transformations in the pretend
play of small children tend to be subject solely to the requirements of
the action plans.[27] Children's pretend play usually does not include a
complex plan which requires objects and settings fabricated specifically for that purpose. They use whatever is at hand as props for pretend
play, e.g., a cardboard box as a house and a mop as a machine gun. In
contrast, Yankees need vehicles and costumes costing a considerable
sum of money, and an urban setting with wide streets, when they act
out the grand plan, "Playing *Bosozoku.*"

Vehicles. The vehicle is an integral component in a Yankee's life-
style. It is quite difficult for Yankees to maintain their action-oriented
life-style with their peers without vehicles. Increased mobility allows
them to widen the territorial scope of their actions. On vehicles they
can easily go to such places as Kawaramachi Avenue, the parks, and
video arcades—"where the action is." With vehicles they can also pick
up girls. Motorcycles and cars provide common topics of conversation
for youths who may otherwise have little to say or to share, particularly if their academic careers or employment have taken divergent
paths after junior high school. The social life and personal identity of
the Yankee are often so closely related that the vehicle becomes an
important mnemonic cue among his acquaintances. Some of his
friends may remember neither his name nor his face but rather the
make and color of his car.

Vehicles are easily available to Yankees. Some obtain money to buy
them from their indulgent parents. Others obtain loans to purchase,
and subsequently modify, their vehicles. Still others may buy them
second-hand, sometimes at very low prices from friends or older group

members; even so, their payments may always be late or indeed never completed. Even if they obtain vehicles by another's money or by a loan, Yankees can present themselves as powerful and discerning consumers by riding in expensive models with many decorative parts and accessories. They can also have the pride of a dilettante of modern technology through the modifications. The vehicle, then, supports a Yankee's sense of masculinity, prestige, and dignity.

Because of this almost symbiotic relationship between the Yankee and his vehicle, the implicit themes (plans) of high-speed driving and sudden acceleration often facilitate his transformation into a *bosozoku*. Through modification of cars and bikes in *bosozoku* style, the Yankee modifies his identity according to the plans implicit in the modified vehicles. Many informants mentioned, indeed, their first purchase of bikes (rather than any psychological strain) as the proximate cause of participation in *boso* driving.

Costumes. *Bosozoku* costumes such as *tokkofuku* (kamikaze party uniform) and *sentofuku* (combat uniform), often combined with characteristic *hachimaki* (headband) and flu mask, have many characteristics in common with Yankee fashion. Both Yankee and *bosozoku* styles are outrageous and "unnatural." They are meant to attract people's attention or to be *medatsu* by offending or intimidating ordinary citizens (*ippan shimin*). Both styles are also an apparent manifestation of exaggerated masculinity or ultramasculinity and embody the theme of "action-seeker."

Bosozoku style is, however, far more theatrical than Yankee style and has the characteristics of stage costumes. Yankee youths take off *sentofuku* or *tokkofuku* in their daily life or when they are off-stage. In other words, although Yankee style itself is theatrical, during adolescence Yankee style constitutes an off-stage attire in comparison with the extremely theatrical stage costumes of *bosozoku*.

Urban Setting. The styles of Yankee and *bosozoku* are, above all, urban phenomena. Anonymous urban space and the existence of a large audience for self-display are prerequisites for the youthful styles. Figures 5.1 and 5.2 show, respectively, the wards and major streets in Kyoto. Although the development of Kyoto as an industrial city has been relatively slow as compared to other major Japanese cities (see appendix A), there are many urban settings in Kyoto for the display of youthful styles by Yankees. Through massive participation in *bosozoku* activities, Yankee boys and girls transform the city into a huge playground.

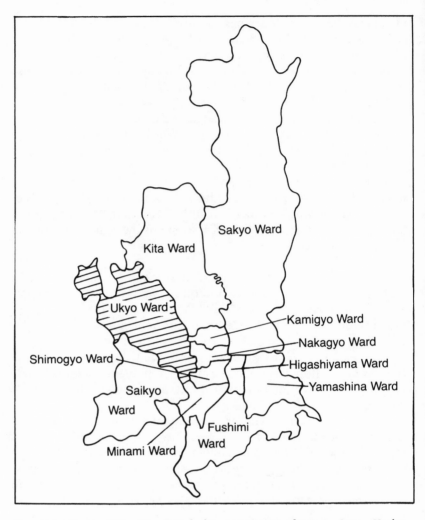

Fɪɢ. 5.1. Kyoto City. (Reprinted, by permission, from I. Sato, *Yankee,* Bosozoku, *Man of Society* [Tokyo: Shin'yosha, 1985], 21.)

Political and commercial activity takes place in three wards, Kamigyo, Nakagyo, and Shimogyo. The rectangular area circumscribed by Kawaramachi Avenue, Horikawa Avenue, Marutamachi Street, and Shichijo Street is particularly important in this regard, and includes city hall, major banks, and the larger stores.[28] These districts and neighboring areas also include numerous bars, taverns, restaurants, and cinema theaters as well as agencies for geisha girls. Al-

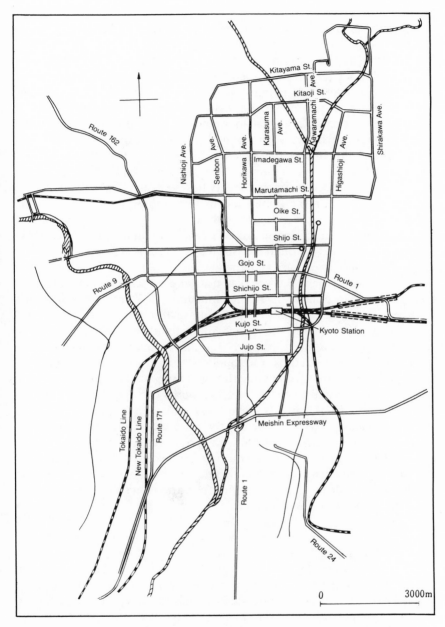

Fig. 5.2. Road Map of Kyoto. (Reprinted by permission, from I. Sato, *Yankee*, *Bosozoku*, *Man of Society* [Tokyo: Shin'yosha, 1985], 21.)

though night life is not so active as in the Shinjuku quarter of Tokyo, or the "Kita" and "Minami" districts of Osaka, the area around Kawaramachi Avenue and Shijo Street is one of the most lively quarters in Japan; it offers youth a splendid stage for self-presentation.

The checkerboard pattern of roads shown in figure 5.2 may give Americans the impression that Kyoto's street system has developed on a level comparable to that in American cities. But in actuality the streets take up only 9.9 percent of the entire area of the city, the smallest proportion among the eleven major cities in Japan. Because Kyoto suffered almost no war damage, there was no need to carry out drastic reconstruction of its streets. Priority has been attached to the preservation of historical monuments, thus restraining rapid street-building and excluding expressways from the city. There are numerous narrow and winding streets branching off from the main thoroughfares. Even the main streets are often interrupted by stores and houses.

Many side streets are so narrow that two automobiles cannot pass each other on them. *Bosozoku* can use them as escape routes when they are chased by police cars. At the same time, the Yankees complain that the absence of expressways precludes extreme forms of high-speed driving. Occasionally, then, they will go to other cities, such as Osaka and Kobe, via Route 1, Route 171, or the Meishin Expressway, to use the expressways in those metropolises.

Still, there are several wide thoroughfares, such as Gojo Street and Horikawa Avenue, where *bosozoku* youths can speed at will around midnight. They can also show off before a large audience on Kawaramachi Avenue. Such observers include *bosozoku* youths and Yankees who are not affiliated with specific *bosozoku* groups, as well as "ordinary citizens." These youths may also participate in the *boso* driving. The structure and coherence of the make-believe world of *bosozoku*, indeed, largely depend upon the cohesiveness of *bosozoku* activity as a collective behavior.

Metamorphosis and Group Process
Mobilization and Involvement

Compliance Relationship. Table 5.1 shows police statistics on the *bosozoku* population in Kyoto prefecture from 1974 to 1984. Although the data do not specify the residences of *bosozoku* youths, the majority of the gangs staged their activities in Kyoto City. According to my informants, between 1979 and 1981, the heyday of the *bosozoku*, many *boso* drives could mobilize more than 100 vehicles. Police reports also show that during this period it was not uncommon for dozens of youths to participate in *boso* driving at any one time.[29]

TABLE 5.1 *Bosozoku* Activity in Kyoto, 1974–84

| Year | Number of Groups | Population | | | Vehicles | | |
		Gang Members	Non-Gang Members	Total	Motor-cycles	Auto-mobiles	Total
1974	30	—*	—*	500**	—*	—*	—*
1975	20	—*	—*	300**	—*	—*	—*
1976	25	—*	—*	300**	—*	—*	—*
1977	7	240	130	370	—*	—*	—*
1978	16	720	275	995	—*	—*	—*
1979	20	—*	—*	1,200**	—*	—*	—*
1980	—*	—*	—*	1,500**	403	369	772
1981	15	—*	—*	1,700**	500**	360**	860**
1982	20	666	247	913	378	251	629
1983	17	553	324	977	436	180	616
1984	9	238	520	758	381	174	555

Source: Kyoto Prefecture Police, *Present State of* Bosozoku, *1974*, 5; idem., *Present State of* Bosozoku, *1984*, Table 5.3.
*Data not available.
**Estimate.

Through massive collective behavior, Yankees may join youths from many parts of Kyoto in creating a make-believe world that constitutes an alternative reality. The grandiose name, "All Japan Kyoto Racing Club" reflects the "reality" of this make-believe world. An underlying uncertainty, however, is concealed by this playlike world. While nominally *bosozoku* groups or confederations may have large memberships, they often resemble phantom organizations where only a few people attend their activities. Many Yankees who joined the *bosozoku* activity may revert to their old life-style if gang activity wanes.

A *bosozoku* group is essentially a spontaneously formed gang whose membership and boundaries are not always clear. It includes many fringe members as well as some dedicated adherents. Involvement in group activities is not necessarily based on clear-cut distinctions of role and status. Furthermore, gang activity is accompanied by considerable risks such as traffic accidents, gang fights, and police custody. Yankees' participation in gang activity and their consequent metamorphosis into *bosozoku* are, then, contingent upon the nature of *bosozoku* groups and their actions. Leaders and executive members of *bosozoku* groups must manage and mobilize followers and uncertain members who are sensitive to the great risks.

Although his analysis is focused on formal complex organizations, Etzioni's typology of the "compliance" relationship can be applied to executive members' strategies of mobilization and to *bosozoku* members' involvement,[30] which in combination support the coherence of the make-believe world of motorcycle gangs. Etzioni classifies the power an organization applies to subordinate participants into three sorts: (1) coercive power, (2) remunerative power, and (3) normative power. He also mentions three types of involvement for subordinate members: (1) alienative involvement, (2) calculative involvement, and (3) moral involvement.

My analysis of the history of the Ukyo Rengo and the All Japan Kyoto Racing Club (hereafter "AJK") shows that the three types of power and involvement form the basis for a Yankee's metamorphosis into *bosozoku*, though the "remunerative-calculative" pair in Etzioni's paradigm mainly refers to extrinsic rather than intrinsic rewards of participation. This analytical framework may take the form of three congruent combinations of power and involvement.

1. Coercive-Alienative
    a) How can the executive members mobilize unwilling members for gang activity through coercive measures?
    b) Why do the members join in the activity in spite of the risks and displeasure involved?
2. Remunerative-Calculative
    a) How can the executive members and gang activity itself offer ordinary members incentives for participation?
    b) What are the incentives of the gang activity for the participants?
3. Normative-Moral
    a) How can the executive members win ordinary members' commitment to gang activity?
    b) What kinds of moral commitment do ordinary members have?

The Heyday of AJK. Figure 5.3 summarizes the history of AJK and its constituent groups. AJK is a confederation of *bosozoku* groups which was said to have once been the largest confederation in Kyoto prefecture, involving more than 300 youths.[31] It was organized under the leadership of Ken'ichi, who was concurrently the leader of the Ukyo Rengo, in July 1980.

Although figure 5.3 may give readers the impression that AJK and Ukyo Rengo maintained their activity for more than four years, there were periods of development and decay in the structure and solidarity of the organizations. In fact, confederations are often formed to hold together constituent groups that have been threatened by police con-

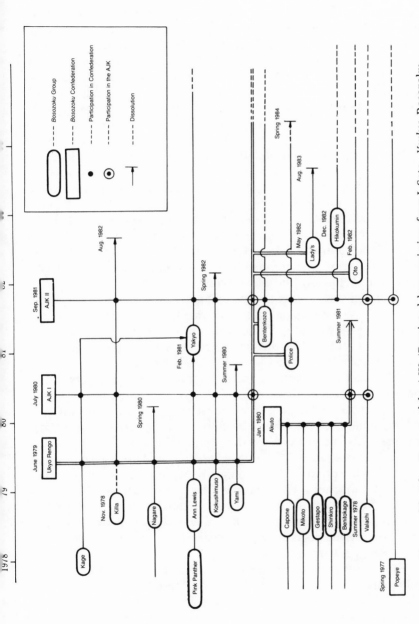

FIG. 5.3. History of the Ukyo Rengo and the AJK. (Reprinted, by permission, from I. Sato., *Yankee*, Bosozoku, *Man of Society* [Tokyo: Shin'yosha, 1985], 49.)

trol or crises of generational succession of membership. For example, the Akuto (Bandit) Association was organized in January 1980 after five constituent groups in southern wards of Kyoto had been weakened by the dissolution of the C. D. (Candies) Association. AJK was organized under Shintaro's leadership in September 1981, after *bosozoku* activity had been curtailed by the extensive application of new traffic laws earlier in the year. By then, many executive members of the AJK had been arrested and sent to correctional institutions, and the confederation existed in name only.

Every time a new confederation was organized, *bosozoku* activity increased to a considerable extent. But such confederations soon became targets of intensive police control. Police measures against leaders and executive members were especially severe. Between July 1980 and August 1984, the Ukyo Rengo had eight leaders who were called *socho* (Maximum Leaders).[32] Among the eight members, Ken'ichi, Shintaro, Masahiko, Saburo, and Taro were arrested on charges related to gang activities. Many ordinary members were also arrested for "collective dangerous behavior," the official name for *boso* driving.

Gang fights with other groups are another risk inherent in *bosozoku* activity. Large-scale gang fights involving the Ukyo Rengo broke out, against the Shiga Racing Club in November 1979,[33] and against the Toryukai (East Side Dragons) in the spring of 1982. In each case more than fifty members of the Ukyo Rengo were involved.

The leader and executive members must persuade others to take part in gang activity despite such risks. They may use coercive measures, such as threatening or administering corporal punishment to reluctant members. Ken'ichi was thoroughgoing in this respect and to a considerable degree succeeded in maintaining group activity. He was a young executive member of a *yakuza* group and imposed quasi-military discipline upon the Ukyo Rengo. He regularly assaulted members for trivial infractions. While he was their leader, the Ukyo Rengo often carried out *boso* driving two times a week. In late November 1979 he was arrested for battery against the leader of Nagare (Flow).[34] After his arrest, many members left the confederation, and the activity of the Ukyo Rengo fell off considerably.

The leaders and executive members also appeal to normative commitments among their members. While Shintaro, like Ken'ichi, used physical punishment to strengthen the group's solidarity, he also emphasized "guts" (*yaruki*) to prod the rank and file forward. Others respected him for his own courage, as well as for his enthusiasm for high-risk driving and great skill at handling vehicles. He not only restored activity among the Ukyo Rengo but also reorganized AJK.

Besides the normative commitments their leaders play upon, group members, especially "regular" participants, hold the common ideal of remaining steadfast in critical situations. Those who are ready to fight opponents, and never confess to the police, are respected and regarded as trustworthy members. The critical difference between *miuchi* or *tsure* (buddies) and *tobiiri* (hangers-on) is based on this stance during critical situations. But this distinction is often ambiguous, and "buddies" may sometimes divulge information about others', as well as their own, crimes under police interrogation. Some "regular" members of the Ukyo Rengo were ostracized by their friends when it was discovered that they had confessed to the police. Although later they were accepted again as "buddies," their acts of betrayal were long remembered.

The age hierarchy within a group has a clear effect upon coercive sanctions and appeals to normative commitments. A *bosozoku* group often has members of different ages who began their relationships during their junior high school days. While the leaders and other executive members may use coercive sanctions against younger members, they rarely take such action against their peers, let alone against older members. More frequently, executive members will appeal to normative values to secure their peers' involvement in group activity. Susumu found himself at a disadvantage in this respect. When he became the leader of the Ukyo Rengo, group activity had diminished considerably after the arrests of Ken'ichi and other executive members. Many members left the group, and only those of Susumu's age continued to participate in activities. Although he was recognized as a skillful and zealous driver, he was also regarded as a weak fighter, and other members did not trust him. Nor was he able to impose coercive measures against peers. The female leader Seiko also found it difficult to keep discipline in the female subsection because most of them were her peers. Junko, who was one year older than Seiko and most other female members, could keep discipline quite effectively.

While coercive measures and appeals to normative values are used mainly with regular members, the third determinant, the use of incentives, can mobilize a wide range of youths, including fringe members and hangers-on. Two major attractions are the intrinsic enjoyment of high-risk driving and the social opportunities offered by collective driving or weekly meetings. In the last analysis, these incentives provide the force that shapes the *bosozoku* organizations and maintains them as groups. Another major incentive is the enjoyment of creating and participating in a make-believe world. The *bosozoku* paraphernalia affirm and reinforce this enjoyment. The presentation of the image of a solidified *bosozoku* group with watertight discipline comes very close to the reality when the group can mobilize its members effectively through such incentives. Coercive measures and normative appeals are effective only when the group can gather a certain number of youths and develop a relatively clear-cut organizational structure.[35]

Despite the great risks of police sanctions, large numbers of youths are mobilized in response to the attractions offered by *bosozoku* activity. During the heyday of the Ukyo Rengo, under Shintaro's leadership, more than 100 youths would participate in a *boso* drive, even with strengthened traffic laws and close police surveillance. Although gang activity in Kyoto as a whole had declined by 1983, in June the Ukyo Rengo could call together more than 60 vehicles for a *boso* drive. The entire event was carefully planned, messages were sent to other groups, and high expectations were raised among all those taking part.[36]

Yankee Cliques and *Bosozoku* Groups

Groups and Cliques. The rise and decline of activity among the Ukyo Rengo make it difficult, sometimes, to distinguish cause from effect in gang activity. In a complex causal chain, incentives, coercion, normative values, risks, and group solidarity inspire collective behavior that consists alternately of groups and crowds. A *bosozoku* "group" thus has the qualities of a spontaneous youth organization whose membership and boundaries are ambiguous.[37]

As a *bosozoku* confederation consists of several constituent groups, each gang includes members of different age groups, and each peer group has cliques of Yankees who hang around together on a daily basis. When the gang activity diminishes, the *bosozoku* confederation or group tends to break down into smaller units, and may exist only as a nominal entity. The weakening of ties among constituent groups further limits gang activity and decreases incentives. There may be some reactivation when police surveillance is relaxed, or when incarcerated executive members are released from custody. When Shintaro reorganized the Ukyo Rengo and AJK, many of his peers had been released from correctional institutions and returned to the "battle lines." They were already over eighteen and had began driving cars, though many of them did not have valid driver's licenses. During this period, other *bosozoku* groups and confederations also increased their activity, and police could not allocate manpower effectively to contain them.[38]

Toshio describes such fluctuations in the level of gang activity as follows,

Any group has its heyday. Even the Toryukai [East Side Dragons] had its prime time. After that, the members are dispersed by police arrests [of some members]. And later, again, they reassemble.

Masahiko was the fourth leader of the Ukyo Rengo. Partly because of his background—he grew up in a southern city of Kyoto prefecture and did not have many personal connections in the Ukyo ward—he could not mobilize members effectively. Gang activity also became risky and fell off after the wholesale arrests of executive members in November 1981. Masahiko talked about his difficulties as a leader:

> To be frank with you, they [other members] were all cold-hearted. They came [to *boso* driving and weekly meetings] just for fun, just to speed. They suddenly disappeared when the police began investigating *boso* driving.

The members who would "disperse" or "disappear" during slow periods of gang activity might often return to the Yankee life-style, unless long-standing members could keep up interest in weekly meetings and *boso* driving. Meetings of groups or confederations serve to reinforce ties among Yankee cliques or *bosozoku* groups.

Table 5.2 shows the number of participants at each weekly meeting the Ukyo Rengo held while I was conducting my field research. Table 5.3 shows the membership structure of the confederation. Only those members who came to the meetings relatively regularly are listed in table 5.3. There were a number of fringe members, who came to the meetings only for the sake of involvement in *boso* driving. As table 5.2 indicates, even the attendance of "regulars" varied when gang activity subsided.

AJK in the Research Period. In July 1983, the leadership and organizational structure of the Ukyo Rengo became ambiguous after several executive members who were seventeen years old, including Taro, the seventh leader, were arrested. They were held on charges lodged during the *boso* drive of June 1983. After their arrests, the remaining members did not carry out any *boso* driving as a group but simply went to drives held by other groups. Although the Ukyo Rengo was the name of a confederation, only members of the Yakyo (Midnight Crazies), the headquarters of the confederation, and a few members of the Police, participated in meetings. Although Kenji and other nineteen-year-olds frequented the weekly meetings, they were about to "graduate" from group activity and came by essentially as observers. While Kenji, the sixth leader, temporarily resumed leadership and de-

TABLE 5.2 Weekly Meeting of the Ukyo Rengo, August 1983–June 1984

Date	Group Activity		Police Control		
	Number of Participants	*Boso* Driving	Police- men	Squad Cars	Police Bikes
1983 August 3	over 30		4	0	3
10	over 35		2	0	2
17	over 25		3	0	2
24	over 55		?	1*	0
31	over 20		2	1	0
September 7	over 20		5–6	1	3
14	—**		?	1*	0
21	15				
28	7–8				
October 5	35				
12	15	X			
19	—**				
26	20				
November 2	27	X	4	0	2
9	34				
16	over 25				
23	15				
30	30	X			
December 7	25		7–8	1	2–3
14	34				
21	31				
28	—**				
1984 January 4	—**				
11	28				
18	21	X			
25	25	X (Jan. 22)			
February 1	28	X			
8	30	X	9–0	1	4
11	22		4	1	0
18	—**		?	2	1
25	22				
March 3	—**				
10	18	X			
17	14				
24	9				
31	6				
April 7	5				
14	9				
21	11				
28	12				
May 31	10				
June 7	7				
28	11				

*Indicates camouflaged patrol cars.
**I could not attend these weekly meetings, for various reasons.

TABLE 5.3 Composition of the Ukyo Rengo: Age, Group, Junior High

| Age | Yakyo | | | | | Police | Bentenkozo | Total |
	Ha. J.H.	Sa. J.H.	U. J.H.	Na. J.H.	Other	Ni. J.H.	Na. J.H.	
19	4	1	0	1	2	0*	0	8
18	0	0	0	0	0	0*	0*	0
17	2	0	5	0	0	6	0	13
16	9	0	3	0	0	3	4	19
Total	15	1	8	1	2	9	4	40

*All members of these categories had disengaged from gang activities by the summer of 1983.

manded that younger members attend such gatherings, he was not very enthusiastic about the group's response.

Taro was released from a Juvenile Classification Home in September 1983. Although he was at first unwilling to resume leadership, he bowed to the wishes of his peers and older members, and succeeded in reactivating the gangs. Under his leadership *boso* driving was carried out seven times, though he later attempted to turn over his position to Tokio, a younger member of the Yakyo. Beginning in October, the Bentenkozo and the Police, as well as the Yakyo, took part in weekly meetings.

After Taro and other members were arrested in late February 1984, however, there was little further activity on the part of the Ukyo Rengo. By that time the older members were already twenty years old (they are the nineteen-year-olds of table 5.3), and had graduated from gang activity. Tokio could not become an effective leader because of his age. Older members (who in table 5.3 are seventeen-year-olds) rarely attended meetings. The Police and Bentenkozo also began to stay away. After late March, weekly meetings consisted almost exclusively of Tokio's associates. Only two new members, who had just graduated from junior high school, were recruited to the Yakyo in April. They carried out only one *boso* drive, a small-scale event. Their meetings were of "*bosozoku* who don't drive" (see chapter 3) or ordinary Yankees. Meanwhile the older members (the seventeen-year-olds of table 5.3) also resumed to the life-style of ordinary Yankees. They returned to their respective hangouts, though occasionally they visited the meeting places they had formerly used as *bosozoku*.

In June Tokio suggested that the Ukyo Rengo be dissolved, since it existed in name only. But he had to withdraw his suggestions because Kenji insisted that the "tradition" of the Ukyo Rengo should not be terminated. Kenji also said the Ukyo Rengo could exist as a group of *gurentai* (hoodlums), if it were not possible to maintain it as a *bosozoku* group. As table 5.1 shows, the activity of *bosozoku* in Kyoto has waned to a considerable extent during the three years between 1982 and 1984. When I left Kyoto in late August 1984, the Ukyo Rengo still had a weekly meeting. Yet it was more like an ordinary "gathering and talking" of Yankees than a regular meeting of *bosozoku*.

Given the existence of *bosozoku* groups in their neighborhoods, and fluctuations in their activities, Yankees may undergo repeated transformation into *bosozoku*. Gang activity provides more than the enjoyment of high-risk driving and social interaction. The heroic image of *bosozoku* disseminated by the mass media and also created by motorcycle gangs themselves provides the youth with an identity that is more appealing than that of a Yankee. When he takes up the mask of a *bosozoku*, the Yankee transforms himself from a somewhat confused "gentleman of the leisure class" into a hero. Even when the mask becomes too risky to wear, he may continue his search for action as an ordinary Yankee. He may turn *bosozoku* again when the situation permits. In most cases, however, there is a definitive end to the natural history of the Yankee's life-style. Just as the heroic drama *"Bosozoku, the Saturday-Night Hero"* has "reaggregation" as the final phase of the pilgrimage of the picaro, the natural history of the Yankee's life-style is terminated with his "graduation" (*sotsugyo*) or "settling down" (*ochitsuku*).

6 From Yankee/*Bosozoku* to "Ordinary Citizen"

> My life's been connected to others. I've gradually noticed that I've been involved in relations with various people. Now that I've noticed that, I'm going to become one of "the public." Once that happens, what can I bet my life on? . . . When I returned to my apartment, Kyoko [his girl friend, who lives with him] suddenly said to me, "Don't you think it's disappointing that everybody gets old? I wish we could live like children forever. . . ." [Silently I told myself] We have to have a wedding.
>
> —Yoshiharu Urita, *Only Saturday Is Left for Us*

The Measles Theory of *Bosozoku*

My contact with the members of the Ukyo Rengo began on June 28 in 1983, when I first met Seiko, the leader of the female subsection of the *bosozoku* confederation, on Kawaramachi Avenue. It was night and she was cruising on her own Kawasaki 400 with Akemi (another female member) on the pillion seat. Both of them wore trousers and sweat shirts and had helmets with the words "Ukyo Rengo" written on them with a marker pen. In our conversation, Seiko told me, "We are already seventeen. We've got to settle down." On August 31, ten members of the female subsection held a party to commemorate the disbanding of the female subsection, and most of them came dressed in skirts and dresses. About half of the ten girls had already disengaged themselves almost completely from gang activity in early August. After the party, the remaining members rarely came to the weekly meetings of the Ukyo Rengo.

Most male members also clearly anticipated their eventual graduation from gang activity, or more generally from the Yankee life-style. The phrase "settling down" (*ochitsuku*) was frequently used to refer to the process of disengagement from the action-seeking life-style, or metamorphosis from Yankee/*bosozoku* to "ordinary citizen" (*ippan shimin*) by age twenty. The police statistics and technical studies on *bosozoku* also show that most *bosozoku* members "mature out" from gang activity by twenty and become conventional adults.[1]

It is widely acknowledged that *bosozoku* is essentially a youthful phenomenon and that few Japanese youths are *bosozoku* after twenty. This public recognition of the "graduation" from gang activity with the attainment of adulthood has led to a folk theory known as *bosozoku hashika setsu* (measles theory of *bosozoku*). This theory views *bosozoku* activity essentially as youthful indiscretion or as a manifestation of the "storm and stress" characteristic of adolescence. It is assumed that youths' participation in gang activity is a sort of youthful fever which can be "cured" by self-healing, as in the case of measles, if one matures enough.

The "measles theory of *bosozoku*" has much in common with "maturation theory" in the field of criminology. It is supposed to explain the curvilinear relationship between age and crime rates, or the crime peak in adolescence and the subsequent decline in crime rates in adulthood.[2] The decline of crime rates with the coming of adulthood is often called "maturational reform." Implicit in the maturation theory is an assumption that one of the major causes of deviant behavior is the immaturity of delinquents. In many cases, the "immaturity" is defined in psychological or biological terms.[3] As Wooton points out, one of the major problems of this theory is its circular argument.[4] Quite often the only evidence offered in support of the assumed maturity of ex-delinquents is the fact that they have outgrown their criminal habits; while conversely, the minority who have not outgrown such habits are recognized as still immature by the very fact that they have not done so. The same is said of the measles theory of *bosozoku*. The general public assumes that ex-*bosozoku* members attained maturity chiefly from the fact that they have disengaged themselves from gang activities.

A number of sociological studies dealing with the curvilinear relationship between age and delinquency suggest that "maturational reform" is a social rather than biological process.[5] These studies argue that an increased stake in conformity rather than biological or psychological maturation is important in maturational reform.

This chapter will show that although my informants have their own version of the measles theory their "maturation" is mainly a social rather than a biological process and that their expectations about "settling down" are closely related to the age hierarchy among Yankees. The mechanism underlying the process of social maturation among

Yankees can be divided into three categories: (1) coercive sanction, (2) age norm, (3) commitment to conventional life-style.[6]

COERCIVE SANCTION
Penal Sanctions

In interview sessions as well as in conversation among themselves my informants expressed strong fear and anxiety about the penal sanctions for adult offenders. In Japan, penal law rather than juvenile law is applied to those over twenty. While most informants do not regard incarceration in the Juvenile Classification Home (*kanbetsusho*—"*kankan*" in their jargon) or juvenile training school[7] (*shonen'in*—"*nensho*") as constituting a criminal record (*zenka*), they consider penal sanctions applied to adult offenders to be a serious stigma.[8]

> AKEMI: You know, if I commit a crime [as an adult], I'll get a record [*zenka*]. After twenty it'll become a criminal record.
> EIKICHI: After twenty. . . . Oh, I can't do that, ha-ha!
> MASAHIKO: After twenty, it's a question of penal laws.
> EIKICHI: Before twenty, we don't get arrested [for most offenses].

Most informants had experienced legal sanctions of some sort during adolescence. Almost everybody experienced police interrogations, and interviews by investigators from the Family Court. Although such sanctions were considered annoying and troublesome, most informants did not consider disengagement from their life-style. What really mattered was incarceration in correctional institutions. Among some seventy informants, at least one had been in prison, two had been placed on adult probation, ten were sent to juvenile training school, and eleven to the Juvenile Classification Home. Those who had no such experience had heard about experiences in these various institutions from their seniors or peers, often in exaggerated terms. Some of those who had been incarcerated in institutions often bragged about their experiences saying, for example, "*Kankan* [Juvenile Classification Home] is just like a kindergarten," or "It was fun to be in the *kankan*." But there were none who said they preferred the institutions to life on the streets.

While informants regarded penal sanctions against minors with relatively little apprehension, they were much less sanguine about the stricter sanctions against adults. They also thought that police investigations were far more thoroughgoing for adult suspects than for minors. Some who were about to turn twenty years old told me in informal conversations, "I'm gonna beat him up before I turn twenty." When they had passed twenty, they said, "I have to be more careful because I'm twenty years old now." In daily conversations at hang-outs, or in weekly meetings, members shared rumors and gossip about seniors who did *not* "settle down" and were incarcerated in prison (*choeki ni iku* in their jargon).

Publicity and Stigma

Media reports, especially newspaper reports, were also regarded as a stigma if one was over twenty. While newspapers preserve ano-nymity in juvenile cases with romanized initials (e.g., "The Boy A who committed the larceny was . . . "), they report adult criminal cases with the real name of the offender and often with his mug shot and exact address. Newspapers, which provide *bosozoku* youths with an important means of getting publicity, then become an agent of serious sanction to those over twenty.

> SHIN'ICHIRO: It's terrible. Until now, I'd be reported as "A" [pseudonym]. . . . Even if my case gets in the paper, I'll be treated as "A," but . . . [after twenty my real name'll be there in black and white].
>
> KENTARO: Oh, it's awful! My mug shot [and real name] will be in the paper. It doesn't matter if they call me "A" or "B" [without mug shot].
>
> SABURO: If I'm arrested [as an adult], my [real] name'll be in the paper together with my mug shot. . . . That's really embarrass-ing. My engagement might be broken off. Who'd marry a guy with a record of having a mug shot in the paper.

My informants' fear about the stigma of a media report is closely re-lated to their perspective about future residence. Most of them considered Kyoto a comfortable place in which to work and live. Some 80 percent of the respondents to the questionnaire expected to be resi-dents of Kyoto City, and 86 percent of them expected to live within Kyoto Prefecture at the age of thirty or forty. During his adolescence, Saburo did not pay much attention to his neighbors' complaints about the loud noise from his and his peers' motorcycles. He was also sent to the Juvenile Classification Home for one period. In 1983, however, he turned twenty years old. He was expected to inherit his father's ship-ping and transport business sometime in the future and live with his parents in Kyoto. Saburo said emphatically,

> I couldn't show my face here, in my neighborhood, in Kyoto. My parents, all of my family, couldn't stay here, if . . . if my mug shot was in the paper. We could never stay here.

AGE NORM
Delinquency and "Mischief"

In the public conception, most of the wrongdoing committed by *bosozoku* youths and Yankees is considered "delinquency" (*hiko*). But my informants often regard their own and their companions' delinquency as *yancha* (mischief), so long as it is within certain limits. In their evaluation of the rank order of wrongdoings,[9] anything less serious than amphetamine abuse is considered *yancha*. They tend to attribute their delinquency primarily to the "storm and stress" of adolescence, over which, according to them, they have little control.[10]

> SABURO: If regulations [against *bosozoku*] are tightened, young people'll vent their storm and stress in other activities.
> SHIN'ICHIRO: I think [if guys can't engage in *boso* driving] they'll turn to amphetamines or inhaling paint thinner.

They perceive the potential for deviance as universal among adolescents and believe that there is an optimal period for expressing that potential. They also believe that if a person fails to express that potential during the optimal period, and does so at a later time, the moral consequence will be worse. The guy who begins a delinquent career at a later time, one whom my informants call a *nariagari* (upstart), fails to acquire immunity to evil urges or to "measles."

> SEIKO: How can I put it. . . ? Well, if you start going wrong early—in junior high school, say—like us, then you'll get settled down earlier [than those who did not].
> SATO: Yeah, I heard about that from other members.
> AKEMI: After all, the ones who turn delinquent after junior high school are more frustrated.
> AKIRA: The ones who start playing [*asobu;* spend one's time in pleasurable pursuits] after getting into college, after they get old, they're more vicious [than us].
> SABURO: Right, exactly! The guys who start playing early settle down early. The ones who study hard and do everything they're told when they're young, once they get a taste of "play," they go crazy over it.
> AKIRA: In general, if a guy starts doing wrong in junior high school, he'll get settled down early because he really knows the drawbacks of that kind of thing. But if he turns delinquent after starting high school, he'll just get worse . . .
> SATO: You mean, one's delinquency will get worse?
> SABURO: They may continue committing crimes until twenty-two, for example! [laughs]

In the mind of my informants, then, their deviant behavior is wrongdoing. They do not share any subcultural norm or ideology which defines their behavior as legitimate or obligatory acts.[11] They do, however, share a subcultural conception that defines their misbehavior as "mischief" or "play" which should be limited to adolescence. In other words, they have their own metaphor, crime as play, which serves to neutralize negative implications of their wrongdoing.

My informants also often regard both the Yankee style and *bosozoku* styles as "stupid stuff" (*ahona koto*), an enjoyable and exciting thing during adolescence but something to be discarded at a certain age. For my informants, the negative moral implications of delinquency are neutralized by the "ludic" metaphor and an "appeal to biological drives";[12] and they believe that delinquency should be age-specific. The generic term used to refer to behavior considered childish for one's age is *"ichibiru"* (doing foolish or childish things). For example, those who drive low-slung cars or participate in *boso* driving after 20 are called *"ichibiri"* (nominalized *ichibiru;* childish guy). Such age norms play a crucial role in the process of "settling down."

Age Norm and Reference Groups

While studies of age norms tend to treat general and abstract norms, or "What most people would expect" in relation to age,[13] the age norms among my informants are subcultural ones and closely related to their conception about "What my buddies would expect." "Buddies" or "reference groups" who define age norms can be divided into three categories—seniors, peers, and juniors. For my informants, the judgment on whether one's graduation from a deviant career is "too early," "too late," or "just on time" depends largely on one's relative position in the age hierarchy of a group and on the behavior of those age groups.

Seniors who have graduated from gang activity to "settle down" provide an important model for one's own graduation in the future. On the other hand, those seniors who failed to make the transition at the proper age and, unlike most of their peers, still remain in the group are regarded as *ichibiri* (childish or foolish guys) and become targets of gossip and ridicule.

> SEIKO: Many senior [female] members who were active members at the age of fifteen or sixteen settled down all of a sudden at seventeen. I want to do it like them. [Seiko was seventeen years old.]
>
> KENJI: When we were sixteen or seventeen you know, when an old guy in his twenties would yell at us, "Let's speed!" I'd think

to myself, "Isn't he stupid!" Even so, I answered, *Osu!* (Yes, sir!) at that time.

The peer group is the most important basis of comparison against which one judges the appropriateness of his behavior in relation to age. Many ex-members said they would join in *boso* driving after twenty only if their peers did so.[14] They also said that they became increasingly uneasy when their peers changed their clothing style or began disengaging themselves from gang activity.

> SEIKO: I'm so nervous about what other people think. Whenever I meet old buddies, they sneer at me and say, for example, "Do you still dye your hair?"
> SABURO: I felt really lonely . . . when none of my buddies came on the *boso* drive.

Juniors are another important source of age-appropriate judgments. A member who has ridiculed seniors still engaging in youthful or "childish" activities may, in turn, become a target of gossip or ridicule if he carries on such activities after a certain age.

> KENJI: Well, nowadays, some are even three years younger than us. I don't want to give orders to them.
> SATO: Really? Why not?
> KENJI: Well, because. . . .
> TAKASHI: Somehow I feel scared about what they think. It's a drag to imagine that they might think, "This old guy is really acting like a kid!"
> SATO: Do juniors really think like that?
> KENJI: Yeah. Even though they bow to you at the time. . . .
> AKEMI: When we were fifteen or sixteen years old, it was embarrassing if our [female] seniors joined a *boso* drive. [We said in secret] "How can they do it when they're so old!" It's our turn now. The juniors're gonna call us *oban* [old ladies].

Among various age-specific kinds of misconduct, paint-thinner inhaling clearly illustrates the relationship between the age hierarchy among youths and the subcultural evaluation of specific misconduct. While almost all of my informants (with the exception of several members of the Bentenkozo) had tried paint-thinner inhaling, they regarded it as "kid stuff" which they should give up by twenty. There were, however, several informants who continued to inhale thinner even after the age of twenty.

Ichiro was a paint-thinner addict and could not commit himself to a job. At one point he asked Mariko (a seventeen-year-old girl) to marry him, and he tried to stop inhaling thinner. He went to work on a regular basis and rarely indulged in his former thinner habit. But their relationship broke off when Mariko and her friends inhaled thinner in Ichiro's room without his permission. Ichiro resumed his habit and reverted to his irregular work schedule. Ichiro was then nineteen, and most of his peers had disengaged themselves from gang activity. Although many of them had inhaled thinner, none of them did so after the age of nineteen.

Ichiro was the only nineteen-year-old who attended the weekly meeting of the Ukyo Rengo almost every week. Although he told junior members that he no longer inhaled thinner, they were well aware of his continuing addiction. The juniors gossiped about him and even made fun of him, openly saying, "Hey! Ichiro. I can smell paint thinner coming from your direction." Although he sometimes became angry about his treatment from his juniors and assumed an aggressive pose, he increasingly lost his prestige among them. To make matters worse, he had assumed the role of dealer, distributing thinner to his juniors. The increased contact with the juniors lessened his prestige among his peers as well.

Ichiro once said to me, "I'll give up thinner when I turn twenty. Anyone who inhales thinner after twenty is a real fool." Actually he continued to use paint thinner after he became twenty, so that in 1984, when I pointed out the contradiction between word and deed, he answered somewhat angrily, "Shintaro also did it when he was twenty-one." But because Shintaro used thinner along with some of his peers, his reputation among juniors didn't suffer quite as much as Ichiro's.

Ichiro himself made fun of Bunzo who, at twenty-four, still inhaled paint thinner. Other ex-members younger than Bunzo ridiculed him openly, not only because he used thinner at his age but also because he often associated with his juniors to do so. Eikichi once commented on Bunzo, saying "How can he inhale thinner when none of his buddies do it?"

Age Norm and Subcultural Artifacts

Clothing style, hair style, and paraphernalia, though not representing misbehavior, are also closely related to age norms based on the age hierarchy among Yankee/*Bosozoku* youths. The youths are expected to adopt a less extreme version of the Yankee or *bosozoku* style when they get old. During the period of my field research, gang members were expected to graduate from motorcycles to automobiles at the age of eighteen, and from low-slung cars to "normal" cars by twenty. Those who drove motorbikes after eighteen or low-slung cars after twenty were openly ridiculed by their seniors and peers. Younger members talked about them behind their backs. As the change in vehicle symbolizes "maturation" or "sophistication," the changes in sartorial and hair styles symbolize the transition from adolescence to early adulthood. As they get older, fewer and fewer Yankees dye their hair, shave their eyebrows, or dress in flashy attire. They move on to conventional perms or other conventional hair styles, and they dress in expensive cloths with subdued colors.

One alternative for Yankee/*bosozoku* youths who want to retain a youthful style after graduating from gang activity is to adopt *saafaa* (surfer) style. "Surfers" in Japan are not necessarily those who actually engage in the sport. Many Japanese surfers never surf; some can't even swim. Rather they dress in a "surfer" style (e.g., open shirts with tropical patterns, cloth shoes) and wear their hair in a distinctive "surfer cut" (straight and combed forward with the back cut short).[15] The nonsurfing surfer is called *oka saafaa* (land surfer).

The surfer style was one of the most fashionable youth styles in Kyoto in 1983 and 1984. My informants generally regarded the surfer style as tame and somewhat effeminate. But they also saw it as more sophisticated than the Yankee style. A considerable number of Yankees graduated from Yankee style to surfer style. Some did so following graduation from junior high school and others did so in their late teens or early twenties. The change in the clothing style was often accompanied by a change in life-style: Yankees who had converted to surfers tended to have more conventional and far less risky lives than before, though they occasionally try to pick up girls at the seaside.

The sequence of life-style from the junior high school version of Yankee style to the style of "ordinary citizen" can be schematically represented, as in figure 6.1. The dotted lines in this figure indicate directions unlikely to be taken. While Yankees may repeatedly become *bosozoku* and vice versa, an ex-Yankee who turns surfer rarely returns to the Yankee or *bosozoku* life-style. Most Yankees/*bosozoku*, as well as surfers, eventually become full-fledged members of adult society when they successfully negotiate several events that mark their passage to adulthood.

COMMITMENT TO CONVENTIONAL LIFE

Yankees do not disengage themselves from "action"-type activities simply because they are afraid of police and media sanctions or because they feel ashamed of engaging in "kid stuff." They also come to have a greater stake in conformity as they get older and experience several events marking their transition to adulthood. While they have little to lose in their adolescence, the situation changes as they move

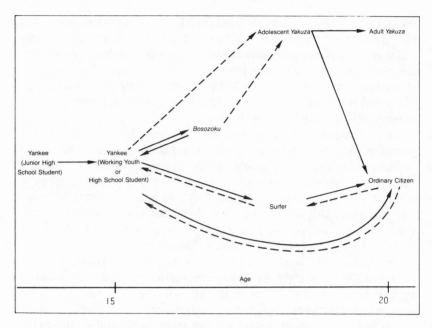

FIG. 6.1. Natural History of Yankee Style.

into adulthood. The transition to adulthood includes the process by which one achieves greater "continuance commitment" to a conventional identity and has a greater "awareness of the impossibility of choosing a different [deviant] social identity . . . because of the imminence of penalties involved in making the switch."[16]

It should be also noted that if they continue to engage in risky activities, both they and their families, stand to lose a great deal. A Yankee's "maturational reform," then, includes the process by which he becomes increasingly involved in the social networks of family and workplace rather than those of peers. Getting a regular job and "going steady," or getting married, are two major events marking a Yankee's transition to adulthood. Both are accompanied by changes in reference groups and alterations in the pattern of allocation of time and economic resources.

Job

For Yankees, the meaning of job changes greatly after they disengage from the action-oriented life-style. During their adolescence, a job was chiefly a means of obtaining enough money for leisure activities; in adulthood it becomes an important means of affirming one's sense of manhood as well as a necessary means of livelihood. The phrase *te ni shoku o tsukeru* (learning a trade) was frequently used by my informants in casual conversations as well as during interview sessions. To learn a trade and become a skilled worker or a self-employed person is the ideal for most informants.[17]

Although the phrase "learning a trade" was used both by informants in their teens and by those in their twenties, the accounts of the former rarely coincided with their behavior. It was rare to hear a younger informant speak with any pride about a current job. On the contrary, younger members often spoke in self-deprecatory terms about their menial job as gas-station attendants or road-construction workers. To them, a "trade" was in many cases a job other than one's current work. They said they would find more lucrative and skilled jobs through repeated trial and error. Some of them also said that a more profitable job would have to wait until they were eligible for a driver's license at eighteen. In this trial-and-error or exploratory period of their occupational career, many regarded their current job as a "mistake."[18] An adolescent could easily quit this kind of job and return to a state of "voluntary unemployment" and to action-type activities. His peers would approve of this kind of job interruption. In fact, they might even reproach him if he used his job to justify either coming late to the weekly meeting or leaving a group activity early.

By contrast, employment took on a serious meaning for older informants. The older informants or OBs (old boys) frequently spoke with pride about their jobs, particularly about how much money they could earn and when they expected to own their own store. On the other hand, older informants also had serious complaints about their jobs. Some complained about the interpersonal relations at the workplace. Others complained about their salary and talked about the possibility of changing jobs.

In many cases, job changes in this period were aimed at higher and steadier incomes. The average monthly wage of the respondent to the questionnaire was approximately ¥107,000 ($428) for those fifteen to seventeen years old, and about ¥157,000 ($628) for those nineteen to twenty-three years old. Nine out of sixteen respondents over nineteen expected that they would change jobs in the future. Some of them thought about becoming self-employed and others anticipated moving to more profitable and stable jobs. While the older respondents mentioned specific job titles and carefully examined the merits and demerits of various jobs, those fifteen to seventeen years old rarely did so. In fact it was common for a younger member to quit a job simply because he had spent the previous night out carousing with the gang.

The attitudes of OB, or ex-members toward their peers' jobs also differed from those of active members. When ex-members occasionally turned up at a weekly meeting or party, after the initial greeting they would often ask, "What are you doing these days?" (meaning, what is your job?). Those who were still jobless or working irregularly were ridiculed or given advice by their peers or seniors. If it happened that someone who had rarely worked in his teens began to take a job, he would likely be teased by his peers or seniors, though not in contemptuous tones. When ex-members heard the news about jobs of their companions who rarely worked during their teens or early twenties, they would also react with facial expressions of disbelief or astonishment, and make comments such as, "I can hardly believe he has a job" or "It's so strange . . . he's got a real job!" To be jobless for over a certain length of time was, indeed, regarded as a serious flaw in one's character. Those who, after twenty, lived off their parents or public welfare were despised and frequently became the object of gossip. During their teens (and in some cases, early twenties), many of my informants were able to spend most of their earnings on leisure activities, because they were being supported by their parents. But they regarded being self-supporting as the ideal and looked down on those who were totally dependent on their parents, even for pocket money. Those informants who did live with their parents proudly told me that they had purchased their vehicles with their own money.

Kentaro's reputation among his peers illustrates the ideal of being self-supporting and the changes in informants' attitudes towards employment before and after their "graduation" from gang activity. Although Kentaro had changed his workplace twice, he had consistently worked as a cook since graduating from junior high school. He participated in gang activity only occasionally because he had to work at night. Partly because of his infrequent participation and also because of his excessive promiscuousness, Kentaro was generally despised by his peers. He was regarded as an "insincere" gang member. Some of his peers and seniors even said, "He's not a member of the Ukyo Rengo at all!" But his peers could not help acknowledging his superiority as a cook. After four years of training, at the age of nineteen, he had acquired sufficient skill to open his own restaurant. Kentaro was, then, a model for being self-supporting, "learning a trade," and becoming self-employed—all of which were ideals among my informants. Although his peers scorned him for other reasons, they could not but recognize, grudgingly, his achievement as a skilled specialist; an achievement which many of them aimed for but had not yet attained.

One of the "job" options open to Yankees after graduating from *bosozoku* activity is to become a member of a *yakuza* organization. An office of the K Family (a *yakuza* branch) was located close to one of the Ukyo Rengo hangouts. While some of the members of the K Family harassed and assaulted *bosozoku* members, others sometimes came to the hangouts of my informants and invited them to "visit our office." Members of other *yakuza* groups also attempted to recruit new members from *bosozoku* members. Several of my informants actually visited the offices of *yakuza* organizations where they helped out with various jobs. But becoming a *yakuza* member was not an attractive alternative to holding down a legitimate job, and most eventually cut ties with the *yakuza*.

Although the situation of the *yakuza* underworld is one of the favorite topics of street-corner narratives among Yankees, it is widely acknowledged that *yakuza* membership does not pay unless one is an executive member or has a special (illegitimate) source of income referred to as *shinogi* (hustle). Most lower echelon *yakuza* members either make their own living or make do with a small "allowance" from their superiors in exchange for services as chauffeurs or bodyguards. Lower *yakuza* members are also obligated to do secretarial work in the offices on a rotational basis virtually without remuneration. To make matters worse, they may have to risk their lives, as *heitai* (soldiers), in gang warfare or in conflicts with the police. My informants obtained this type of information through personal experience or rumors about their acquaintances who had become *yakuza* members. Some of the *yakuza* members had been incarcerated for assault or use of firearms. Others had defected to other prefectures to evade police investigation or pursuit by *yakuza* organizations.

Threats and flattery are used to recruit new *yakuza* members. A *yakuza* organization attempted to recruit one of my informants with threats of violence as well as with offers to offset his amphetamine debts to their organization. Once, when I was drinking with the informant and several other ex-*bosozoku* members, one of the ex-members strongly recommended that my informant not give in to *yakuza* threats. This informant later told me that he was working in a supermarket as a sales clerk.

In the jargon among my informants, *kata ni hamerareru* (getting molded into the [*yakuza*] pattern) refers to the process by which one is forcibly recruited by a *yakuza* organization. They generally regard those who "got molded into the *yakuza* pattern" as lacking courage and personal integrity. Several active and ex-members who frequented the *yakuza* offices were openly ridiculed by peers and seniors. The son of a *yakuza* boss was also frequently teased by his peers. When he was asked sarcastically whether he would inherit his father's organization, he replied somewhat angrily, "Never! Not that!" though he later owned a house of prostitution. Another informant had *sujibori* (a "contour line" tattoo) on his left thigh and concealed it with a jockstrap when he wore short pants. (Some *yakuza* fringe members or delinquents have contours of tattoos which are not filled in, either because they do not have enough money or because they hesitate to have such a stigma on their own bodies.) His peers and seniors sometimes jumped on him and exposed the tattoo to make fun of him. But when another informant, who was not a member of a *yakuza* organization, showed up with his shoulders completely tattooed, his peers and seniors worried about him because a tattoo was regarded as something shameful that was hard to efface.

Marriage

Most informants said that marriage is (or will be) the most important determinant of their disengagement from an action-oriented life-style. Toshio insisted that "We are guys, you know. We're still young after twenty-five," and he continued, "Until you get married, until marriage, you're still young." Also, among the choices in a questionnaire item regarding determinants of "settling down" the one about marriage received the largest number of responses.

In August 1984, four male informants got married (two were twenty-two years old and the other two were twenty-one), a twenty-one-year-old was engaged, and two (one twenty-one, the other twenty) were living with girlfriends. Among the four informants who were married, one had two children and two had one each. All of these seven informants who were either married or about to marry appeared only occasionally at weekly meetings of the Ukyo Rengo. They associated with their peers far less frequently than before.

Most of the informants who were nineteen years old and had girlfriends or "steadies." When I asked them about their preferred type of spouse, they generally said that they would not marry a Yankee girl.

> KENJI: I'll choose a girl for my wife who's different from us. I don't like the girls who've done the same things as us. After all, straight girls, I . . . Let me tell you how it is, I'm a stupid guy, you know. But it's because I know I'm stupid that I want a smart girl.
>
> ICHIRO: Those girls I picked up. . . . Suppose that I go steady with one of them; I'd be worried about her past, for sure. For example, I'd think she might've been picked up by other guys before me. My head would be full of those kinds of thoughts. So, I wouldn't choose a girl I picked up.

Most other informants who were under nineteen also said that they would prefer "ordinary" girls to Yankee girls, not to mention female *bosozoku* members. But my informants' negative comments on Yankee girls were often contradicted by their actual choices. Kenji boasted in an interview session that he had a few girl friends and that he would never marry an ex-*bosozoku* girl because, "the baby would be born dressed in *tokkofuku* [*kamikaze* party uniform!] [laughs]" A few months later, however, he started living with a girl who had been known as a tough fighter in her junior high school days and frequently participated in *boso* driving after graduating from junior high school. Ichiro's intended bride was also a Yankee girl who sometimes joined in *boso* driving. Toshihiko's girlfriend was a member of the female subsection of the Ukyo Rengo. Hirokichi's former "steady" was another female *bosozoku* member. She later began living with Takamitsu and, according to his peers, might eventually marry her. Michio's "steady" roommate and later his fiancée was a girl who used to be the leader of a female *bosozoku* group in a southern ward of Kyoto.

Therefore, although male informants generally have negative stereotypes about Yankee and *bosozoku* girls, they tend to consider their own girlfriends as exceptions. It does seem plausible that boys and girls of the same social type would tend to associate with each other and eventually marry each other.

The problem of marriage seems more serious for female *bosozoku* members than for male members. The label of "*bosozoku* girl" or "ex-*bosozoku* girl" was regarded as a more serious stigma than "*bosozoku* boy" or "ex-*bosozoku* boy." Table 6.1 shows the distribution of responses to Question V-5 "What will be your response to your child if he (or she) says he (or she) will become a *bosozoku?*" The results suggest that *bosozoku* youths themselves in general do not regard *bosozoku* activity as desirable and that a stronger negative stereotype is imputed to female *bosozoku* members than to male members by *bosozoku* youths themselves.

In fact, female *bosozoku* members are sometimes openly teased or even criticized by male members in weekly meetings about their "unladylike" behavior, including participation in *boso* driving. In casual conversation with me, several male informants over twenty said that the existence of the female subsection was deplorable and that, formerly, girls never used to get out of their boyfriends' cars even when they joined in *boso* driving. After the female subsection was organized, several male and female members became involved in relationships with each other. From that point on, the "boyfriends" adopted a strict stance toward their girlfriends and refused to allow them to join in *boso* driving, though some girls joined in secretly.

TABLE 6.1 What will be your response to your child if s/he says s/he will become a *bosozoku*?

Questionnaire Item	For a Son		For a Daughter	
	Male Respondents	Female Respondents	Male Respondents	Female Respondents
I will give my approval to him (her)	2	0	1	0
I will let him (her) do what s/he wants to do	22	8	5	2
I will try to persuade him (her) not to become *bosozoku*	18	2	7	3
I will definitely not allow him (her) to become *bosozoku*	14	0	43	4
N.A.	0	0	0	1
Total	56	10	56	10

Female members were offended by the gender stereotype and the discriminatory treatment by male members. But, at the same time, they shared the stereotype with the male members. They said that they could understand the boys' negative attitudes toward the *bosozoku* girls. When I said to Seiko and Naoko that the boys who disliked *bosozoku* girls were a bit self-centered, Seiko answered, "You're right. But I understand how they feel about us. If I was a boy and my girlfriend was a *bosozoku* member, I'd feel lousy." Naoko agreed with Seiko, "Me too. I wouldn't have a *bosozoku* girl as a girlfriend if I was a guy."

It was generally acknowledged among female informants that the approximate age for "settling down" was seventeen for females and nineteen or twenty for males. They were clearly aware that, as *bosozoku*, they were a minority even among Yankee girls. While most male members graduated from junior high schools in Ukya ward, only three *bosozoku* girls came from junior high schools in the same ward. The rest of the girls came from other wards. Recognition of negative stereotypes for female *bosozoku* and a limited "marriage market" are probably two major reasons why the "graduation" of *bosozoku* girls is earlier than that of *bosozoku* boys. In Junko's words:

When you get right down to it, a woman plays the passive role in getting married. A woman is given away [to her husband's family]. If a girl gets detained in a training school or Juvenile Classification Home because of *boso* driving, . . . it'd be a serious disadvantage for her marriage prospects.

Changes in Life-Style

The transition to adulthood for my informants was closely related to a change in reference groups and daily way of life, or more specifically, "how they spend their time and resources, with whom and for whom." Many informants mentioned a decrease in contact with their peers as the most significant difference between their life-style before and after "settling down." They explained that once they settled down, *asobikata* (literally "how to play," or how one spends one's leisure time) would change radically and they would meet with peers only for occasional drinking parties or for an outing at the seaside or some other place a couple of times each year.

A seventeen-year-old informant described how he spent his time: "We sleep in the daytime, get up when the night starts, and then fool around until morning. Yeah, we just keep repeating the pattern. So the distinction between Sunday or something [weekdays] doesn't matter at all. We can't tell which day of the week it is." This statement describes fairly well the life-style of many informants, especially those who were jobless. Many ex-members also lost their jobs several times when they were "young" because they had been drawn into the life patterns of their jobless peers.

Yankees are able to spend their time in a leisurely manner because they are not yet firmly embedded in the institutional framework of occupation and family. Their expectations of relatively abundant job opportunities also tend to make them indifferent to the risks of unemployment and optimistic about the future. They think the time for "settling down" has not yet arrived because their peers are also still playing around, although they realize that, eventually, they will have to leave their life-style behind. Increased commitments to a job, which is seen as profitable and stable, and to a steady girlfriend force a maturing youth to work his schedule around the requirements of his workplace and his girlfriend. After he marries, he has to take responsibility for the allocation of his income for the household budget, childbearing, mortgage payments, etc.[19] It becomes quite difficult for him to spend both time and money with his peers. His past companions also come to hangouts only rarely, and when they do make an appearance, they leave earlier than before. The change in social interaction at hangouts makes those who are still jobless feel uneasy and encourages their transition to adulthood.

A number of ex-members occasionally appeared at the weekly meetings of the Ukyo Rengo. They rarely got out of their cars unless their peers or seniors were there. Even if they did get out and talk to their peers or seniors, they rarely stayed until midnight. In many cases, they left, saying they had to get up early the next morning for work. In addition, most ex-members rarely stayed late even at the parties for "old boys" ("alumni association") of the Ukyo Rengo. At the parties, an ex-member would occasionally get up to make a phone call to his superior at work. Only a few ex-members would join those who went on to a secondary party. Most of those who declined the invitation to the second party mentioned their jobs as the reason.

At a year-end party in 1983, Masahiko went home with his younger brother before midnight even though his peers insisted he stay a while longer. He said he had to wake up for work at 7:00 A.M. Actually he had called his boss from the party to confirm his work schedule for next day. Masahiko was the son of a well-to-do business executive and rarely worked until he got his job as steeplejack in the autumn of 1983 when he was twenty-two. During the summer he sometimes visited weekly meetings of the Ukyo Rengo as an "old boy," but he rarely attended after he got the job. I once asked him after an interview whether he thought he finally had settled down since getting the job. He answered, "Not yet. I'll be able to say that I've finally settled down when I see my buddies less." He also said that he had really learned lessons from his experience in training schools where he had been detained twice and that he thought he should get married as soon as possible if he wanted to really settle down.

Yasuhiro was one of Masahiko's peers and occasionally came to weekly meetings together with Shintaro. He ran a small restaurant and on weekdays he sometimes went drinking with Shintaro and other peers at a bar. But he rarely associated with his peers after his wife gave birth in June 1984. In anticipation of the new baby, in December 1983, he and his wife moved from a room over his restaurant to a small house. When I helped them move, along with one of Yasuhiro's friends, Yasuhiro complained about the high cost of childbirth and said he might become a truck driver in the near future, a profession that would pay better than his restaurant, in order to support his family.

Expectations About Transitions

My informants' expectations about the ages at which various events signifying the transition to adulthood would take place were

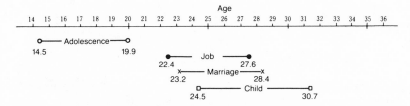

FIG. 6.3. Expectation of *Bosozoku* for Age at Transition Events, and Maximum Ages: Female (N = 10). (Reprinted, by permission, from I. Sato, *Yankee, Bosozoku, Man of Society* [Tokyo: Shin'yosha, 1985], 221.)

relatively unanimous. They also believed that there were certain maximum ages for these events, after which the events would be judged "too late." Questions V-1, 2, and 3 in the questionnaire were designed to estimate the expected age for each event and its maximum age. Figure 6.2 shows schematically the mean of responses to each question. According to the figure, male informants anticipated that their transition to adulthood would take place during their early to middle twenties. They felt obligated to begin regular employment and get married before thirty, though they believed it was acceptable to have their first child after thirty. The results of the interviews and conversations after the administration of the questionnaire confirmed that thirty was regarded as an age-limit and that they expected to get a regular job and to marry sometime in their early twenties.

Figure 6.3 shows the means for female informants' responses to similar questions.[20] Although there were a limited number of respondents (N = 10), results show that girls expected that they would marry and have their first child at age twenty-one and twenty-two respectively; this was about one year earlier than the expectations of male informants. The maximum ages for the two events were also younger for female respondents than for males. Thus, for girls the age range allowed for the two events was relatively shorter. The range between the averages of expected and maximum age for marriage is about five years for boys, but it is less than four years for girls. For a first child, the range is more than six years for boys and approximately three and half years for girls.

These results give support to the hypothesis that consideration of the "marriage market" is crucial in the relatively early transition of girls from the action-oriented life-style: girls are obliged to settle down earlier than boys because they may otherwise lose the opportunity for marriage. To a lesser degree, male informants' expectations about appropriate ages for transition events and their recognition of maximum

FIG. 6.3. Expectation of *Bosozoku* for Age at Transition Events, and Maximum Ages: Female (N = 10). (Reprinted, by permission, from I. Sato, *Yankee, Bosozoku, Man of Society* [Tokyo: Shin'yosha, 1985], 221.)

ages for the events seem to reflect a similar awareness of the disadvantages of an anomalous transition pattern.[21] Males as well as females stand to face a shortage of potential spouses if they are unable to marry by a certain age. Males' occupational careers will be severely damaged if they have not yet established themselves in a stable job by the age of thirty; employers are generally not willing to employ those who are over thirty and have irregular employment records. Irregular employment will also jeopardize their marital life. Although many male informants felt that they had the option of continuing a youthful (but less risky) life-style after disengaging themselves from full participation in the group, even that option disappeared by age thirty. They explained that they had to "settle down" in the true sense of the word, i.e., marry and get a stable job, before thirty. The possibility of not doing so was almost unimaginable for them. The age of thirty was, then, regarded as the end point of their participation in the youth "leisure class."

SUMMARY

Yankees are liberated from many conventional institutions upon graduation from junior high school or after dropping out of high school. They are "gentlemen of leisure" who are able to pursue an action-oriented life-style which includes great risks as well as opportunities for thrills and excitement. They have little familial obligations during adolescence. In addition, their occupational careers are not jeopardized by their deviant activities as seriously as is the case with those who aspire to higher education. Yankee youths can become unemployed when they are "too busy" with leisure activities to continue work. While they are minors, the penal sanctions are relatively lenient. When situations are favorable, they even dare to participate in *bosozoku* activities involving great physical risks as well as the risk of apprehension by the police.

Yankees are, however, reincorporated into conventional society around their late teens or early twenties by the institutional framework of a conjugal relationship and job, as well as by the strict penal sanctions applied to those over twenty. The age norms proscribing the continuation of "childish" activities and the change in the social-interaction patterns among peers also encourage the disengagement from the action-oriented life-style. By their early twenties Yankees graduate from risky undertakings to become "ordinary citizens," whose life-style is almost totally alien to participation in *bosozoku* activities.

The process of "settling down" or "role exit" from *bosozoku* to ordinary citizen is, then, a semi-institutionalized one, including the characteristics of "group exit." Most Yankees regard the role exit as irreversible and socially desirable. Though the designation "ex-*bosozoku*" has negative implications, the *bosozoku* role is not considered a "master role" which is central to one's self-identity and needs a complex procedure to quit.[22]

Bosozoku and Yankees are not the only youth styles in Japan. Numerous youthful "tribes" (*zoku*) have proliferated amid the unprecedented affluence. With their explicitly deviant styles and spectacular performances, some of the youth tribes incite public outrage and moral panic. The next chapter will deal with societal contexts of the emergence of *bosozoku* and social reaction against them.

III   *Context of Play*

7   Through the Looking Glass: Social Context of *Bosozoku* Play and Moral Panic

With great numbers of both the educated and the ignorant, the play-attitude towards life of the adolescence has become permanent. . . . [W]e have already alluded to the prevalence of state of mind which might be called one of permanent adolescence. It is characterised by a lack of sense of decorum, a lack of personal dignity and of respect for others and the opinions of others, and an excessive concentration on self. The general weakening of judgment and of the critical impulse had prepared the soil for the spread of this attitude. . . .

In this world full of wonders man is like a child in a fairy tale. He can travel through the air, speak to another hemisphere, have a continent delivered in his home by radio. He presses a button and life comes to him. Will such a life give him maturity? On the contrary.

—Johan Huizinga, *In the Shadow of Tomorrow*

BOSOZOKU AS A MIRROR FOR JAPANESE SOCIETY

In 1976, a large-scale mob outbreak took place in Kobe involving a crowd of more than 10,000 people. The mob scene originally began as high-speed racing by motorcycle gangs. Shortly after the incident, the Japanese Cabinet decided to organize a committee to restrain *bosozoku. Bosozoku* activity was at a new peak in 1980, and an article titled "Youths with No Future: For the Elimination of *Bosozoku*" appeared as the feature article in the *White Paper on the Police* published in 1981. In the same year, special committees were organized in thirty-eight of forty-seven prefectures to cope with the *bosozoku* problem. Governments of twenty-one prefectures and 591 cities, towns, and villages passed resolutions for the *tsuiho* (expulsion) of the *bosozoku*.[1] By that year, thirty-one local governments had instituted prefecture-wide regulations against the use of motorbikes by high school students. In 1982 the Japanese PTA Union passed a resolution for a complete ban of applications for licenses or the use of motorcycles by high school students. In 1983, unions of garage owners in thirty-six prefectures carried out campaigns against illegal modifications of vehicles. During the same year, unions of gas station owners in thirty prefectures conducted campaigns against supplying fuel to modified vehicles.[2] During those years, one could see numerous signboards, posters, and stickers from these campaigns on city streets, garage walls, and in gas stations across Japan. Such words as *konzetsu* (extermination), *zetsumetsu* (eradication), and *kaimetsu* (annihilation) were frequently found on such placards.

While *bosozoku* youths defined their own gang activity as play, the general public defined it otherwise. In media reports as well as in the public mind, miscellaneous crimes including theft, glue sniffing, drug abuse, battery, rape, and murder were attributed to *bosozoku*. *Bosozoku* were also said to be the first reserve for *yakuza*. An article in a national paper even attributed one-fourth of all criminal offenses committed in a year to *bosozoku* and concluded that the offenses by *bosozoku* made the "record of juvenile delinquency in the past year [1980] the worst in history."[3] Strangely enough, the *bosozoku* was also often characterized as a pitiable victim who suffered from chronic frustration and an inferiority complex. In such a pathetic characterization, the "real" origin of the evil forces was attributed to adverse social conditions such as meritocratic society and "academic-pedigree-oriented society." In short, while motorcycle gang activity might be play for most Japanese youngsters on the street, it meant a grave threat to the social order or a manifestation of social maladies for the general public.

The diabolical and pathetic characterizations of the *bosozoku* were, in many cases, achieved by arbitrary and all-inclusive use of the term *bosozoku*. The nebulous use of the term also led to unfounded inferences from official reports and statistics. The official documents themselves were often constructed in misleading ways. It seems to me that the media reports and official documents reveal much more about moral confusion in Japanese society than about the social background of motorcycle-gang activity.

In Part I of this volume I examined the text of *bosozoku* play. Part II was devoted to a description and analysis of the natural history of the Yankee's life-style as a context of social play. Here in Part III I will examine much broader social, economic, and cultural backgrounds which engendered *bosozoku* play and societal definitions of the social play. *Bosozoku* and societal reaction against motorcycle gangs will be taken as a "mirror" for Japanese society during the period of the mid-1970s to the early 1980s.

The mirror metaphor used in this chapter is somewhat different from the familiar metaphor the news industry employs when it treats the relationship between certain forms of deviance and their social background. Deviance is, indeed, a "sign of the times," because deviant acts, in their social context, cannot but reflect their social background. It should be noted, however, that the various organs of the media themselves in their responses to deviance can be also compared to reflections in a mirror. We can often find public anxieties and obsessions reflected in the media treatments.[4] In such cases, delinquency becomes a sort of inkblot test upon which people project their own conception of what is normal and what is aberrant.

YOUTHS' ADVENTURES IN WONDERLAND
Affluence and Changing Life-Styles

If the first three decades of the Showa era (from 1926 to the mid-1950s), the era of Emperor Hirohito, is characterized by misery and poverty amid struggle for industrialization and the aftermath of World War II, the second three decades (from the mid-1950s to 1989) may be marked by the rapid economic development and the emergence of a mass-consumption society. The rapid postwar development of Japan coincided with similar worldwide trends from the 1950s to the early 1970s. The average growth rate of the gross national product in Japan was 8.3 percent during the 1950s and 10.5 percent during the 1970s. Although economic growth slowed down considerably due to the oil crises of 1973 and 1978 and the subsequent worldwide recessions, Japan negotiated the economic crises with relative success. The average growth rate for the GNP was recorded at 3.7 percent during the ten years from 1974 to 1983. Japan has even expanded its share in several sectors of the international market since the oil crises. Japan has now grown into an advanced industrial nation which sometimes boasts of itself as an economic "superpower." It has even been criticized by Western nations, notably the United States, as a consequence of severe trade imbalances since 1977.[5]

What is remarkable about the postwar economic development in Japan is that it was achieved with remarkably low levels of unemployment and relatively even income distribution. With a booming economy and great demand for labor, the unemployment rate decreased from a 2 percent level between 1955 to 1960 to less than 1.5 percent between 1961 and 1974. Even during the recession following the oil crisis, the demand for labor in the service sectors had kept the unemployment rate below 2.5 percent, although there was an increase to 2.6 percent in 1983.[6] Japanese workers are not only "fully" employed but also relatively equally paid. There was a narrowing of distinctions in income during the 1960s. The interquartile variation in average wages of all male workers declined to 0.52 in 1973 from 0.73 in 1954.[7] The Gini index of household income, after income taxes were subtracted, was 0.1775 in 1982, compared with 0.1890 in 1965.[8]

Affluence and the relatively even distribution of wealth have led to improvement in the material standard of living and abrupt changes of life-style for people in many sectors of the economy. While in 1955 the average household allotted 46.9 percent of its consumption expenditure for food, 28.2 percent of its spending went for this purpose in 1982. By contrast, the proportion of spending for "miscellaneous items" (grooming and hygiene, transportation and communication, education, culture and recreation, and entertainment) rose from 30.4 to 49.5 percent during the same period.[9] Meanwhile Japanese families had purchased a great number of durable goods. In 1958, 24.6 percent of Japanese households owned washing machines and only 3.2 percent owned refrigerators. By the mid-1970s, almost all households had washing machines, color TVs, vacuum cleaners, and refrigerators.[10] The consumerism that has developed since the 1960s has featured the automobile as the symbol of the good life. Through appeals to their youthfulness and resourcefulness, Japanese youngsters are attracted to the automobile, which is now easily available to them.

Material affluence has also increased the importance of leisure and recreation for people's lives. Technological innovations in industrial production and the demands of unions for fewer working hours have reduced working time since the early 1970s. The average weekly time spent for recreational activities by all age groups increased from about five and three-quarter hours in 1970 to about six and a half hours in 1980.[11] The money spent in real terms for recreational activities increased by 140 percent from 1965 to 1980.[12]

The transformation of Japan from a production-oriented society of scarce consumer goods to a consumption-oriented society of abundance was especially evident between the mid-1960s and the early 1970s. A temporary recession occurred in 1957–58 as a result of monetary restraint; the *White Paper on the Economy 1959* cited the sharp increase in individual consumption as a crucial factor in the ensuing economic recovery in 1958. In turn, increased spending was largely for the purpose of electrical appliances and clothing made from synthetic fibers. The white paper called this trend in spending for new commodities the *shohi kakumei* (revolution in consumption) and this phrase was taken up instantly. In the mid-1960s the further development of affluence and consumerism produced another catchword—*Shohi wa bitoku* (Consumption is a virtue).

After the oil crisis of 1973 there was a recession, many firms went bankrupt, unemployment mounted, and the prevailing euphoria subsided. Nonetheless, Japan remained a relatively affluent, mass-consumer society during the ten years between 1974 and 1983. This was a time, however, when Japanese society had to confront new problems that would have been almost unimaginable during the critical postwar period of starvation and poverty. For example, obesity instead of malnutrition, and "excessive" rather than limited amounts of leisure time, became national concerns in contemporary Japan. Youth problems, especially the "third wave of delinquency," the upsurge in delinquency beginning in the early 1970s, were a social concern of an affluent society. Older generations had difficulty in making sense of such matters. Material affluence seemed to have brought forth societal anomy, which had produced moral confusion and an overreaction against the "social problem." More generally, the increased affluence of young people had led to various types of experimentation among Japanese youths.

Consumption and the Styles of Affluent Youths

Affluent Youths. In a society of widespread affluence, the individual and social life of Japanese adolescents and young adults is inseparably bound up with leisure, consumption, and the mass media. Technological innovations, economic development, and a quasi-mystical or fanatical belief in the "academic pedigree" have led to high rates of enrollment, after the required period of compulsory education, in high schools and colleges. As a consequence, many youths do not work. In 1984, more than 94 percent of the graduates of compulsory junior high schools entered senior high schools. Among high school graduates, 36 percent went on to colleges.[13]

Although until the mid-teens many youngsters are given relatively large allowances,[14] most of them are quite busy studying and preparing for entrance examinations.[15] It is not rare that junior high school students (or even primary school students) stay at *juku* (cramming classes) until 9:00 P.M. or later. The situation changes dramatically once the Japanese youngsters are liberated from the "examination hell" and enter colleges. Japanese college students, who have few academic obligations in order to graduate, have abundant free time. They can earn sizable sums of money from *arubaito* (part-time work, from the German "Arbeit"), mostly as tutors for schoolchildren or in service industries.[16] Many of them also use credit and loans for recreational purposes. Generally their parents pay for their tuition and often given them considerable sums of allowances. Ordinary students have their own electrical appliances, such as color televisions and hi-fi sets, and they may travel abroad. Many of them have automobiles, although for most purposes there is a well-developed, safe public transportation system. Parking space is a serious problem at many colleges and often faculty find students' cars that are more expensive than their own and sometimes are imported from foreign countries.

The affluent life-style continues between graduation and marriage. Young professionals or white-collar workers have far less free time than during their college days; nonetheless, reduced working time, the widespread five-day work-week, occasional national holidays, and summer vacations allow them to spend their incomes and bonuses on recreational activities. With their great purchasing power and their pursuit of leisure activities, unmarried young professionals or white-collar workers in Japan have been called the *dokushin kizoku* (unmarried aristocrats), a phrase first used in 1977.[17]

Working youths without a college education can earn as much as educated workers, and differences in income remain small until workers are about 30 years of age. Between the ages of 20 and 24, high school graduates earn about 92 percent as much as those with college degrees, and incomes are about equal for those between 25 and 29.[18] Working youths may also use credit and loans to purchase commodities, especially expensive items such as automobiles. Although the available statistics do not make distinctions as to levels of education, among unmarried male workers less than 19 years old, 53 percent own television sets, 54 percent own stereo sets, and 55 percent own cars. Of those between 20 and 24 years old, 60 percent have televisions, 58 percent own stereos, and 55 percent possess automobiles.[19] With fewer hours on the job, working youths also enjoy much free time. In addition, with a relatively high demand for labor, it is possible for them to temporarily leave their work and "have fun" for a while. In spite of moderate economic growth during the ten years between 1974 and 1983, there had always been more jobs than applicants for positions ordinarily offered to junior and senior high school graduates.

Behaviors and tastes of affluent Japanese youths are influenced to a considerable degree by the youth-oriented media, though the youths often have an influence on the media and trends in the consumer market. Weekly (or biweekly) news magazines directed at young people started in the 1960s: *Heibon Punch* was first produced in 1964, and *Weekly Playboy* appeared in 1966. Such publications feature color photographs of nude or seminude pinup girls and are concerned entirely with consumption and leisure, dealing extensively with fashions, entertainment, sports, pop music, cars, and sex. Their circulations vary from some 450,000 to about one million.[20] The youth-oriented consumer goods presented in such magazines and other media, including television, movies, and radio, create a sizable market and have great impact on the Japanese cultural scene. A considerable portion of the market for pop music is dominated by *jaritare* (kid singers) whose musical talents are comparable (or in some cases even inferior) to those of amateurs. Still, their songs frequently rank at the top of the hit charts. The commercial success of the youth-oriented media also has a great influence on the publishing world. Shueisha sold 2.9 million copies of one issue of a weekly comic magazine called *Jump* in 1979.[21] Several major publishers who used to publish exclusively academic and literary books (e.g., Kadokawa, Chuokoron, Kawaide) followed the lead of Shueisha and turned to publication of comic books. Now some 40 percent of weekly magazines and 20 percent of monthly magazines are comic magazines in Japan.[22]

Taste Cultures. College students and professional or white-collar workers with college degrees on the one hand, and working youths on the other, constitute the most conspicuous "leisure class" in Japan. But the tastes of these two groups often show significant differences, especially in their most conspicuous manifestations by the fashion leaders of the respective groups. College students and urban "unmarried aristocrats" hold sophisticated dandyism as an ideal (here only male tastes are concerned) and display it through moderate forms of "showing-off."[23] The "proper" and most fashionable coordination of product brands, especially of American or European goods, is the norm among these youths. An outmoded or incongruous combination with specific brand names brings forth ridicule and contempt. Such combinations are regarded as evidence of poor taste, of showing-off through unsophisticated mimicry. The youths of this sophisticated group prefer the masculine themes expressed in athletic activities requiring self-control, such as skiing, tennis, and surfing.

By contrast, the fashions of a considerable portion of working youths tend to manifest outright showmanship tinged with deliberate vulgarity. Many of them wear clothes of garish colors and have short permanent waves. On formal occasions they may also wear vertical-striped, double-breasted coats. Others may regard their attire as vulgar and coarse. The working youths also tend to engage in "conspicuous consumption." While particularly affluent college graduates and "aristocrats" may use European cars, working youths who are well off may buy American sports cars such as Camaros, Firebirds, and Corvettes; these vehicles are generally regarded as evincing bad taste on the part of Japanese owners. Conspicuous display with unabashedly vulgar overtones exemplify the rough and tough masculinity, indeed the thematic virility of working youths' taste, which provides the prototype of Yankee style. This style is also imitated by junior and senior high school students who adopt deviant styles called *tsuppari* (flamboyant defiance), and commit offenses such as paint-thinner inhaling, vandalism, violence at school, and shoplifting. Many of them join in the style of working youths after they enter the work force, following graduation from junior high school or withdrawal from senior high school.

Differences in the "taste cultures,"[24] though they do not necessarily indicate exact coincidence with class or ethnic divisions, in the case of Japan, sometimes produce antipathy or contempt between educated and working youths. The working youths may sneer at the "effeminate" or "affected" poses of college students and young "aristocrats."[25] Urita, the ex-leader of a large *bosozoku* confederation, writes in his memoirs, *Only Saturday is Left for Us,*

> The college boy "dudes" dress themselves up with baggy pants and high-heeled shoes, and pass by with contemptuous eyes on us. I feel like a complete stranger in Roppongi. I hate this town. Of course, I have no taste for high-class restaurants or cozy, classy snack bars [with a youthful clientele].[26]

On the other hand, college students and "unmarried aristocrats" are contemptuous about the "vulgar," "coarse," and "rustic" taste of working youths. They may be offended by working youths' intrusion into their favorite resorts. *The Official Mie Hand Book* [sic], which is a parody version of *The Official Preppie Handbook* and exemplifies the taste of college boys, contains the remark:

> Let's expel those who come to Shonan [a pleasure resort suitable for surfing] with dyed hair and surfboards on a low-slung [Nissan] Laurel.[27]

Youthful Tribes and Social Reaction. The conflict between the two taste cultures of the young is far less conspicuous than the adult-youth conflict manifested in the form of adults' antipathy against and anxiety about youthful stylistic innovations. This adult-youth conflict is, in many cases, represented through the mass media. The prolonged schooling, rapid sociocultural change in the postwar period, the afflu-ence of youths, and the development of youth-oriented media have resulted in increased age segregation[28] between adults and youths in postwar Japan. As in many other industrial nations, age rather than socioeconomic status or communal units often becomes an important criterion for role or status definition, the basis of social interaction, and sometimes mobilization at the societal level.[29] The Japanese public, especially adults, have often expressed antipathy, indignation, or dis-may at the conspicuous manifestations of age segregation, and have criticized the "rebellious," "flamboyant," "degraded," "selfish," or "hedonistic" attitudes of the young. Both the development of dis-tinctive adolescent life-styles, and societal reactions against them have been promoted by the growing mass media, which have identified sev-eral youthful "social types."[30] "Youth problems" have often been represented by the visual or pictorial images of youths with distinctive appearances and characteristic labels.

The numerous youthful *zoku* (tribes) who appeared in the postwar period are a typical example of such youthful social types. In postwar Japan the suffix *zoku* frequently has been used, both by the mass media and among the general public, to categorize groups, particularly of young people, with distinctive life-styles. Many youthful *zoku* bor-rowed styles from their counterparts in Western nations, especially the United States, which has provided models for consumer life and pop culture for the Japanese. Among them were the beat-*zoku* (who first appeared in 1959), Ivy-*zoku* (1964), high teen-*zoku* (1964), *ereki* (elec-tric guitar)-*zoku* (1965), hippie-*zoku* (1967), *angura* (underground)-*zoku* (1968), psyche(delic)-*zoku* (1968), and rock'n'rollers (1980). One of the most notable instances was *taiyo-zoku* (the sun tribe) in the mid-1950s, the first youthful *zoku* in postwar Japan. The *taiyo-zoku* was considered to exemplify irresponsibility, impulsiveness, and anti-adult character—the features of what Parsons and others called "youth culture."[31] The "sun tribe," indeed, marked the emergence of spec-tacular youth culture in the developing consumerism and age segrega-tion in Japan.

On the one hand, the images of these *zoku* or youthful social types and their distinctive styles serve to give order and meaning to other-wise boring and purposeless adolescent lives. In many cases, the novel style and identity may also offer opportunities for youths to have fun, thrills, kicks, and excitement. On the other hand, such styles are re-garded, especially by adults, as the manifestations of subcultural traits, of the sort displayed by an alien "tribe." The news industry often expresses moral indignation and mockery, as well as curiosity and fascination with such novel styles. Designations formed with *zoku*, then, in many cases reveal the cognitive and moral systems of a society at large which revolves around the fear that "extreme differences in performance style may lead ultimately to disastrous societal or personal consequences."[32] The social representation of such youths serves as a mechanism for social control and suggests a guideline for mobilization of social control agencies, though these measures may sometimes have unanticipated consequences.

The *kaminari-zoku* (thunder tribe), circuit-*zoku*, and *bosozoku* were stylistic deviations which involved three components characteristic of a mass-consumption society—affluent youths, the media, and vehicles—and exemplified social reaction against youthful experimentation. Through inclusion of a great portion of the youth population and intensification of conflict with social control agencies, motorcycle gang activity increasingly acquired the tastes of working youths, involving the theme of outright defiance and manifestation of rough and tough masculinity.

FOLK DEVILS AND MORAL PANICS: THE CREATION OF THE *BOSOZOKU*
The "Moral Passage" of Motorcycle Gangs

The "play" of motorcycle gangs was not a completely novel phenomenon of the *bosozoku* period. Motorcycle gangs have existed in Japan since the mid-1950s. But it was not until the mid-1970s that such gangs became a serious public concern, and societal reaction assumed unitary and nationwide proportions.

When motorcycle gangs first appeared in the mid-1950s, those youths who drove motorcycles in a group were not members of clearly defined groups. They often defined themselves as *otokichi* (motorbike maniacs or sound freaks), and an encounter in a certain place was enough reason for group driving. It was the public and mass media that imputed the assumed characteristics of collective enterprise by giving the label *kaminari-zoku* (thunder tribe). This label derived from the loud exhaust noise emitted from their mufflerless motorcycles. Those youths who were called *kaminari-zoku* were in most cases either sons of wealthy families or auto mechanics. They had access to motorcycles that were still to expensive for ordinary youths.

Since the mid-1960s, motorization in Japan advanced, and automobiles as well as motorcycles came to be used by gangs.[33] Three names were applied to the gangs during this period: thrill-*zoku*, mach-*zoku*, and circuit-*zoku*, the last name being the most popular. A relatively large number of youths from various socioeconomic backgrounds joined in the gang activities. Toward the end of this period, several incidents occurred in which large groups with an audience watching the gang activities gathered in parks and streets. The audience varied from a few hundred to about a thousand. These incidents were easily suppressed by the police force and did not grow into mob scenes.

During the five years form 1967 to 1972, several events occurred in some western prefectures in which motorcycle gangs and their audience grew into mobs that destroyed cars and stores. The most serious was the *Toyama Jiken* (Toyama Incident) in 1972, in which over 3,000 observers joined in the mob and 1,104 people were arrested. After that incident, the attention of the mass media was attracted to the motorcycle gangs, and the name *bosozoku* (out-of-control tribe or violent-driving tribe) came into wide use. Many similar episodes followed throughout Japan, and the number of youths joining *bosozoku* groups increased. The groups came to have relatively articulated organizational arrangements. Even intergroup confederations were formed. The number of members was estimated at about 40,600 in 1981, while it was estimated at about 12,500 in 1973.

In the *kaminari-zoku* period (from the mid-1950s to the mid-1960s), motorcycle gangs were treated as a "bunch of noisy kids." Occasional traffic accidents, and others' annoyance with exhaust noise, sometimes attracted media attention and led to calls for strengthened police regulation. But the gangs were often viewed as "victims" entrapped in behavior emphasizing "speed and thrills."[34]

This treatment was still predominant during the circuit-*zoku* period (from the mid-1960s to the mid-1970s): The term *kaminari-zoku* was used as frequently as circuit-*zoku*. Several mob outbreaks, which occurred mainly between 1967 and 1972, gradually changed the image of motorcycle gangs. News reports portrayed the groups involved as rioters or as a hot-blooded, disorderly crowd. Nonetheless, deviant behavior among the gangs was attributed to "crowd psychology," and spectators as well as gangs were blamed.

The situation changed "dramatically"—i.e., drastically and in dramaturgical form—in the *bosozoku* period (from the mid-1970s to the early 1980s). Crimes committed by individual *bosozoku* youths, as well as *boso* driving and gang fights, began to appear in headlines. The expressions "criminals," "delinquents," and "criminal group" were frequently used in news reports. Motorcycle gangs appeared as full-fledged villains, or indeed as devils who should be "expelled" or "eradicated." During this period, the social drama featuring motorcycle gangs increasingly acquired the overtones of a morality play or "sacrificial" drama,[35] though pathetic characterization of *bosozoku* often appeared in combination with the diabolical depiction.

The Natural History of Morality Play

Figure 7.1 shows the number of articles about *bosozoku* that appeared in three major newspapers from 1973 to 1984.[36] Variations in the numerical frequency of articles reflect fluctuations in *bosozoku* activities. Several circuit-*zoku* mob incidents from 1967 to 1972 preceded the increased attention given to such groups in 1974. After the Toyama incident of 1972, flagrant and destructive outbreaks of this sort took place in twenty-four of the nation's forty-seven prefectures. It was during this year that the police conducted their first survey of motorcycle gangs. Three large-scale confrontations between motorcycle gangs or between gangs and the police took place in Kanagawa, a prefecture adjacent to Tokyo, in January 1974 (Hitler vs. Alleycats), January 1975 (Kanagawa Racing Club vs. Kanagawa Prefecture Police), and June 1975 (Tokyo Racing Club vs. Kanagawa Racing Club); all of them attracted media attention and contributed to the vilification of the *bosozoku* image. But it was, above all, the Kobe Festival incident in 1976 that gave the word *bosozoku* wide currency. At that time, a "circuit game" took place throughout the festival (14, 15, 16 May), and culminated in a mob scene on May 15. A crowd of more than 10,000 people joined the rioters, destroying taxicabs and patrol cars, and stoning and burning police stations. The incident gained further notoriety when a crowd pushed a police truck into a cameraman and killed him.[37] More than one-third of all the newspaper articles about *bosozoku* in 1976 dealt with this incident.

Variations in the number of articles from subsequent years roughly correspond to the fluctuations in *bosozoku* activity shown in police surveys. The smaller number of articles in 1979 corresponds to the decline in *bosozoku* activities after new traffic laws, which made the very act of collective driving illegal, took effect in December 1978. In 1979 the number of participants and vehicles in *boso* driving and gatherings declined by more than half. But the *bosozoku* became more active in 1980, when it was generally known that the laws had relatively weak deterrent effects. Attention of the mass media turned again to crimes, as well as gang fights and *boso* driving, which were attributed to "revived" and "more wicked and worse" motorcycle gangs.

The decline in the number of articles after 1982 reflects a corresponding reduction in *bosozoku* activity since the revision of the traffic laws in 1981, reinforcing the penal sanctions against collective driving. During the four years from 1980 to 1983 the number of partici-

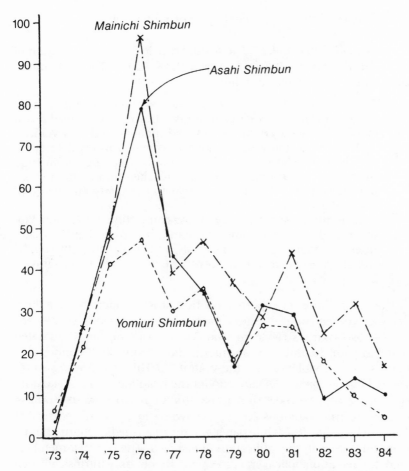

FIG. 7.1. Number of Newspaper Articles about *Bosozoku*, 1973–84.

pants and vehicles in *boso* driving had fallen by more than half. The number of youths involved in gang fights in 1983 was less than one-seventh of that for 1980. Although newspapers occasionally reported *bosozoku*-related incidents after 1982, media attention has been attracted to "novel types" of motorcycle gang activities among loosely organized groups since that year. Among them are *zeroyon* (drag racing)-*zoku*, *kyoso-zoku* (racing tribe), and circuit-*zoku*.

Bosozoku, who soared to stardom as social devils in the mid-1970s and "revived" in 1980, have been mentioned rather infrequently during the last seven years and thus have been "exorcised" or "expelled" from media reports and the public mind.[38]

Shapes of the Devil: Techniques of Vilification

The Label "Bosozoku." The feature article of the 1981 edition of the *White Paper on the Police,* "Youths with No Future: For the Elimination of *Bosozoku,*" begins as follows:

> *Bosozoku,* who have been condemned as antisocial groups, have become even more vicious recently. They not only speed down city roads as if they owned them, and endanger ordinary vehicles and residents, but also repeatedly commit various delinquent acts, including ferocious and violent ones. In particular, in 1980 the power and activity of *bosozoku* reached unprecedented expansion and became a great threat to the safety and peace of citizens' everyday life.
> In addition, *bosozoku* have a close connection with school violence and *yakuza.* On the one hand, by promoting the delinquency of violent groups in schools, and, on the other, by supplying a source of recruitment for *yakuza, bosozoku* further aggravate both problems.[39]

The *Asahi Shimbun* reported on this article under the headline, "BOSOZOKU BECOMING CRIMINAL GROUPS/THE WHITE PAPER ON THE POLICE—BOSOZOKU ALSO PULL THE WIRES OF SCHOOL VIOLENCE," and stated that "In sum, *bosozoku* are an intermediate group with connections both to school violence and the *yakuza.*"[40] This article was also reviewed by the *Yomiuri Shimbun* under the headline, "[THEY] PROMOTE SCHOOL VIOLENCE—HALF OF THEM CONNECTED WITH YAKUZA/TAKE A SCALPEL TO THE FEROCIOUS BOSOZOKU—WHITE PAPER ON THE POLICE."[41] The article in the 1981 white paper and the mass media reports about it were final steps in the vilification of *bosozoku.* The *bosozoku* members were treated as diabolical creatures who are not only intrinsically evil but who conjure up other devils in a conspiracy to bring calamities into the world.

Arbitrary and all-inclusive use of the term *bosozoku* contributed considerably to the vilification of motorcycle gangs. In reports about crimes, the word *bosozoku* may have any of five meanings: (1) *bosozoku* groups themselves; (2) youths who are affiliated with a specific group; (3) youths who occasionally participate in *boso* driving or other activities; (4) youths who, because of their appearance or paraphernalia, resemble *bosozoku* members; and (5) youths who used to be *bosozoku* members. The word is, then, often used as a generic term to refer to youth crimes in which vehicles are involved, whether or not the youths have any affiliation with specific groups or any such self-image. Youth crimes associated with the use of motor vehicles become, by definition, *bosozoku* crimes. The term becomes very supple, with many applications, and the designation *bosozoku* becomes a catch-all category that retains any of a number of negative images.

Headlines are quite misleading in this respect. In many cases, when a careful reader moves beyond the headlines, he finds that the articles themselves deal with "crimes of *bosozoku*" that were neither committed by active gang members nor associated with specific groups. In news stories involving crimes by "ex-*bosozoku*," the prefix "ex-" (*moto*) is frequently set in much smaller type than the rest of the headline. In some cases, the prefix is completely omitted.

In one of the most notorious "*bosozoku* murder" cases in 1976, an ex-*bosozoku* formerly of the "Mad Special" group, ran down and killed a drunken person who had kicked his car. This incident was frequently cited by journalists and in academic works as a typical case revealing the "*bosozoku*'s abnormal attachment to cars."[42] Among the three major newspapers, only *Yomiuri Shimbun* mentioned the fact that the offender had withdrawn from *bosozoku* activity three months before the incident; but even this paper called one traffic violation and one count of theft by the ex-*bosozoku* member a "ferocious criminal record."

More extreme examples are found in headlines dealing with crimes and youths who, because of their appearance or paraphernalia, look like *bosozoku*. In the story under the headline "A MAN IN CRITICAL CONDITION/BEATEN BY BOSOZOKU,"[43] the "*bosozoku*" were, in fact two men who were about twenty years of age and drove "a modified car producing great exhaust noise." Similarly, in an incident of "*bosozoku* murder" in 1978, the culprits were defined as "*bosozoku*,"[44] or "ferocious *bosozoku*,"[45] on the grounds that they used modified cars.[46] This incident, as with the murder case in 1976, was said to be an instance of *bosozoku*'s "abnormal attachment to their cars."

Even for crimes committed by active *bosozoku* members, the news industry uses the word *bosozoku* in misleading ways and furthers vilification. Mundane day-to-day crimes (such as shoplifting, vandalism, ordinary traffic violations), which otherwise usually do not attract media attention, become newsworthy if they are committed by *bosozoku*.[47] Through such reports, the label *bosozoku* increasingly has acquired its own explanatory potential.[48] Seemingly plain, factual statements, such as "*Bosozoku* boy found shoplifting" comes to imply "A boy committed a crime *because* he is a *bosozoku*" rather than "A boy committed a crime. He happened to be a *bosozoku* member." Other possible attributes of the boy (he might be a high school boy or a factory worker) are ignored because they have little news value and explanatory potential. Through these reports, the label *bosozoku* has become a deviant "master status trait" which has a generalized symbolic value "so that people automatically assume that its bearer possesses other undesirable traits allegedly associated with it."[49] To put it another way, this designation has acquired predictive as well as explanatory potential: "He will engage in shoplifting, for he is (or was or looks like) a *bosozoku* member."

Official reports and statistics are not immune to this type of arbitrariness. On the contrary, the official definition of the *bosozoku* itself includes ambiguities and has led to the characterization of *bosozoku* as "criminal groups" in the mass reports and academic works.[50] This is clearly seen in the argument of "overrepresentation." Using police statistics, Ikeda points out that the rate of arrest for the *bosozoku* population (276 per 1,000 members) is remarkably higher than that for the entire population of that age group (17.1 per 1,000 youths) and characterizes *bosozoku* as a "delinquent group."[51] Such an argument of overrepresentation, and the characterization of *bosozoku* as "criminal groups" are questionable in several respects. First, the police statistics do not distinguish between crimes committed by members of specific *bosozoku* groups and those of nongang members. Nor do the statistics consider differences between crimes related to gang activities and those committed by individuals. The police survey itself shows that nongang members have made up a relatively large portion of that part of the youth population officially defined as *bosozoku:* while this portion made up some 21 to 27 percent in the period between 1976 and 1980, it jumped to 35.7 percent in 1981, and reached 52.4 percent in 1983.

The official definition of *bosozoku* is given in the 1974 police memorandum, "On Strengthening the Regulation of *Bosozoku*":

> *Bosozoku* are those who drive cars and collectively engage in *boso* behavior such as exceeding the speed limit, ignoring traffic signals, and driving illegally modified vehicles.[52]

In the daily work of policemen, subjective judgment plays a crucial role; sartorial styles, forms of vehicle modification, and driving patterns become important criteria.[53] These relatively loose points of reference explain the high proportion of youths who reportedly do not belong to specific *bosozoku* groups but are defined in police surveys as part of the *bosozoku* population.[54]

Whether in official reports or media reports, the label *bosozoku* becomes increasingly absorbent the more it is used, and is imbued all the while with negative images. People may expect that if they could eliminate ("expel," "exterminate," or "eradicate") this diabolical figure, steeped in sin and impurity, they could have a clean and peaceful world.

Visualization of the Devil. As compared with reports about "crimes by *bosozoku*," news reports on *boso* driving and gang fights are less likely to abuse the term. In reports of this sort, sensational headlines using exaggerated expressions suggest a state of anarchy or internal disturbance.

BLAZING FLAMES, FURIOUS CROWD—TURMOIL IN KOBE
ANARCHY LASTS UNTIL MIDNIGHT
THREE YEARS OF STREET RACES—FINALLY A DEATH[55]

BOSOZOKU GANG FIGHTS IN THE CITY CENTER OF TOKYO

[O]n this night the *bosozoku* gatherings included 11 groups, 1,600 vehicles, 3,500 youths on the Ohi Wharf in the city center; there were three groups, 500 vehicles, and 1,500 youths at Jindai-ji Park in Chofu in the Tama district.[56]

Boso drives and gang fights include, indeed, several newsworthy features which are rarely found in activities of other types of youth gangs, such as: large groups, outright attacks on the police, conspicuous paraphernalia, high mobility, and very high noise levels. Photographs constitute an integral part of reports on such activities. While mug shots, pictures of victims' faces, and photographs of the scenes of crimes typically accompany reports of *bosozoku* crimes, pictures of driving or fighting gangs and burning, incinerated, or smashed vehicles are frequently featured with newspaper and magazine reports of *boso* drives and gang fights. These social devils are portrayed at the very scene of their wrongdoing. The evil image is further accentuated by depictions of *bosozoku*'s appearance and paraphernalia—intimidating costumes and "grotesquely" modified vehicles.

Television is the most appropriate medium for reports in this category: it can not only convey a sense of motion more vividly than newspaper and magazine photographs, but it also supplies sound recordings from its coverage of incidents. During the heyday of *bosozoku*, *boso* driving frequently went on the air in special documentary programs as well as in ordinary news programs. The documentary programs may have heightened the emotional involvement of the general public, and quite effectively involved it in the morality play. But they also inspired deeper involvement of the "devils," who were enthusiastic about publicity or notoriety. The documentaries were frequently made at the request of *bosozoku*.[57] The vilification of the *bosozoku* sometimes led, ironically, to "deviance amplification"[58] not through the process of "self-labeling" by deviants, as the labeling perspective on deviance predicts,[59] but through "counter-labeling" and the creation of a counter-identity as the romantic picaro.[60]

Images of the Victim

Once reports on *bosozoku* turn away from gang activity and crime and attend to youths as individuals, a different character image emerges: the *bosozoku* as victim. Mutually contradictory phrases such as "Eliminate *bosozoku*" and "*bosozoku* as pitiable victims" often appear together in the same articles. The coexistence of the two characterizations attest to the moral confusion of the general public. The nebulous connotation of the word *bosozoku* accounts for this coexistence. In the phrase "Eliminate *bosozoku*" the emphasis is on group activity, while the other expression refers to individual *bosozoku* as victims. The representation of *bosozoku* youths as victims of adverse social conditions has become a cliché in public statements and mass media reports.[61] The pathological interpretations of *bosozoku* activity and subculture mentioned in Parts I and II are typical examples of the cliché.

The following excerpt from one article in a series of articles on *bosozoku* in the *International Association of Traffic Safety Science Review* was cited verbatim in the *Yomiuri Shimbun.*[62] This excerpt, though lengthy, shows the typical mixture of the pathological and pathetic views of the *bosozoku:*

> [I]n general, the adolescents who engage in *bosozoku* activity are those junior or high school students who had to choose the vocational career course and give up entering schools of higher grade because of their poor academic achievements. In the case of working youths, they are mostly unskilled manual laborers who belong to the lower social positions. Because they dropped out of competition for higher education in a meritocratic and competitive society, they have a deep-seated self-consciousness as outlaws. They are also victims of an inferiority complex and sense of defeatism in comparing themselves with students of high achievement and with social elites. Furthermore, they are suffering from frustration and irritation due to a frustrated desire for self-realization. Therefore, they have a deep-seated antipathy against social elites and authority, and eagerly seek opportunities to show themselves off in a grandiose manner. It is the "car" and "the feeling of togetherness" with their fellows (who share the same lot) that compensate for this frustration.[63]

In the pathetic characterization of the *bosozoku,* it is often assumed that there are "real" origins for psychological strains which can be attributed to societal pathology. The social symptoms commonly mentioned include oppressive features of the *kanri shakai* (managed society), spiritual poverty in industrial society, alienation in urban settings, and the dysfunctional nuclear family. Defects of the Japanese educational system are typified by such expressions as *gakureki shakai* (academic-pedigree-oriented society), the "examination hell," and *ochikobore* (dropouts, laggards), which are most frequently mentioned as *the* leading causes of *bosozoku*. The *bosozoku* youth is said to have a sense of inferiority, whether as a student with a poor academic record or as a working youth with a poor academic pedigree.

Although the news industry has portrayed *bosozoku* as victims of adverse social conditions since it first applied the term to motorcycle gangs, it was academic and quasi-academic works on *bosozoku* which gave authority to the pathetic image. Media reports often quoted such academic studies or just announced that "many scholars" had pointed out the psychological strains of *bosozoku*. When compared with journalists' reports about *bosozoku*, these academic studies are free from impassioned and grandiloquent expressions such as "ferocious criminals," "blazing flames of burning vehicles," and "evil *bosozoku*." Moreover, many studies state specifically the means of data collection and techniques of analysis, or have references to previous studies. Many also include numerous statistical tables, and some use sophisticated techniques such as tests for statistical significance and multivariate analysis. In such studies, it may seem that the conclusions are written in "neutral language" and do not create or construct the very reality they seek to describe and analyze.[64] This is probably one of the reasons why the news industry frequently refers to "many scholars" as an authoritative source.

A close examination of the works by these "many scholars," however, reveals that these generalizations for the most part are based on shaky evidence and that the "neutral language" is, indeed, another technique of dramatization. Using the technique, the authors of such technical works create a coherent and clear-cut image of *bosozoku* youth out of ambiguous and complex reality, and thus affirm the public stereotype.

Some scholars simply do not mention any empirical findings when they describe the psychological makeup of *bosozoku* youths. Their descriptions seem to be based on inferences from impressions of *bosozoku* activities, and thus are tautological.[65] Several other writers, as a preface to their own descriptions of motorcycle groups, state that "many scholars" have already depicted the psychological traits of *bosozoku* youths; but they do not mention any references.[66] Even in studies that include considerable statistical information about *bosozoku*, the data showing "inferiority complexes," or "frustration" because of poor academic pedigrees, as prevalent among the gang youths tend to be rather shaky. In almost all cases, psychological strain is merely inferred from the statistical data on youths' academic pedigrees.[67]

While in academic studies descriptions of *bosozoku* under psychological strain are relatively long, consideration of adverse social conditions is often quite short and cursory. In most cases, social pathology is taken for granted and is described simply in short phrases such as "examination hell," "managed society," "adverse consequences of urbanization," or "defects of the meritocracy." Virtually no evidence is provided concerning the relationship between adverse social conditions and the activity of specific *bosozoku* groups or the life histories of specific youths. *Bosozoku* activity itself is the only observed evidence presented as a manifestation of any social pathology.[68]

In sum, it seems that academic studies representing *bosozoku* youths as being victims of psychological stress are nothing more than rephrased versions, using "scientific" language, of public stereotypes.

The pathetic image of the *bosozoku* has coexisted with the diabolical image partly because the word *bosozoku* refers both to youths and to their activities. But a more essential reason for this terminological ambiguity is the dichotomy between public vilification of *bosozoku* based upon common images and society's reaction to real and tangible youths. It seems no accident that the conception of *bosozoku* as pitiable victims has been supported by the authors of technical studies of motorcycle gangs. Many of the authors of these studies are staff members of judicial or correctional institutions, and in the course of their work meet *bosozoku* youths firsthand. These people have opportunities to express their own views independently from the views of law enforcement agencies, which are more concerned with the restoration of social order. For their part, journalists must also be well aware of the difference between real young people and their own portrayal of *bosozoku* youths as abominable devils. In mass media reports about accidental deaths of *bosozoku* youths, they are treated not as "dead devils" but as unfortunate victims of traffic accidents. The pathetic image also makes the *bosozoku* seem less terrifying to the public. Here he is not a senseless rogue but a pretty hoodlum with understandable motivation.

Whether it is diabolical or pathetic, any clear-cut characterization of the *bosozoku* makes it possible for the general public to make sense of what appears to be beyond their understanding. The Japanese, indeed, have difficulty in making sense of various types of delinquency that have emerged in the midst of their material affluence. In the early 1980s, they also experienced a vague anxiety about the future of Japanese society.

THE HUNTING OF THE *BOSOZOKU:* THE CONTEXT OF MORAL PANIC
The Third Wave of Delinquency

The vilification of *bosozoku,* accompanied by the seemingly contrasting pathetic image, began in earnest in 1976, when the upsurge in delinquency came to attract increasing media attention and the phrase "the third wave of delinquency" was first used.[69] As compared to the first and second waves of delinquency, the third wave had peculiar characteristics in that it occurred amid widespread affluence. The "first wave," during the aftermath of the Second World War, reached its peak in 1951 and apparently resulted from poverty, starvation, hardship, moral confusion, and disruption in the functions of social control agencies. The sources for the second upsurge of delinquency, which reached its peak in 1964, are usually attributed to social disorganization related to rapid urbanization and the massive participation of postwar "baby boomers" (who were born between 1947 and 1951) in criminal activities.[70]

Official statistics published by the National Police Agency and the Ministry of Justice show that rates of juvenile delinquency for the period between 1978 and 1983 exceeded the highest levels reached during the previous two delinquency waves. This problem, of higher juvenile delinquency rates, may also be adduced from the publications of several institutions (e.g., Ministry of Education, Office of the Prime Minister). As with the *bosozoku* problem, the news industry and scholars used statistics of this sort to dramatize development of the "third wave of delinquency" or the "third peak of delinquency." Numerous popular, academic, and quasi-academic works about delinquency were published. In bookstores, books on delinquency might occupy as much as one-fourth of the "education" or "youth problem" section. Some of these books sold by the million. Juvenile delinquency also became a popular topic of daily conversation among Japanese adults. Numerous campaigns were organized for the treatment and prevention of delinquency.

It is against this backdrop of society's preoccupation with the upsurge in delinquency, marking "the worst record in history," that the *bosozoku* played a role in the drama of scapegoating and redemption. A closer examination of the characteristics of juvenile offenses constituting the third wave, however, reveals that the rise in delinquency was not as serious as the news industry proclaimed. It also suggests that a large portion of the delinquent acts resulted from increased age segregation amid affluence and consequent moral "drift" of a sizable number of younger adolescents, who had less of a stake in conformity than other age groups.

First, the majority of the offenses comprising the third wave were petty thefts. During the ten years from 1974 to 1983, over 70 percent of the juveniles arrested had been charged with larceny; in 1983 as much as 77.2 percent of the charges were for larceny.[71] Petty thefts such as shoplifting and theft of vehicles for joyriding accounted for most of the "larceny." It is widely acknowledged among policemen as well as judicial and correctional officers that most shoplifting has been committed not for the material support but for thrills and excitement or in response to pressure from peers for whom theft is a sort of game.[72]

Second, data concerning the ages of offenders show that increased delinquency does not involve those who have an obstinate, long-standing "criminal predisposition." The rates for adult offenders have declined almost steadily since 1951. The majority of delinquents are between fourteen and seventeen years old. The crime rates for those eighteen to twenty-four years old have remained almost constant. It would seem, then, that at the age of eighteen or nineteen the great majority of adolescents "mature out" from delinquency.[73]

Third, a cross-national comparison also shows that Japan has a remarkably low crime rate compared with other advanced industrial nations. In 1980, proportionately four to five times as many crimes occurred in each of four countries—the United States, Britain, France, and West Germany—as in Japan.[74] There were also remarkable differences between Japan and the United States in the rates of serious offenses. In Japan, for every 100,000 people there were about 1.5 homicides, 2.0 rapes, and 1.9 robberies in 1982; for the United States the proportional rates were 9.1 homicides, 33.6 rapes, and 231.9 robberies.[75]

Even if for Japan crime and delinquency are not such serious problems as in other advanced industrial nations, and even though most juvenile offenses are petty thefts, any perceived increase in aberrant behavior among adolescents will certainly lead to public anxiety. As with the social dramas featuring *bosozoku,* the news industry dwells upon the seriousness of the third wave of delinquency and arouses moral panic in the public. Some spectacular cases have lent themselves to such media treatment, which in the process has intensified public anxiety.

In the news media's coverage of the third wave of delinquency, violence in the family,[76] violence in the schools, and misdeeds of the *bosozoku* have attracted special attention since the mid-1970s. From around 1976 these three types of delinquency had been treated under distinctive designations;[77] at that time the phrase "third wave of delinquency" was first used.[78] While violent offenses had comprised less than 15 percent of all crimes during the decade before 1983 and had not increased markedly, official publications, as well as the news industry, often paid special attention to any short-term increase in violent crimes, and depicted them as the most important feature of the delinquency wave. The feature article in an evening edition of *Mainichi Shimbun* discussed the *White Paper on the Police 1982* under the headline "DRASTIC INCREASE IN JUVENILE DELINQUENCY," and declared that, "[W]ith regard to delinquency involving violence, violent offenses increased by 21.6 percent *as compared with the previous year.*"[79] Thus, the official and media reports gave their readers the impression that delinquent acts had increased both in number and in level of violence.[80]

Although violence at school and in the family aroused some sensational coverage, other forms of delinquency were also treated as though such crimes could occur in many places. First, it was frequently reported that younger adolescents were committing delinquent acts. In 1983, among all adolescents above the age of fourteen, those fourteen and fifteen years old committed 56 percent of the reported offenses; this group was responsible for 25 percent of all offenses, including those charged to adults. This increase in younger offenders is called the *teinenreika* (juvenescence; increase in younger people) of delinquency.

Second, it was also frequently reported that more and more girls were committing crimes. While 27,638 girls were arrested on criminal charges in 1976, in 1982 the number increased to 45,918. The press often reported this "drastic increase in delinquency by girls," though the majority of the offenses by girls were petty thefts and girls were still a minority in the delinquent population.

The third feature of recent delinquency, the increase in such acts among adolescents of "ordinary" families, was often discussed under the phrase *ippanka* (generalization). In 1955 the public prosecutor-general's office determined that 70 percent of all delinquents were from families that were "poor" or "needed welfare support"; only 13 percent of all delinquents came from such families in 1981. On the other hand, the proportion of delinquents from "ordinary" families rose from about 30 to 84 percent during the same period.[81]

To the public, then, the third wave of delinquency appeared to threaten three otherwise protected groups: innocent children, obedient and virtuous girls, and diligent middle-class adolescents. Delinquency no longer seemed limited to specific adolescent groups. Fears of increased violent offenses, the ubiquitous presence of factors leading to crime and to confusion of traditional moral values lent a sense of urgency to the search for the "real cause" of crime, for an identifiable villain who was the master of all the evil forces.

The news industry and those who had written about delinquency had searched for *the* cause for the problem. Numerous factors had been mentioned as *the* central issue. Among the sources given for this problem were postwar modernization, urbanization, westernization, or more specifically Americanization; diversified value systems; the detachment of kinship relationships from the nuclear family, the symbiotic relation between mother and child, and the loss of parental authority leading to a "fatherless society"; a dysfunctional educational system; a harsh and impersonal meritocracy, and the oppressions of a "managed society"; and even the excessive consumption of sugar accompanied by vitamin or calcium deficiencies. As with publications about *bosozoku*, news reporters, scholars, and social commentators who cited these factors rarely provided reliable empirical data as substantiation. Even if the public derived temporary catharsis from the "explanations" or "interpretations" in the works of social commentators, they seldom found means for the resolution of such problems. On the contrary, with so many factors to choose from, people developed anxiety and felt that delinquency was "only the tip of the iceberg," a symptom of general societal disorganization. Indeed it would be difficult to come to terms with many of the societal "causes" over a short period. Many of these problems, which figure in the crude assumptions of "evil causes evil," seemed to reinforce each other and wreaked havoc in the world. A scapegoat was needed, one who could die and leave this world, taking with him all the sins he had brought.

Over a short period the *bosozoku* seemed almost ideal for the role as a villain in this seemingly endless drama, providing the scapegoat for the evils of social disorganization. He had a conspicuous, bizarre, and intimidating costume, and he proclaimed his presence with cacophonic noises from his grotesque and fierce-looking motorcycle or automobile. He was extremely audible, as well as visible, as *the* devil and seemed to embody the evil forces which should be "eliminated" or "exterminated." Moreover, unlike violent children at home, or students who were disruptive in the schools, *bosozoku* acted outside of accepted settings, in the impersonal and anonymous vastness of Japanese cities. While violent or wayward children should be "treated" or "cured," *bosozoku* should be "expelled." The designation of *bosozoku*, or "out of control tribe," was, indeed, suitable for a devil who acts at the margins of moral boundaries. He was betwixt and between those figures too anthropomorphic to be expelled and those societal maladies that were too impersonal and distant to be identified with specific persons (e.g., "managed society," "harsh meritocracy"). He was, as it were, at an "aesthetic distance" from the audience and served to provide a cathartic experience.[82]

As *the* devil, the *bosozoku* was "exorcised" or "expelled" from media reports and the public mind by about 1982. But delinquency is still a lingering question in Japan. The problems of delinquency frequently mentioned in the media include amphetamine abuse, the "drastic increase" in delinquent girls, and *ijime* or the bullying of weak school-children by strong ones. None of these involve a clearly drawn diabolical figure. It is likely that future events will produce another scapegoat, because the overreaction against the *bosozoku* and against the upsurge in delinquency seem embedded in the general public's anxiety about the future of Japan.

Overconfidence and Anxiety through the Looking Glass

Delinquency was among several social problems which had attracted media attention during the period between the mid-1970s and the early 1980s. Other noteworthy concerns, which frequently received wide news coverage, include increases in the divorce rate, the many bankruptcies of business firms, rising unemployment, the increasing number of elderly people living alone, and discontent with the academic-pedigree-oriented society. In many cases, the United States is mentioned as the basis for comparison, and events there are taken as foreshadowing the future of Japan.

Since the beginning of modernization in Japan, the United States and other Western nations have been often taken as both mirror and model for the Japanese people, but the images reflected have changed greatly during the past two decades. In 1968 Japan had the third largest GNP of any nation, just after the United States and the Soviet Union. It has also achieved marked improvement in its material standard of living despite the oil crises. On the economic front Japan has, indeed, "caught up" with Western nations, even superseded many of them. Along the way several advanced nations seem to have developed debilities such as the "British disease" or more generally *senshin-kokubyo* (disease of advanced nations). Whether or not the Japanese people generally speaking wanted to "catch up" with other nations as the political leaders advocated, they have a great deal of confidence, perhaps too much, in the achievements of their country.

More recently, particularly since 1977, this national self-assurance has grown, in the wake of a favorable trade imbalance with the United States and in response to works dealing with Japan's "success" as a nation. The news industry often carries articles about advanced technology in Japan, and sometimes about principles of management and interpersonal relationships within firms supporting the development of such techniques. The news industry also makes much of crime con-

trol, stable family relationships, a developed a relatively cheap medical
insurance system, and the educational achievements of Japanese children, when it addresses such issues or compares Japan to the United
States and other Western nations. Thus the Japanese public has built a
sense of pride in their country as a "superpower" with relatively few
social problems. The extreme popularity of a number of books written
by Western authors about the sources of the nation's achievement[83]
also attests to the overconfidence of the Japanese. Vogel's *Japan as
Number One: Lessons for America* is typical of this genre. The Japanese
edition of this book received its forty-fifth printing in 1985 and, according to an announcement by the Japanese publisher, it sold more
than 600,000 copies in Japan.[84]

The popularity of positive treatments such as this one by a Western
author seems to attest to the Japanese people's pride and confidence in
what is Japanese and what is traditional; although it is not often clear
whether the "Japanese" or "traditional" traits refer to aboriginal sociocultural traits or traits which support the status quo of specific firms
or Japanese society as a whole. Indeed, recent popular works in Japan
tend to reconsider "traditional" institutions (e.g., loyalty to one's own
firm, harmonious senior-junior relationships), and regard them as
positive influences rather than sources of backwardness, as many Japanese used to think in former days.

Still, the perception of "catching up" and of an improved material
standard of living will make people more alert to domestic problems.
They are also more likely to question the value of affluence. Since the
mid-1960s such problems as pollution of the environment and "spiritual poverty amid material affluence" have attracted wide public
attention.[85] More recently, however, it seems that the Japanese have
developed a more serious but vague anxiety about the future, and feel
that their country is approaching a critical turning point. Economic
prospects are mixed at best. Particular concerns include modest economic growth; increased unemployment, which in 1983 surpassed
2.5 percent,[86] the highest rate since rapid growth began; a saturated
domestic market for monetary investment and an urgent need for expansion of foreign investment; and, in 1983, the highest level of
bankruptcy of the postwar era.[87] Among the social problems that are
considered most pressing are demographic disparities, particularly
those involving older people: one projection shows that over 15 percent of the population may be over sixty-five by the turn of the century);[88] the decline of the *nenko* system (seniority system of wage increase) because of the changing age groups employed and the general
improvement of basic salaries and wages. Apart from the representa-

tion of these issues by the media, many problems of this sort actually influence the lives of a considerable number of people. Few "advanced nations" can achieve fully effective solutions to such problems. Nor do they augur well for Japan's future. Other advanced nations—whose "development" may converge with that of Japan—present the dismal prospect of affluent societies stricken with moral confusion and numerous social problems.

It is against this backdrop of a vague anxiety amid overconfidence that the Japanese public, as well as the media, have reacted to new types of delinquency that have arisen in an affluent society. People are astonished that criminal acts are committed in situations of affluence as well as poverty. They learn from media reports, as well as from incidents in their own schools or neighborhoods, that juvenile misconduct is quite possible in a society of affluence and mass consumption. Girls from "ordinary" homes engage in shoplifting for thrills and excitement; fourteen-year-olds commit acts of wanton violence. The Japanese people are also taken aback by the "hedonistic," seemingly anomic and amoral, attitudes revealed by juvenile offenders' own accounts of their actions. News reports quote them as saying, for example, "Everyone shoplifts. Why should I be the only one arrested?" "No specific motives. It was just for fun." "It [battery, which resulted in a murder] was play."[89]

The identification of "new" types of delinquency, and attitudes suggesting hedonism on the part of offenders, led to the phrase *asobigata hiko* (playlike delinquency) around 1970. This state of mind, which is said to affect the majority of Japanese delinquents, is often contrasted to *dentogata hiko* (traditional delinquency),[90] which is committed by poor people or those with serious psychological disturbances. Such concepts may allow people to make some sense of new forms of delinquency, and thus provide some relief when they assume that the sources of delinquency in most cases are not long-lasting problems.

Nonetheless, the increasing number of total offenses and "drastic" increases in violent offenses, as well as amoral and hedonistic attitudes among delinquents, have magnified public concern. Anxiety and moral panic have been especially intense since the mid-1970s, when three types of violence—that in the family, that in the schools, and the violence of *bosozoku*—emerged as basic problems. The public as well as the media have been fearfully preoccupied with the "worst record" yet of delinquency. Juvenile offenses do not seem to be "mere play" any longer. The National Police Agency stopped using the word "playlike delinquency" in 1982 for fear that such terms would understate the seriousness of the problem.[91]

While delinquents themselves may define their misconduct as "play," the general public has become increasingly intolerant of their hedonistic pursuits and have defined them otherwise. The Japanese public and the news industry questioned the morality of *bosozoku* activity by asking "Is this play?" They then defined the situations in terms of interdictions, such as "This is not play" or "This should not be play." Three days after the Kobe Festival incident, the *Asahi Shimbun* published an editorial titled "WIPE OUT THE *BOSOZOKU* DRIVING ON THE WEEKEND." It said,

> Their [*bosozoku's*] activities have come to resemble those of *yakuza*. In fact, there are some *bosozoku* groups which have contact with *yakuza*. Some *bosozoku* were also involved in rape cases. *Their activities have already gone beyond the stage of children's play.* . . .There is only one thing to do, that is, thoroughgoing regulation.[92]

Public anxiety about "Crime in an Affluent Society"—the subtitle of the 1984 *White Paper on Crime*—arouses concern about problems endemic to a prosperous nation, and leads people to reflect on the values lost in their pursuit of material well-being. Malfunctions in the academic-pedigree-oriented society are only some of the problems mentioned in this search for the causes of societal anomy. Advanced Western nations can no longer offer models to solve such problems. On the contrary, they suggest that worsening conditions lie ahead for Japanese society. As in the analysis of the "secrets" of economic success, the Japanese media, and ordinary people, suggest traditional solutions for Japan's failure to achieve societal control over adolescents. Such measures include firmer paternal authority, a Spartan educational regimen, and adolescent groups organized around morally dependable youngsters.

On the other hand, many of the causes of delinquency mentioned by the journalists, social commentators, and scholars are construed to be "traditional," especially the symbiotic or overly close relations between mothers and children, which yielded the catchword *bogenbyo* (diseases originating in the mother).[93] Excessively supervised schools and the academic-pedigree-oriented society are also "traditional" causes of delinquency. Former Prime Minister Nakasone's plan for educational reform was advanced partly to deal with problems of increasing delinquency and the malady of excessive emphasis on academic achievement.

The news industry criticizes or praises such educational projects on an ad hoc basis. For example, while increased supervision is meant to prevent school violence, it is also said to be the source of such problems. Whereas strong emotional ties between mothers and children are regarded as an underlying factor in juvenile violence in the family and indeed elsewhere,[94] it is also often mentioned as a crucial factor in the high educational achievement of Japanese schoolchildren. Such concerns on the part of the media for specific but widely separate problems sometimes further aggravates moral confusion in Japanese society.

Although *bosozoku* has been exorcised from the media and the public mind, vague anxiety remains and delinquency is still a lingering prospect. It seems that moral confusion about education and delinquency will never end, until and unless Japan as a nation finds measures for the social control and socialization of youths who are somehow disoriented, bored, and adventuresome in a society of affluence and increasing age segregation. Until that time, a considerable number of Japanese youths will continue to experiment with styles which sometimes entail serious consequences.

Conclusion: Parody and Anomy in Affluent Japan

> Fear prophets, Adso, and those prepared to die for the truth, for as a rule they make many others die with them, often before them, at times instead of them. Jorge did a diabolical thing because he loved his truth so lewdly that he dared anything in order to destroy falsehood. Jorge feared the second book of Aristotle because it perhaps really did teach how to distort the face of every truth, so that we would not become slaves of our ghosts. Perhaps the mission of those who love mankind is to make people laugh at the truth, *to make truth laugh*, because the only truth lies in learning to free ourselves from insane passion for the truth.
>
> —Umberto Eco, *The Name of the Rose*

CRIME AND PLAY

"One day I'll be back on the streets and I'm gonna be hard, hard—one mean son of a bitch ready for action." So said Michael Hagan, a Los Angeles gang member or "home boy," who was sentenced to the maximum of twenty-seven years to life for first-degree murder. He was twenty-three years old when he sprayed a junior high school girl with bullets from a semiautomatic rifle and killed her on a Los Angeles street. The murder of the girl, who never had belonged to any gang, is reported to have happened as a consequence of intended assault on a rival gang. *Time*, reporting this gang-related murder case, also describes critical changes in American ghettos.[1] It is reported that the burgeoning trade in crack cocaine has transformed "gangs from

This chapter is adapted from my "Play Theory of Delinquency: Toward a General Theory of Action," *Symbolic Interaction* 11 (1988): 191–212, and is used with permission of the publisher, JAI Press. © 1988 by JAI Press, Inc., Greenwich, Conn.

stray hoods into multi-million-dollar enterprises." It has also changed gang activity from an adolescent pastime to full-time work that includes those in their twenties and thirties.

Gang activities in many American cities seem, then, to be "fun" no more. This impression is strengthened when one reads Jack Katz's recent book, *Seductions of Crime*. Quoting numerous ethnographic materials, Katz describes the ways in which street-corner boys in American cities attempt to display the symbols of terrifying evil in earnest. According to Katz, to avoid being thought of as engaging in child's play, they attempt to convince others that they "mean it" through the actual practice of violence.[2] It seems the same in the U.K. The so-called "Birmingham school" of sociologists study expressive, and often deviant, "leisure" pursuits of working-class boys in England. The youths depicted in their monographs seem preoccupied more with resentment against their inferior position in the stable class structure than with the pursuit of fun as a "leisure activity." In these studies, the stylistic deviations of English working-class boys are said to be symbolic rebellions against dominant values.[3] Needless to say, most of the scholars who hold the strain theory or cultural deviance theory discount the playlike quality of delinquency. They treat delinquency either as the behavioral expression of frustrated wants and needs or as an almost automatic response to subcultural imperatives. Even the social control theory, especially its recent versions, cannot fully appreciate "fun" in doing evil. If, as this theory implies, delinquency is the rein of hedonistic impulses liberated from any kind of control, it will lead to total anarchy or chaos, and eventually to dread and anxiety, rather than enjoyment.

I have depicted Yankee/*bosozoku* youths quite differently in this volume. They may appear excessively carefree and almost cheerful to American and British readers. Why are they so different? Does the difference between Japanese Yankees and American and British corner boys reflect actual differences in life on the street in their societies? Or does it merely reflect the obsession and guilt feelings of American and British sociologists about the failed American dream and the stable class structure in the U.K.? Does this volume tell, boastfully, another success story of Japan as an affluent society with few social problems? What would be the general implications of the findings about Yankees/*bosozoku* for an understanding of the relationship between crime and play? This concluding chapter provides tentative answers to these questions and presents an "attraction theory" (as against "reaction theory") of gang delinquency which, as Bordua pointed out nearly three decades ago, had been in abeyance since Thrasher's work.[4]

ACTION ON THE STREET

Hagan, posing in an oblique stance in a photograph in the *Time* article and sporting a blue bandanna, a gang insignia, and signaling with a tattooed hand, says that his delinquent career was "fun" when he was younger. Even after he "got into the radical stuff" he had never dreamed of, he found the dangers of the street "exciting." Yet, the radical stuff was addictive.

Urban ethnographers who frequently observe life on the street first-hand note that many wrongdoings are committed "just for the hell of it." Ethnographers note and describe thrills, kicks, and excitement in street-corner activities, including legitimate and semilegitimate, as well as explicitly illegitimate, ones. What Downes calls the "attraction theory of delinquency" is inspired by the findings of ethnographers. The ethnographic studies[5] suggest that there are two types of action, which correspond to the two different meanings Hagan gives to the thrills and excitement in the Los Angeles ghetto.

Ethnographic Studies

During the 1920s and 1930s, Chicago-school sociologists, notably Shaw, McKay, Thrasher, and Tennenbaum, investigated the natural history and activities of spontaneously formed adolescent play groups. According to them, the play groups emerge in social milieus characterized by social conflict and disorganization, family weakness, and attenuated neighborhood controls. These play groups later grow into gangs in response to intergroup conflict and the youths' struggle against the restraints adults seek to impose.[6] Through intensive case studies of delinquents and extensive analysis of the social milieu of urban areas, Shaw and McKay see the first step in a delinquent career as a playful act or a kind of game.[7] Similarly, on the basis of thoughtful observations of 1,313 youth groups in Chicago's gangland, Thrasher argues that gang activity both satisfies and instigates an adolescent's cravings for thrills, excitement, and new experience.[8] Among other studies by Chicago-school sociologists, Thomas's *The Unadjusted Girl* and Cressey's *The Taxi-Dance Hall* see a "desire for new experience" or girls' quest for a romantic and thrilling way of life as a critical factor for the career of young prostitutes and female "taxi" dancers.[9]

During the late 1950s and 1960s, when poverty was "rediscovered" in the United States,[10] a number of sociologists and anthropologists investigated the life-styles of adolescents and young adults who were from slum, lower-class, or working-class neighborhoods. Some of these investigators dealt with various community groups of youths or young adults who were considered to exemplify subtypes of certain life-styles. These subtypes include the "action-seeker," the street-corner boy, and the "street corner man."[11] Other studies focused on specific social types, such as black drug-users, lower-class youths, and street-corner gangs.[12] These researchers view "kicks," "fun," and the excitement of street-corner activities as the keynote for each life-style.

More recently, several British scholars, as well as some American ones,[13] have published ethnographic studies that deal with playlike deviance among youths who seek active life-styles. Among such studies are those often referred to as the "Birmingham school." They depict British youths' search for action as an attempt to create meaningful experience amid pervasive boredom, or as an expression of resentment arising from life in deprived neighborhoods and from class antagonism.[14] Among other British scholars who are not considered members of the Birmingham school, Cohen discusses the Mods and Rockers, and Marsh, Rosser, and Harré analyze the subcultural styles and behavior of football hooligans. Cohen's view is that the participants in the collective behavior schemes are seeking "opportunities for excitement, autonomy and sense of action."[15] Similarly, Marsh, Rosser, and Harré argue that football fans seek a "chance to escape from the dreariness of the weekday world of work or school to something which is adventurous and stimulating."[16]

Serious Action and Playlike Action

"Action" is the key word in understanding the thrills and excitement of life on the street described in the ethnographic literature and displayed in the active life-style of Yankees/*bosozoku*. Goffman defines action as "activities that are consequential, problematic, and undertaken for what is felt to be their own sake."[17] A review of the ethnographic works and the results of my field research on *bosozoku* suggest that there are two types of action: playlike action, which is carried out literally "just for the hell of it"; and serious action, which provides thrills and excitement but also serves other purposes.

Delinquency and other legitimate and semilegitimate activities on the street assume the character of "playlike action" most typically when they are essentially adolescent experimentation. Street-corner kids who are engaged in this type of action have, as in the case of most *bosozoku*, a more or less clear expectation of their eventual graduation from their action-oriented life-style. In fact, by common consent many young "action-seekers," upon maturity, exchange their life-style for that of "routine-seekers."[18] Many young prostitutes who began their deviant careers from the "impulse to get amusement, adventure, . . .

freedom in the larger world, which presents so many allurements and comparisons," anticipate settling down as ordinary housewives who achieve their "desire for security" rather than "desire for new experience."[19] Youthful search for action will be defined, then, as "kid stuff" or "mere play," and it can provide "fun" when it is playlike.

Depending upon their eventual consequences, however, the active pursuits sometimes lose most of their playlike quality and become "serious action." Many black boys from slum areas may hope eventually to retire from their action-oriented careers and establish stable households as they enter adulthood. But it is also likely that economic insecurity and peer pressure will compel them to lead outwardly cheerful but internally anxiety-ridden lives as "street corner men," "hoodlums," or "wineheads."[20] Similarly, the dancer in a taxi-dance hall anticipates getting married and settling down, disengaging herself from a romantic and adventurous existence that lies midway between legitimate work and prostitution. Otherwise, she is likely to assume progressively lower positions at seedier dance halls until she ends her working life as a prostitute.[21] The *bosozoku* fails to become an "ordinary citizen" if he "gets molded into the *yakuza* pattern." The life of a street corner man, prostitute, or *yakuza* may be replete with thrills and excitement, yet it lacks "fun": playlike quality. Deviance is no longer "mere play" and often becomes a more "serious business" through habituation to the criminal way of life.[22] In such a case, search for action often becomes an obligatory behavior prescribed by subcultural codes.

The distinction between these two types of action is not absolute but relative. Playlike action that provides intense enjoyment has an inherent tendency to become serious action. Life on the street includes both types of action and youths vacillate between the two, as they do between fiction and reality or between play and the mundane world.

CORRUPTION OF PLAY
Serious Action and Corruption of Play

Huizinga defines play as a "voluntary activity or occupation executed within certain fixed limits of time and place, according to rules freely accepted but absolutely binding, having its aim in itself and accompanied by a feeling of tension, joy and the consciousness that it is 'different' from 'ordinary life'."[23] In Caillois's definition of play, too, circumscription within time and space and separation from ordinary life are crucial criteria.[24] Play, indeed, should be insulated or "framed"[25] from everyday life in order for it to create its own reality.

If play is contaminated by ordinary life, its very nature is destroyed and what Caillois calls "corruption of play" ensues.[26] Similarly, action ceases to be playlike and becomes serious when the boundary separating it from ordinary life is disrupted. Thrilling excursions into the world of action may end with the total loss of freedom to choose possible realities. *Agon* (competition) results in accidents, crippling injuries, or death. Belief in *alea* (chance) leads to superstition or a bankrupt fatalism. What began as playful *mimicry* ends with a fixed deviant role, such as that of the mobster. Excessive pursuit of *ilinx* (vertigo) makes one an addict.

Many types of playlike action presuppose a precarious balance between the tendency toward corruption of play (or the contamination of the play "frame" by the primary reality) and the control capacity of playlike definitions of the situation. By defining a certain action as "kid stuff," "make-believe," or "mere play," the playlike definitions of the situation provide institutional discipline for overinvolvement in or overflow from the play "frame." In other words, the playlike definitions have boundary-setting functions. The subculture of action-oriented people, then, tends to include assumptions about the limits of playlike deviance and about eventual graduation to everyday life. Among American delinquents, there may be shared assumptions about an "optimal range of delinquent behavior" within which actions are "deviant enough to establish a negative identity but not so deviant as to repel significant others."[27] Street-corner gangs may develop a tacit consensus by which they avoid fights with each other and maintain prestige by proscribing conflict because of age difference or on other grounds; in many cases there are rumors and street-corner narratives of gang fights that did not take place.[28] *Bosozoku* subculture emphasizes the expressive nature of motorcycle gang activities in extremely repetitive and redundant ways. It also includes a "death and rebirth" theme on the basis of which the *bosozoku* youngster makes sense of the marginality of his activity and eventually gets rid of his negative identity upon the attainment of adulthood.

The playlike definitions of the situation, however, cannot entirely keep playlike action from becoming serious. Unlike "domesticated" and "tame" leisure, such as the vicarious enjoyment of watching a movie, action often produces deep enjoyment, especially when it approaches the pole of serious action and creates a truly engrossing alternative reality. In such a case, corruption of play and irrevocable consequences often ensue. There are at least three elements in action which lead to this corruption of play: collective encouragement, intense involvement, and a challenge to reach the limit.

Collective Encouragement

An audience and fellow actors are needed if a youth's exploratory behavior is to create an alternative reality and produce an enhanced sense of self; thus collective action is essential. Language, clothing, and gestures, as well as behavior, are regulated by subcultural codes, which have as an important element a distinctive style.[29] In many cases, this style allows considerable latitude for creativity and improvisation.

Because an alternative definition of the situation is established— and participants feel that "everyone does it"—each individual is not troubled by fears that he is insane or deviant to an extreme degree.[30] Collective participation, then, permits active pursuits on a massive scale, so that one may feel that certainty exists in the alternative reality.[31] Collective behavior that leads to action on a grand scale often induces participants to exceed a critical limit and suffer irrevocable consequences. Active pursuits, then, may generate a momentum of their own, beyond the anticipation and control of participants. Many of the gang fights that lead to eventual murders have this quality.[32]

A former executive member of a motorcycle gang called the Moko (Fierce Tigers), which in 1978 was the largest motorcycle-gang confederation in Kyoto, told me that once he abruptly became frightened when the number of participants in a *boso* drive exceeded 300. His anxieties were well-founded and turned to reality, when a large *boso* drive in Shiga Prefecture and a confrontation with the police led to an assault on a squad car and a police station. He was arrested on charges arising from this incident, along with twenty other members, and was sent to prison.

Intense Involvement

The alternative reality constructed by playlike definitions of the situation may be far more compelling than conventional and official definitions, because that reality is ordered, like a game, by a set of simplified goals and rules. It may also induce spontaneous involvement free from the overtones of unwilling conformity that youths associate with the monotony, boredom, and seeming endlessness of everyday life. In other words, playlike action provides youths with "psychological flow." They can feel that they are the moving agents of their own behavior rather than the objects of others' intentions. To a certain extent, they can devise variations in performance styles where conventional standards allow little scope for individual preferences.

In most cases, action of this sort, undertaken in a spirit of play, is performed in a delimited temporal and spatial context. Thus circumscribed, behavior may be ordered according to goals and rules that are simplified to permit full engrossment. The clear contrast between action and excitement in an alternative reality and the drabness of mundane, everyday life also heightens involvement in active pursuits. But at times participants' engrossment precludes other concerns, and past a certain point what began as play becomes an obsession or addiction. Boys who "play Indian" may eventually burn their companions at the stake.[33] The high-risk *boso* drive provides intense involvement and excitement. Many of my informants were involved in serious traffic accidents and suffered severe injuries. Some of their friends died during such activities. Still the enjoyment of *boso* driving exceeds the consideration of great risks, and some even joined *boso* driving wearing plaster casts on their legs.

Challenge to Reach the Limit

Although action includes legitimate and semilegitimate pursuits, as well as explicitly illegitimate undertakings, truly exciting and engrossing pursuits often test and challenge conventional standards to their limits. Explicitly deviant styles and outright defiance are among the most effective means of getting thrills and kicks, and of experiencing the joy of showing-off.

Thrasher points to a similar aspect of the image projected by adolescent gangs in Chicago:

> The gang . . . however, not having their cultural detachment, usually accepts the code of society but is in rebellion against it. In fact, the diabolical character of disobeying the social codes appeals to gang boys. While they accept the moral authority of the community, still it is external to them and they get a "kick" out of their attitude of disrespect for established rules.[34]

Indeed, evil is often "fun" exactly because it is evil and can provide the excitement of transgression itself. Duncan maintains that,

> [O]nce "do" and "do not," "shall" and "shall not," "is" and "is not," becomes "mine and thine," then all the power of the forbidden arises. The neighbor's wife we must not covet becomes glamorous because she is forbidden, a strange and mysterious creature who haunts us in acts, which to her husband are familiar and even tedious.[35]

While doing my field research, I was dismayed but at the same time impressed when an informant commented on the subjective experience of high-risk driving on a city street: "It's rather like raping a girl. It's the terribly thrilling feeling of doing something wrong, with the thought in mind, 'Hell, I'm doing something terribly wrong! Can I really do it?' "

In transcending the boundary of conventional norms and getting "kicks" out of it, one steps into the other source of corruption of play: the sacred.

PLAY AND THE SACRED

If play is to be really playlike, it should be insulated from the sacred as well as from ordinary, "profane" life. Action becomes serious when it is contaminated by the sacred as well as by the profane. As Caillois argues in his *Man and the Sacred*, although both play and the sacred are and should be insulated from everyday life, they are opposed to each other in other respects. Man worships the sacred. He is defenseless and at the mercy of the sacred. In contrast, man is master of destiny in play. Play enables him to keep a distance both from the fear of the sacred and the necessities of the profane (or practical life) and thus allows him to reflect critically upon them.[36]

When action becomes of the "serious, heroic, and dutiful kind" it serves purposes other than the intrinsic enjoyment of thrill-seeking: i.e., to support certain moral and sacred values and gain social rewards from one's support for such values.[37] Goffman, in his seminal essay "Where the Action Is," argues that action is a means of acquiring and maintaining "character" and is an end in itself only in relation to this purpose.[38] He even says that statements that say that action is an end in itself should be taken as "locutions."[39] He argues,

> If society is to make use of the individual, he must be intelligent enough to appreciate the serious chances he is taking and yet not become disorganized or demoralized by this appreciation. Only then will he bring to moments of society's activity the stability and continuity they require if social organization is to be maintained. Society supports this capacity by moral payments, imputing strong character to those who show self-command and weak character to those who are easily diverted or overwhelmed.[40]

Goffman goes on to say that it is because we respect strong character that we half-admire an immoral deed which is accomplished by a well-executed plan that excludes impulsive temptations. The culprit (or the picaro) is regarded as "a very *bad* character even while it is appreciated that he is not a *weak* one."

In a similar vein, Katz, in his *Seductions of Crime*, deals with the moral quality of serious action and its relation to the sacred. Through examination of records of criminal cases, autobiographical data, and various ethnographic and journalistic materials, he points out that the image of "violent hardman" or "bad nigger" have a great appeal to street-corner kids and ghetto men in the U.S. By presenting himself as "bad," as transcending good and evil and being untractable, one can dramatize his strong character and transcend a humiliating self-image as a "petty hoodlum" or a man in a subordinate racial position. By the practice of violence, he can also show that his posture is not a mere pretense but that he "means it."[41] In short, he presents himself as a Nietzschean superman who transcends conventional rationality and morality and is empowered by the forbidden power of "the impure": i.e., the fraternal twin of "the pure" included in the sacred.

It seems that the aura of serious action and bad (but strong) character provides cultural themes with which street-corner boys engage in playlike action play so as to improvise fictive images of the mystic action-seeking hero: e.g., "cat," "big shot," "hustler." As we have seen in earlier chapters of this volume, Yankees borrow the aura of action from such characters as the *yakuza*, the *uyoku*, or the *koha* in creating the image of untractable *bosozoku* of strong character. The moral overtone of the images of character is an indispensable ingredient for the "kicks" of self-presentation on the street or through the mass media. As long as the self-presentation remains a parody or fiction, the search for action is playlike. Yet the fiction or parody sometimes turns to reality. Nightmare instead of fantasy becomes reality in a situation such as a bitter gang-fight which includes heavy casualties. Action becomes even more serious when it becomes a fixed way of life extending to adulthood. Search for action becomes a moral obligation supported by subcultural codes of the underworld. The deviant character with the aura of action is no longer a fictive role to be "played at" but a fixed social role which should be "enacted." It seems, then, that the profane and the two components of the sacred—the pure and the impure— often collude to corrupt the playlike quality of action.

ANOMY AND PARODY IN THE AFFLUENT SOCIETY

Goffman says, "Although every society no doubt has scenes of action, it is our own society that has found a word for it."[42] If, as Goffman argues, gambling is the prototype of action, Las Vegas (or modern American society as a whole) may be the prototype of an action-generating social milieu in modern, urbanized, and westernized (or "Americanized") society. Not only "action" and related terms have spread from the gaming tables in Las Vegas to American society as a whole; various active life-styles and a considerable portion of the vocabulary associated with active pursuits also have diffused from the U.S. to other societies. *Akushon* (action) is a loan word widely used in Japan. Many Japanese *bosozoku* groups hang around McDonald's and Kentucky Fried Chicken shops. Coca-Cola is one of their favorite beverages. And, as we have seen, a term given to Japanese street-corner boys and girls is "Yankee"!

It should be noted, however, that the diffusion of the action-related styles and vocabulary from America to other countries is not independent of changes in socioeconomic structures in those countries. It seems to me that an affluent modern society has an inherent tendency to allure a wide variety of people into action. If gambling is the prototype of action, action is the prototype of the life-style in demystified, modern urban societies around the world.

Losing (or liberated from) an overarching symbolic universe of discourse of religion or detached from firm communal and familial ties, modern people are confronted with abundant possibilities leading to anomy or parody.[43] Some people may find this situation extremely anomic as well as chaotic and feel anxiety and frustration. Terrified by the existence of too many behavioral options and the sense of "homelessness,"[44] they may join some cult, gang, or fascist group, seeking to escape from freedom[45] or to find answers for perennial problems of human existence.[46] Such groups may provide these disoriented people with a sense of firm identity supported by some sacred symbols. These people may occasionally seek action and praise the moral values associated with the image of a man of character who is dedicated to the sacred symbols.

Others, however, may find "escape from *boredom*" more compelling[47] and view the anomic situation as a chance for "parody" or playlike action; and playlike action often includes deviant undertakings. When conventional institutions do not supply certain groups of people with a sense of meaning and purpose, they will experience pervasive boredom and monotony in ordinary life and seek activities in which goals and rules are decidedly unconventional. The inadequacy of surveillance and coercive sanctions will tempt the group further into exploratory undertakings. Such activities also attract those who find it demeaning to seek conventional forms of social prestige, although a sense of inferiority is not the only reason alternative standards are sought.

Exploratory behavior is especially playful when each of the participants finds it possible to create his own version of the definition of the situation. Urban areas, with their mobility and anonymity, are the most likely stages for exploratory and playful undertakings that lead to improvisational performances. Among the urban population taken as a whole, adolescents who are not fully assimilated into conventional social institutions are most likely to become "action-seekers." They are also most likely to form interactional settings where they "hang around" with no specific purpose and wait for something to happen. The urban and suburban areas include many places suitable for such social gatherings: street corners, barrooms, discotheques,[48] wide thoroughfares to speed on and large parking lots to gather in.

People engaged in playlike action are not fully committed to either the official definition of the situation or the alternative, playlike definitions of the situation. They vacillate (or "drift")[49] between the two (or more) perspectives, and full but temporary engrossment is obtained more frequently with the alternative definition of the situation. While the playlike definitions can provide a sense of meaning and purpose or a chance to escape from boredom, excessive commitment to the definitions sometimes leads to fatal and irrevocable consequences.

When action becomes serious rather than playlike, one is at the mercy of an alternative definition of reality. Detached or liberated from traditional institutions and sacred symbolism, he may have originally engaged in action-seeking as a way of escaping from boredom. But he may, at the end of his search for new freedom, find himself entrapped in the web of a quasi-sacred and quasi-mystical symbolism of a cult, fanatic ideology, or criminal underworld.

In the final chapter of *Homo Ludens* and throughout *In the Shadow of Tomorrow*, Huizinga bitterly criticizes and laments the decline of the play element in modern mass society. Without the sacred, without festival, and without play, modern people not only lose the spirit of fair play and noble attitudes but also lose fixed moorings for their identity.[50] The resultant anomic situations occasionally conjure up an element of the sacred that is a fraternal brother of the pure: i.e., the impure. The awe, dread, and fascination associated with the image of ferocious rogues, charismatic cult leaders, and men of character in the criminal underworld seem to be related to the resurrection of the sacred in this seemingly demystified modern society.[51]

Japan has been relatively successful in containing youthful search for action within the limit of play, as compared to the U.S., U.K., and several other Western nations. In addition to the low levels of the general crime rates, it has diminished the size of *yakuza* organizations, which would provide fixed deviant roles as career criminals.[52] Japan is also relatively immune to three recent developments which tend to make action serious: AIDS, drugs, and guns. Most people engage in sexual experimentation with little fear of AIDS. Experimentation with drugs stops, in general, at amphetamines and does not extend to cocaine or heroin. Gang fights among adolescents do not usually involve handguns or even switch-blade knives, not to mention automatic or semiautomatic rifles. The situation, however, may change in the future. While Japan has caught up with Western nations in the sphere of industrial production, the Japanese have just recently come to learn from Western nations, especially from the U.S., how to consume on a massive scale and how to live in material and economic affluence. When disoriented Japanese youths experiment with further deviant pursuits, and if adults and youths themselves cannot restrain tendencies toward the corruption of playlike action, youths may lose their freedom and become "out of control."

Appendix A
Research Methods

ANALYZING FLOW EXPERIENCE

A semistructured interview and a questionnaire were the two major techniques employed in order to obtain my informants' own accounts of their experience and motives for engaging in *boso* driving. (Appendix B provides the interview used.) Questions about flow in the *boso* driving were asked during interview sessions in which other questions, concerning the history and structure of the *bosozoku* group or personal data, were asked as well. All of the interview sessions were tape-recorded and transcribed verbatim. In the thirty-three interviews, thirty informants answered almost all items in the interview schedule. The mean age of the thirty informants was 17.9, with a range from 15 to 21. Six were female; twenty-four were male. After the results of the questionnaire were computed, more narrowly focused interviews were administered to some additional twenty informants. (All were males.) Causal conversations and discussions with informants during weekly meetings and other more informal occasions were further sources of information.

As can be seen in appendix C, the questionnaire included two items about subjective experience in *boso* driving. These were filled out by informants on the occasion of a year-end party of the *bosozoku* group or during interview sessions. As a result, sixty-six of the seventy questionnaires were usable for analysis. The mean age of all respondents was 17.3, with a range from 15 to 24. Ten were female; fifty-six were male.

Direct observation of *bosozoku boso* drives was another source of information. *Boso* drives were carried out by the group nine times during my field research (see table 5.2). I observed four of them. In addition, I was a passenger when some of my informants raced each other on city streets. These were not considered *boso* drives, but they did exhibit to me some acrobatic driving techniques. Although I did not participate in a *boso* drive, these experiences gave me some personal sense of it.

ANALYZING GROUP NAMES

The two major techniques employed for the decoding of group names were the compilation of *bosozoku* names from all over Japan and interviews

223

with gang members. More than 1,800 group names were taken from two books written on *bosozoku* by journalists called Group Full Throttle (*Bore Up! Bosozoku* and *Bosozoku Archipelago '81;* see chapter 3). Each group name was written on an index card. Some of the entries were filed in several different categories according to criteria such as linguistic origin of characters, peculiar orthography, pronunciation, and meaning of word(s). Several tentative hypotheses were repeatedly revised when negative cases were found as the number of items in the categories increased. The hypotheses were also checked by interviews and causal conversation with informants. The basic procedure, therefore, resembles what is called "analytic induction," though the premise of "perfect fit" does not necessarily apply in this case. See Florian Znaniecki, *The Method of Sociology* (New York: Farrar & Rinehart, 1934).

ESTIMATING SALES OF *BOSOZOKU* BOOKS

Three publishers, namely Rippu, Kadokawa, and Shinko Gakufu replied to some of my inquiries concerning the circulation of their publications. Tairiku Shobo declined to give me such information, and the other three firms did not respond to either of the two letters I sent to them. The replies from the three responding companies showed that *The Bosozoku Boy, Shakotan Boogies,* and *Don't Mess Around with Me!* had been produced, respectively, in printings of 9,000, 12,000, and 335,000 copies by March 1984. Rippu also indicated that the first two printings of *The Bosozoku Boy* were of 7,000 and 2,000 copies. Shinji Sagawa, "We Can No Longer Ponder the Measures to Be Taken for *Bosozoku,*" *Shonen Hodo* September (1981): 38–41, reports that by 1981 *Bosozoku Archipelago '80* had 70,000 copies in print. The only other information that may be used to determine the total distribution of books is the number of editions or printings. For example, *Only Saturday Is Left for Us,* which was originally published in 1975, had reached its twelfth printing in 1980, and could still be obtained in this form during the summer of 1984. I would estimate that, in all, from 100,000 to 130,000 copies of this work were published.

RESEARCH SITE: KYOTO AND UKYO WARD

Most of my informants live in Ukyo Ward in Kyoto. Kyoto is the name of both a prefecture and city. It is primarily within the city, which is situated inland on the northern portion of the Kyoto fault basin, that Yankee/*bosozoku* youths seek "action." On this site the capital city, Heiankyo, was founded in 794, and this urban area has been continuously inhabited for nearly twelve centuries. But the modernization and urbanization of Kyoto began around 1870, after the Meiji Restoration. When the modern legal system was adopted in 1889, the city's area was delimited at about 30 square kilometers (about 11.4 square miles). On more than ten occasions neighboring cities, towns, and villages were annexed, until Kyoto grew to be the third largest city in Japan, with 611 square kilometers (about 232 square miles). While the city proper occupies only 13 percent of the area, it has some 1.5 million inhabitants or 60 percent of the prefecture's population (2,424 people per square kilometer). As the city expanded, the number of wards increased, from only Kamigyo and Shimogyo in 1929, to eleven in 1976 (see figure 5.1). The rate of population growth, however, has not been as rapid as that of the other ten major cities in Japan—Tokyo, Yokohama, Osaka, Nagoya, Sapporo, Kobe, Kawasaki, Fukuoka, Kitakyushu, Hiroshima. The textile industry, which is still basic to the city's economy, has not recently employed additional workers in large numbers. In October 1983 Kyoto ranked sixth in population among Japanese cities.

Ukyo Ward is located in the western part of Kyoto City and has been characterized by a rapid population increase. While the population of the city as a whole has increased by approximately 20 percent during the last thirty years, the population of Ukyo and Saikyo Wards combined (Saikyo Ward was a part of Ukyo Ward until 1976) has increased by about 150 percent. During the same period, the number of households in the two wards combined has increased by approximately 290 percent, whereas the total number of households in Kyoto City has increased by about 90 percent (Kyoto City Office, *1960 Census Data on Kyoto City,* 1; idem, *Commerce in Kyoto,* 3). The relatively wide farming areas Ukyo Ward used to enclose have been converted to residential areas following on the area's rapid population growth and residential development. Many areas in Ukyo Ward have been characterized as "commuter towns": over 50 percent of the working persons in the ward have jobs outside Ukyo Ward (Kyoto City Office, *1980 Census Data on Kyoto City,* 402–4).

Among subsections of the ward, the population increase was especially rapid in the area where most of my informants live; this area includes census tracts whose populations have more than tripled during the last three decades. Several features characteristic of newly peopled districts in Japan are found in this area, i.e., various newly constructed stores including family restaurants and fast-food stores, numerous apartment buildings, small houses that are built close to each other. Most of my informants graduated from Ha, Sa, or U Junior Highs located in this area. Sa and U were established originally as branch schools of Ha after Ha had the largest number of students among all junior high schools in Kyoto Prefecture.

This information suggests that urbanization or suburbanization of this area has led to weakened community control over adolescents. My informants considered Ukyo Ward as an urbanized area and viewed adult residents in their community basically as "others," although they mind neighbors' views of themselves once they turn twenty. No adult groups except the police and *yakuza* intervened in the activities of the Ukyo Rengo. But my hypothesis or hunch about the relationship between attenuated neighborhood control and *bosozoku* activity or delinquency in general is not conclusive. It was impossible for me to examine the impact of urbanization on delinquency in this area from official data, because available police statistics do not provide data about a regional differential in crime rates for the period of rapid population increase. Nor could I obtain adult residents' or police officials' statements on this issue because of limited time for research and because I feared such contact with adults would damage rapport with my informants.

Appendix B
Flow Interview Schedule

Please try to imagine yourself when *boso* driving is going well.

1. How does it feel?
2. How does this feeling get started?
   What do you do to get it started?
   Can it happen anywhere, any time?
3. What keeps it going once it starts?
4. Once this feeling starts, do you have to make an effort to keep your mind on what you are doing?
   What kinds of things distract you?
   How often do you feel distracted?
   How do you avoid distraction?
5. Can you think about other things beside *boso* driving, once this feeling starts?
   If not, why not?
   If yes, what sorts of things?
6. Does anything happen to the way time passes for you?
   Does it seem to go slower or faster than usual?
7. Do you usually know the right thing to do?
   How do you know when you are doing the right thing?
8. What happens if you don't do something right?
   How does it feel?
9. When *boso* driving is going well, do you feel any different?
   1) Do you feel more aware of your body, or less?
   2) Of yourself?
   3) Of your problems?
   4) Do you feel differently about your buddies?
   5) About your vehicles and other "things"?
   6) What is the difference in feeling between solo driving and *boso* driving?
10. Do you feel in control of yourself?
    Of the things around you?

Less or more than usual?
Why?
11. Do you ever think back on the experience afterwards?
 If you do, how does it make you feel to remember it?
 Does it affect the rest of your life (e.g., job)?
 How?
12. Does *boso* driving ever get boring?
 When? Why?
 What do you do when it gets boring?
13. Do you ever worry or feel anxious when you are on *boso* driving?
 When?
 What do you do then?
14. Now try to imagine yourself when *boso* driving is not going well.
 Do you stop right away?
 If yes, how can you stop participating in the drive?
 If not, why not?
 (If answer is "No," ask questions 1 to 11 above.)
15. Have you ever thought about giving up *boso* driving permanently?
16. What other activity is similar to the feeling of *boso* driving?

Appendix C
Questionnaire on Adolescence in Kyoto

What is *seishun* (adolescence) for us? What meanings will it have for our future life? We are carrying on an investigation into such issues in order to publish a book. The results of this questionnaire will be tabulated in the form of graphs and tables. They will become important information for the book. We appreciate your kind cooperation.

Name (   )

Age (   )

Male/Female (check one)

OB [Old Boy]/Active Member (check one)

I. Enjoyment of *Boso* Driving

    1. Please rank the following components of enjoyment in *boso* driving. Rank as 1 the most important, the next 2, and so on, from 1 to 9.

                                                              Rank

Friendship, companionship . . . . (   )

Competition, measuring self against others . . . . (   )

Development of personal skills . . . . (   )

Medatsu koto (Being seen) . . . . (   )

The activity itself, getting involved in the world peculiar
to *boso* driving . . . . (   )

Sukatto suru koto (Emotional release) . . . . (   )

Prestige, regard, glamour . . . . (   )

Experience of speeding, use of driving skills . . . . (   )

Challenging one's own limitations and/or ideals . . . . (   )

    2. In *boso* driving, I . . . (check one)

        (   ) almost always drive by myself.

        (   ) often drive by myself.

        (   ) sometimes drive by myself and sometimes ride on a fellow's vehicle.

(   ) often ride on a fellow's vehicle.
(   ) almost always ride on a fellow's vehicle.

II. Image and Feeling of *Boso* Driving

If you were to describe your feelings during *boso* driving, how are they similar to the feelings of the activities listed below? or how are they dissimilar to these feelings? Please check appropriate column.

	Very similar	Similar	Neutral	Different	Very different
Listening to good music					
Running a race					
Parachuting from a plane about to fail					
Playing a game (*shogi, go, ocero*, etc.)					
Deep-sea diving for treasure in shark-infested waters					
Making love					
Driving too fast					
Assembling equipment					
Watching a good movie					
Entering a burning house to save a child					
Playing a competitive sport					
Solving a riddle					
Designing or discovering something new					
Swimming too far out on a dare					

Playing cards or mah-jongg					
Exploring a strange place					
Appearing on a TV program					
Betting a great deal on a horse race or bicycle race					
Being with a good friend					
Reading an enjoyable book or cartoon					
Playing a theatrical role before a large audience					

III. Fashion, Life-style
   Are you a Yankee now? (check one)
   (   ) People may think I am a Yankee. So do I.
   (   ) Although I don't think of myself as a Yankee, other people
             may think so.
   (   ) Although people may not think I am a Yankee, I think of
             myself as one.
   (   ) People do not think I am a Yankee. Neither do I.
IV. Occupation
   1. Do you currently have a job (including part-time job)?
                    ┌ Have not——Student/Unemployed (check one)
   Check one-   │
                    │
                    └ Have——a) What is it? (   )
                            b) Full-time/part-time (check one)
                            c) Monthly salary—about (   ) 0,000 yen
                            d) Who mediated the job? (check one)
                               Family   Part-time job magazine
                               Relative   Newspaper
                               Buddy   Neighbor
                               School   Public employment agency
                               Other (   )

e) Do you intend to stay with this job for some time?

(   ) Yes

(   ) No. I will get another job.

    —What kind of job do you hope to get as a regular job?

    (   )

(   ) No. After quitting the job, I will not get another job.

    —Why? (e.g., I will become a house-wife.) (   )

Other (   )

2. What kind of job do you think you will have and where do you think you will be, when you are 30 years old?

Where? (check one)
- Kyoto City
- Kyoto Prefecture
- Somewhere in Kansai region except Kyoto
- Other (   )

Doing What? (   )

3. What kind of job do you think you will have and where do you think you will be, when you are 40 years old?

Where? (check one)
- Kyoto City
- Kyoto Prefecture
- Somewhere in the Kansai region except Kyoto
- Other (   )

Doing What? (   )

4. Are you currently enrolled in school, or have you graduated? (check one)

Junior High School	Full-time High School	Part-time High School	Vocational School	College	Other
└ graduated	|—currently enrolled	|—currently enrolled	|—currently enrolled	|—currently enrolled	( )
	|—taking leave of absence	|—taking leave of absence	|—taking leave of absence	|—taking leave of absence	
	|—left before graduation	|—left before graduation	|—left before graduation	|—left before graduation	
	└ graduated	└ graduated	└ graduated	└ graduated	

5. Among the things you learned in school what has been the most useful for your current job? Write about it briefly.

(   )

V. Your Future (1)

1. Please specify the ages of the beginning and the (prospective) end of your *seishun* (adolescence)?

From (   ) to (   )

2. At what ages do you expect the following to occur?
   Getting married   (   )
   Having your first child   (   )
   Getting a regular job   (   )
3. What are the maximum or latest ages by which you will have attained
   the following?
   Getting married   (   )
   Having your first child   (   )
   Getting a regular job   (   )
4. How many children do you expect to have?
   (   )
5. What will be your response to your child if s/he says s/he will become
   bosozoku? (check one)
   1) Son
        (   ) I will give my approval to him.
        (   ) I will let him do what he wants to do.
        (   ) I will try to persuade him not to become *bosozoku*. But if
                       he insists on that, I will let him do what he wants to do.
        (   ) I will definitely not allow him to become *bosozoku*.
   1) Daughter
        (   ) I will give my approval to her.
        (   ) I will let her do what she wants to do.
        (   ) I will try to persuade her not to become *bosozoku*. But if
                       she insists on that, I will let her do what she wants to do.
        (   ) I will definitely not allow her to become *bosozoku*.
6. What type of spouse do you hope to have? Please describe briefly your
   ideal spouse.
   (   )

VI. Your Future (2)
   1. Do you think you are currently settled down (as an adult)? (check
      one)
             (   ) No—I will get settled down by (   ) [age]
             (   ) Yes

   2. What has caused you to | What will cause you to settle
      settle down? Choose the | down? Choose the
      appropriate answer(s) | appropriate answer(s) from
      from the following | the following choices.
      choices. |

      Check all the appropriate choices by the sign "X." Check the most
      important ones by the sign "XX."

      (   ) Getting engaged, getting married, thinking about girl (or
                    boy) friend seriously

(   ) Becoming nervous about what people might say about me
(   ) Lessons learned from police sanctions
(   ) Thinking that I have exhausted what I can do during adolescence and had enough fun
(   ) Having a child
(   ) Thinking about my own future seriously
(   ) Devoting myself to a job
(   ) Becoming nervous about injury and accidents
(   ) Getting old enough to settle down
(   ) Losing contact with peers
(   ) Thinking seriously about what my family members or relatives say
(   ) Lessons learned from injury and accident(s)
(   ) Losing physical strength and energy
(   ) Getting nervous about police sanction

Thank you for your kind cooperation. Please reexamine your answers from the beginning to end to see if you have left any questions unanswered. If you have any opinions about this questionnaire and/or about the attitudes of the general public toward the *bosozoku*, write it briefly below.

Appendix D
Bosozoku Argot

abunomi   shock absorber only; suspension system with no suspension coils; also *nosasu*.

amepato   an American patrol car; a patrol car with an oblong light on its roof.

ampan   paint thinner.

ampura   a stupid person.

ashi   foot; any means of transportation.

atama   the head; the leader of a *bosozoku* group.

bakku   back; backer, fixer.

ban o kiru   to dominate the gangs within a school as the maximum leader; also *ban o toru*.

baribari   (onomatopoeia) extremely, vigorously; extreme, vigorous.

bibiru   to become frightened.

bokkoboko   (onomatopoeia) to "beat up" someone severely.

bontan   black baggy pants used in combination with *Gakuran*.

boyan   *bosozoku*.

chaina   a Chinese dress.

chaka   a handgun.

charimen   a driver's permit for small motorcycle (50 cc).

charinko   a bicycle.

chikuru   to inform the police.

chinkoro   the act of informing the police.

choran   a modified school uniform (jacket) with a medium-length hem.

churan   a modified school uniform with a minimum-length hem.

daburu akuseru   double acceleration; to race engine twice while driving a motorcycle.

darui   to become sick of something.

dasai   styleless, outmoded, rustic; also *mosai*.

dasshoku   to bleach hair.

dosoku genkin   "No Outdoor Shoes Allowed" (Phrase on stickers often put on a modified automobile.)

dotsubo   terribly disappointing.

egui   extreme, radical, extremely ugly.

embure   engine brake.

fukuro   to gang up on somebody and beat him up.

futsu no ko   an ordinary, non-Yankee girl.

gaikotsu burashi   a skeleton brush; a hair brush with sparse, thick bristles.

gakuran   a modified school uniform; see also *choran, churan, yoran*.

gasaire   house search by the police.

gasupaku   to steal gasoline.

genchari   motorcycle of small displacement; also called *zerohan*.

gingin   (mimesis) extremely.

gokibai   a cockroach bike, a medium-size motorcycle (90 cc or 125 cc) used by the police; also called *gokiburi* (roach) and *buriburi*.

gombo   gang rape, rape.

haifura   high flasher; a relay which regulates flickering of a light.

hakonori   box riding; to expose one's body from the window of a moving automobile (see photo 1 and fig. 3.7).

haku   to vomit; to confess to the police under interrogation.

hamigo   ostracism of disloyal gang member; also called *haneko*.

hanabi   fireworks; to make sparks by striking an asphalt pavement with the kickstand of a motorcycle.

haneko   *see hamigo*.

happa   leaf; marijuana.

hashiriya   a street racer.

hatamochi   the flag holder; a person who holds a group flag during a *boso* drive (*see* photo 1).

heitai   a soldier; a *bosozoku* member of a low echelon.

henzuri   masturbation.

hetare   sissy.

hetautsu   to make a mess of something.

hishi   rectangle; the Yamaguchi family—the largest *yakuza* organization, whose insignia is rectangular.

ichibiri   foolish guy, childish guy.

ichibiru   to play about, to do a childish thing.

ikeike   youthful, vigorous, active.

ikiru   to bluff.

iku   to fornicate, to beat up, to use amphetamines.

imo   potato, unsophisticated person, rustic person.

imohiku   to become terrified, to become scared.

ippansha   an ordinary vehicle, a vehicle driven by a non-*bosozoku* driver.

ippan shimin   an ordinary citizen, non-*bosozoku*, law-abiding person.

iwasu   to beat up, to steal, to rape; any type of "action."

jikoru   to cause a traffic accident.

kama kiru   to drive zigzag.

kamashi   bluff.

kankan   Juvenile Classification Home.

kantera   a light; a light on the roof of a police squad car.

kata ni hamerareru   to become molded into a pattern, to be forcibly recruited by a *yakuza* group.

katsuage   extortion.

ketsu   ass; the pillion seat of a motorcycle.

ketsu furu   same as *ketsu makuru*.

ketsu makuru   to hinder chase by police cars by zigzagging; also *ketsu furu*.

kinkin   heavily dyed (hair); also *makkinkin* (onomatopoeia).

kippu   a ticket, traffic ticket.

kiru   to make an abrupt turn.

kitaizoku   curiosity-seekers.

koha   a young tough.

koki   traffic squad police.

kyokudo   an extremely ugly girl.

maddo makkusu   Mad Max; to make a circle of burned rubber by braking the front wheel of a motorcycle and swinging the motorcycle around.

mappo   cop.

marusa   *bosozoku* (from police jargon).

mempato   a camouflaged patrol car.

menchi kiru   to stare at someone; also *menta kiru*.

mukatsuku   to become offended, to get irritated.

mumen   to drive a vehicle without a license.

mushiokosu   to feel like using amphetamines.

nanpa   a skirt-chaser, ladies' man; to "pick up" a girl.

nariagari   an upstart; a person who began a delinquent career after graduating from junior high school.

nensho   Juvenile Training School.

nezumi   *maddo makkusu* by automobile.

noheru   no helmet; to drive a motorcycle without a helmet.

nomaru   normal; a vehicle with no modification.

nosasu   see *abunomi*.

oban   old woman; a girl too old to be a delinquent.

odoru   to dance, to fight in a duel.

okama   homosexual, sissy.

okama horu   anal sex; to collide with a car from behind.

onna   girlfriend, female lover.

otoko   boyfriend, male lover.

pacchi haku   to take a commission as the third party in the trade of a vehicle or other things between one's friends.

pachiki   shaved hairline; to give a butt of the head.

paka   a police patrol car.

pakuchari   a stolen bicycle; to steal a bicycle.

pakugasu   to steal gasoline.

pakuru   to steal, to arrest.

panpan   a prostitute, a promiscuous girl.

papparapan   a stupid girl who is easily "picked up."

pattsun   a patrol car.

pijan   a receiver that can receive the short-wave broadcasts of the police.

pin hiiru   pin heels; women's sandals with thin heels.

pon   (meth)amphetamine.

pori   a policeman, the police.

poribus   police bus, police wagon.

pori bokkusu   police box.

raida   a rider; ordinary motorcyclist.

raida chenji   rider change; to interchange riding positions with a passenger while driving a vehicle.

ranto   a rumble.

rairiru   to become intoxicated by inhaling paint thinner.

redisu   ladies; female *bosozoku*.

renchan   to participate in *boso* driving day after day.

ridasha   the lead vehicle; the vehicle of the *bosozoku* leader.

sabui   cold, risky; also *samui*.

satsueikai   photo-shooting meeting; a meeting to take photos that are supposed to appear in journalists' books on *bosozoku*.

senko   teacher.

sentosha   front vehicle; the vehicle at the front position of the band of a *boso* drive.

shakotan   (onomatopoeia) low-slung automobile; also *pettan, petako, gotton*.

shateko   a protégé in a *yakuza* group.

shibaku   to beat up someone.

shibui   stylish, trendy, urbane.

shigasaku   a rustic Shiga bum; "Yankee" in Shiga Prefecture; also *kenmin*.

shijuhachi   forty-eight; detention in a police cell for forty-eight hours for interrogation; also *yompachi*.

shikatosuru   to ignore adults' orders and suggestions; to ignore someone or something.

shiki o toru   to lead; to organize and lead a *boso* drive.

shinchu   a paint-thinner addict.

shingo heisa   intersection blocking; to block the traffic intersecting the course of a *boso* drive by making loud exhaust noises and sounding horns.

shinogi   an illegal means of earning; a "hustle."

shiposhipo   (onomatopoeia) a pump used in stealing gasoline from others' vehicles; steal gasoline by a pump; *see gasupaku*.

shirokoi   mischievous; to tell a barefaced lie.

shirigaru   a promiscuous girl.

shokku   a shock absorber.

shugo   a custom header pipe.

shukai   meeting; weekly meeting of a *bosozoku* group.

shukai boso   a *boso* drive carried out on the occasion of a weekly meeting.

sotsugyo   graduation; to disengage oneself from *bosozoku* activity.

sutoreto   straight hair; a non-Yankee girl with un-permed, straight hair.

taiko   the opposite lane.

taiman   a duel.

tamasarau   to abduct a member of an opponent gang to intimidate him or to beat him up.

tarai   a gang rape.

tobiiri   opportunistic participants in a *boso* drive.

tokko, tokkofuku   a kamikaze party uniform.

tonko suru   to escape.

tontsu   a muffler without diffuser pipe and fiber-glass packing.

tsubo fumu   to make a blunder.

tsure   a buddy.

unko suwari   shit-squatting (see figs. 3.9–12); also called *yankii suwari*.

utau   to sing; to confess to the police.

wappa   a pair of handcuffs.

waru   delinquency, a delinquent.

yaki, yakiire   torture, corporal punishment.

yankii   Yankee; delinquent, street-corner boy.

yankii suwari   see *unko suwari*.

yompachi   *see shijuhachi*.

yonshasen kama   to zigzag across four lanes.

yoran   a modified school uniform with the maximum length of hem; see *choran, churan, gakuran*.

zeroyon   a drag race.

zoku   *bosozoku*.

zubozubo   (onomatopoeia) a promiscuous girl.

Notes

Short titles have generally been used for works cited in the notes. Works frequently cited have been identified by the following abbreviations.

AJS	*American Journal of Sociology*
AS	*Asahi Shimbun*
ASR	*American Sociological Review*
BA	Group Full Throttle, eds. Bosozoku *Archipelago*. Tokyo, Daisan Shokan, 1979, 1981, 1982.
BB	Group Full Throttle, eds. *Bore Up!* Bosozoku. Tokyo: Daisan Shokan, 1980.
BBA	Mihaly Csikszentmihalyi. *Beyond Boredom and Anxiety*. San Francisco: Jossey-Bass, 1975.
B100	Hiroshi Nakabe, ed. *The* Boso *Driving of 100* Bosozoku *Guys*. Tokyo: Daisan Skokan, 1979.
BDI, II, III	Jiro Ueno, Bosozoku *Documentary I, II, III*. Tokyo: Futami Shobo, 1980.
JSY	Office of the Prime Minister. *Japan Statistical Yearbook*. 1962–84.
KS	*Kyoto Shimbun*
MS	*Mainichi Shimbun*
SA	Economic Planning Agency. *Statistical Abstracts*, 1966–83.
WPC	Ministry of Justice. *White Paper on Crime*, 1976–84.
WPP	National Police Agency. *White Paper on the Police*, 1976–84.
WPYA	Office of the Prime Minister. *White Paper on Youth and Adolescence*, 1976–84.
YS	*Yomiuri Shimbun*

Titles of Japanese materials are translated in notes. For original titles, see References.

INTRODUCTION

1. *AS*, 4 July 1981.

2. *WPP, 1981; WPP, 1983; WPP, 1984; WPC, 1983*.

3. See Travis Hirschi, *Causes of Delinquency* (California: University of California Press, 1969); and Ruth Kornhauser, *Social Sources of Delinquency* (Chicago: University of Chicago Press, 1978).

4. See D. Downes, *The Delinquent Solution* (New York: The Free Press, 1966), 81.

5. Frederick Thrasher, *The Gang* (Chicago: University of Chicago Press, 1927); Gresham Sykes and David Matza, "Juvenile Delinquency and Subterranean Values," *ASR* 26(1961): 712–19; David Matza, *Delinquency and Drift* (New York: John Wiley,

1964); Downes, *Delinquent Solution;* Jack Katz, *Seductions of Crime* (New York: Basic Books, 1988).

6. Herbert Gans, *The Urban Villagers* (New York: The Free Press, 1962); Gerald Suttles, *The Social Order of the Slum* (Chicago: University of Chicago Press, 1968); Ulf Hannerz, *Soulside* (New York: Columbia University Press).

7. For the original formulation of the concept of "definition of the situation" and its later development, see William Thomas and Florian Znaniecki, *The Polish Peasant in Europe and America* (New York: Alfred A. Knopf, 1927); William Thomas, *The Unadjusted Girl* (New York: Little, Brown, 1923); Florian Znaniecki, *Cultural Sciences* (Urbana, Ill.: University of Illinois Press, 1952); Donald Ball, "The Definition of the Situation," *Journal of Social Behavior* 2 (1972):61–82; R. Perinbanayagam, "Definition of the Situation," *Sociological Quarterly* 15 (1974): 521–41; and Robert Stebbins, "The Definition of the Situation," in *Social Behavior in Context,* ed. Adrian Furnham (Boston, Mass.: Allyn and Bacon, 1986), 134–54.

8. See Thomas and Znaniecki, *Polish Peasant,* 1831–1914; and Morris Janowitz, *The Last Half Century* (Chicago: University of Chicago Press, 1978), chap. 2.

9. For the use of metaphor in sciences, literature, and everyday life, see Richard Brown, *A Poetic for Sociology* (Chicago: University of Chicago Press, 1989); Paul Ricoeur, *The Rules of Metaphor* (Toronto: University of Toronto Press, 1977); and George Lakoff and Mark Johnson, *Metaphors We Live by* (Chicago: University of Chicago Press, 1980).

10. Merton's strain model does not necessarily presuppose that structural strain is always to be translated into psychological strain. See Downes, *Delinquent Solution.*

11. Clifford Geertz, "Deep Play," in *The Interpretation of Cultures* (New York: Basic Books, 1973), chap. 15.

12. See Helen Schwartzman, *Transformations* (New York: Plenum, 1978).

13. See William Thomas and Dorothy Thomas, *The Child in America* (New York: Alfred A. Knopf, 1928), 572; Erving Goffman, *The Frame Analysis* (New York: Harper, 1974), 1–2; idem, "Reply to Denzin and Keller," *Contemporary Sociology* 10 (1981): 60–68; and Warren Handel, "Normative Expectations and the Emergence of Meaning as Solutions to Problems," *AJS,* 84 (1979), 864–65.

14. Brian Sutton-Smith and Diana Kelly-Byrne, "The Masks of Play," in *The Masks of Play,* ed. Brian Sutton-Smith and Diana Kelly-Byrne (New York: Leisure Press, 1984); Catharine Garvey, *Play* (Cambridge, Mass.: Harvard University Press, 1977).

15. Although the three sets of studies share the emphasis on the role of symbol and meaning in culture and/or human action, they, even within each set of studies, differ considerably with regard to other assumptions: e.g., the role of human volition in symbolic construction and transformation, definition of "drama." This study employs each perspective mainly for interpretation of empirical instances rather than for testing the possibility of theoretical synthesis, and thus it is admittedly eclectic, theoretically as well as methodologically.

16. Gerald Suttles, "Urban Ethnography," *Annual Review of Sociology* 2 (1976), 3.

17. Raymond Gold, "Role in Sociological Field Observations," *Social Forces* 36 (1958): 217–23; Norman Denzin, *The Research Act* (New York: McGraw-Hill, 1978), chap. 7.

18. Hunter Thompson, *Hell's Angels* (New York: Ballantine, 1966), 66.

CHAPTER ONE

1. The diverse activities of *boso* driving can be divided roughly into two categories: *tsuring* (touring; group tour) and *shinai boso* (*boso* driving on city streets). Analysis in this chapter is mainly concerned with the experience in the second category of *boso* driving, and with those drives that are relatively well organized.

2. This word and other Japanese words mentioned in this section have no other metaphorical meanings.

3. *MS*, 12 June 1978; emphasis mine.

4. Yoshiichi Kaneto, *"Bosozoku"* in *Violence of Adolescents* (Tokyo: Tachibana Shobo, 1981), 212.

5. See, for example, Masayuki Tamura and Fumio Mugishima, "The Present State of *Bosozoku*," *Kagaku Keisatsu Kenkyujo Hokoku* 16 (1975): 38–72; Kazunori Kikuchi, "A Treatise on *Bosozoku*," *Katei Saibansho Geppo* (July, 1981): 10–25; and Yasunori Chiba, *Bosozoku* (Tokyo: Nihon Keizai Shimbunsha, 1975).

6. Tamura and Mugishima, "Present State of *Bosozoku*"; see also Yasuhisa Nagayama et al., *Report on* Bosozoku *Problem* (Osaka: Osaka Bosozoku Mondai Kenkyukai, 1981), 29–30.

7. Tamura and Mugishima, "Present State of *Bosozoku*," 70; Masayasu Taniguchi, *"Bosozoku,"* in *Playlike Delinquency,* ed. Kazunori Kikuchi and Mamoru Horiuchi (Tokyo: Gakuji Shuppan, 1982), 128.

8. See for example, *B100; BD I; BD II;* and *BD III.*

9. Mihaly Csikszentmihalyi et al., *Flow: Studies of Enjoyment,* PHS Grant Report, 1974: *BBA.*

10. *BBA,* 36.

11. *BBA,* 38–48.

12. See Hannerz, *Soulside;* Matza, *Delinquency and Drift;* and James Leary, "White Guys' Stories of the Night Street," *Journal of the Folklore Institute* 14 (1977): 59–71.

13. Gregory Bateson, "A Theory of Play and Fantasy," in *Steps to an Ecology of Mind* (San Francisco: Chandler, 1972), 177–93; Goffman, *Frame Analysis.*

14. *WPP 1984,* 205.

15. *WPP 1981,* 30.

16. Cf. M. Balint, *Thrills and Regressions* (London: Hogarth, 1959).

17. Ikuya, Sato, *An Ethnography of* Bosozoku (Tokyo: Shin'yosha, 1984), 33.

18. *BBA;* Richard Mitchell, *Mountain Experience* (Chicago: University of Chicago Press, 1983).

19. *BBA,* 83–84.

20. *BBA,* 47.

21. *BBA,* 42–44; Cf. George Mead, *Mind, Self, and Society* (Chicago: University of Chicago Press, 1934), 273–81.

22. Emile Durkheim, *The Elementary Forms of the Religious Life,* trans. J. W. Swain (New York: The Free Press, 1912).

23. *BBA,* 14.

24. See chap. 2.

25. See chap. 5.

26. Csikszentmihalyi, personal correspondence, 2 September 1983.

27. *BBA,* 107–8.

28. See R. Bauman, "Verbal Act as Performance," *American Anthropologist* 77 (1974): 290–312.

29. Leary, "White Guys' Stories," 61.

30. See chap. 4.

31. See chap. 3.

32. Mihaly Csikszentmihalyi and Reed Larson, *Being Adolescent* (New York: Basic Books, 1984), 246–49.

33. Victor Turner, *Dramas, Fields, and Metaphors* (Ithaca, N.Y.: Cornell University Press, 1974), 274.

34. Victor Turner, *The Ritual Process* (New York: Aldine, 1969), 194.

35. *BBA*, 49–50.

36. *BBA*, 29–33, 52–53.

37. This process of "graduation" is partly based on the age norm pertaining to the use of cultural artifacts. See chaps. 2 and 5.

38. *BBA*, 81–82.

CHAPTER TWO

1. Thompson, *Hell's Angels*, 17.

2. Kikuchi, "A Treatise on *Bosozoku*," 10.

3. Yoshinobu Tazaki, "*Bosozoku* Are a Manifestation of Motorized Society," in *The Present State of* Bosozoku *and Countermeasures to Be Taken*, ed. Hyogo Kenkei (Kobe: Hyogo Kenkei, 1981), 44; Yasunori Chiba, *How to Prevent Youth from Becoming* Bosozoku (Tokyo: Kumon Sugaku Kenkyu Senta, 1981), 25.

4. See for example, Shiro Hiyama and Mori Yamazaki, *The Background of Youthful Violence and Its Prevention* (Tokyo: Gyosei, 1981); Kaneto, "*Bosozoku*"; and Kikuchi, "A Treatise on *Bosozoku*."

5. See for example, Tamura and Mugishima, "Present State of *Bosozoku*," 146; Taniguchi, "*Bosozoku*," 128; and Ken'ichi Tsuruoka, "Play and Delinquency," *Choken Kiyo* 30 (1981), 82.

6. Tamura and Mugishima, "Present State of *Bosozoku*," 146.

7. See for example, *BA '80* and *BB*.

8. *B100*, *BB*.

9. *BB*, 112–33.

10. Georg Simmel, "Fashion," *AJS* 62 (1957); 541–58; Herbert Blumer, *International Encyclopedia of the Social Sciences*, s.v. "Fashion"; idem., "Fashion," *Sociological Quarterly*, 10 (1969): 275–91; Thomas Smith, "Aestheticism and Social Structure," *ASR* 39 (1974): 725–43.

11. Blumer, "Fashion," 290.

12. Paul Willis, *Profane Culture* (London: Routledge & Kegan Paul, 1978); Peter Marsh, Elizabeth Rosser, and Rom Harré, *The Rules of Disorder* (London: Routledge & Kegan Paul, 1978); Dick Hebdige, *Subculture* (London: Methuen, 1979); Edward Hall and Tony Jefferson, eds., *Resistance through Ritual* (London: Hutchinson, 1976).

13. Harold Finestone, "Cats, Kicks, and Color," *Social Problems* 5 (1957): 3–13; Suttles, *Social Order of the Slum*.

14. Gary Fine and S. Kleinman, "Rethinking Subculture," *AJS* 85 (1979): 1–20; Gary Fine, "Small Groups and Culture Creation," *ASR* 44 (1979): 733–45.

15. Dennis Brissette and Charles Edgley, *Life as Theater* (Chicago: Aldine, 1975), 5; Fine and Kleinman, "Rethinking Subculture," 12.

16. Tamura and Mugishima, "Present State of *Bosozoku*," 59.

17. The exchange rate during the research period of 250 yen to the dollar will be used throughout this volume, unless otherwise indicated.

18. *WPP 1976*, 246; *WPP 1981*, 24.

19. Cf. Gene Balsley, "The Hot-Rod Culture," *American Quarterly* 2 (1950); 353–58.

20. See Simmel, "Fashion," 54; Suttles, *Social Order of the Slum*, chap. 4; Willis, *Profane Culture*, chap. 3; and Marsh, Rosner, and Harré, *Rules of Disorder*, passim.

21. Csikszentmihalyi and Csikszentmihalyi, *Optimal Experience*, 86.

22. Georg Simmel, *The Sociology of Georg Simmel*, trans. Kurt Wolff (New York: Free Press, 1950), chap. 4.

23. See chap. 4.

24. Many informants compared their cars to their private rooms. They required fellow passengers to take off their shoes. Most Japanese don't take off their shoes in cars, as they do at home. *Bosozoku* often put on stickers with the phrase "No outdoor shoes allowed." I was notorious among them for my insensitivity on this point. They often complained that I entered their cars with my shoes on.

25. See chap. 5.

26. In Japan, the market for accessories in also highly developed and differentiated. The *Showa 58 Nen Jidosha Nenkan* (1983 Automobile Yearbook) estimates the size of the market at between roughly two and three trillion yen ($80 to 120 billion). Each parts-maker spends a sizable amount in advertising its brand names. *Bosozoku* youths learn about such accessories from advertisements in motorcycle and automobile magazines (as well as from other gang members). Among magazines popular with *bosozoku* (such as *Holiday Auto, Young Auto*), almost half of each issue is taken up by advertisements for and articles about parts. Many advertisements feature attractive pictures of accessories with numerical specifications in accompanying captions. Such magazines also produce expensive special issues of catalogues of parts, with colorful illustrations.

27. See Takeshi Dojo, Bosozoku *Documentary* (Kobe: Kobe Shimbun Shuppan Senta, 1982).

28. Blumer, "Fashion," 342.

29. Daniel Boorstin, *The Image* (New York: Harper & Row, 1961), 222–24.

30. Cf. J. Scott and E. Vaz, "A Perspective on Middle-Class Delinquency," *Canadian Journal of Economics and Political Science* 29 (1963): 324–25.

31. See chap. 6.

32. Tamura and Mugishima, "Present State of *Bosozoku*," 69–70.

33. Cf. Jack Katz, *Seductions of Crime*, chaps. 3 and 4.

34. Kenneth Burke, "Dramatism," in *International Encyclopedia of the Social Sciences*, 450; Mary Douglas, *Purity and Danger* (London: Routledge & Kegan Paul, 1966); Hugh Duncan, *Communication and Social Order* (London: Oxford University Press, 1968), 220–21; Katz, *Seductions of Crime*, passim.

35. Kunio Tsukamoto, *The Pleasure of Wordplay* (Tokyo: Kadokawa Shobo Shinsha, 1980), 112.

36. Cf. Mikhail Bakhtin, *Rabelais and His World*, trans. Helene Iswolsky (Cambridge, Mass.: MIT Press, 1968).

37. See, for example, Albert Cohen, *Delinquent Boys* (New York: The Free Press, 1955); and R. Cloward and L. Ohlin, *Delinquency and Opportunity* (New York: The Free Press, 1960).

38. Cohen, *Delinquent Boys*, 28.

39. M. Rotenberg, "Self-Labeling Theory," *British Journal of Criminology* 15 (1975), 365.

40. Bateson, "Theory of Play and Fantasy."

41. Cf. Stephen Tyler, *The Said and the Unsaid* (New York: Academic Press, 1978), 168–81; George Lakoff, *Women, Fire, and Dangerous Things* (Chicago: University of Chicago Press, 1987), passim.

42. See Simmel, *Sociology of Georg Simmel*, 332–33, 364–65.

43. Milton Yinger, *Countercultures* (New York: The Free Press, 1982), 161–71.

44. See chap. 7.

45. *BA '80.*

46. *B100; MS*, 4 November 1978; 24 June 1979; *BA '82*, 64–75.

47. See chap. 3.

48. Thompson, *Hell's Angels*, 100.

49. Ibid.

50. Hedbige, *Subculture,* 90–92; Marshall Sahlins, *Culture and Practical Reason* (Chicago: University of Chicago Press, 1976), 72–73.

51. See Brissette and Edgley, *Life as Theater,* 5.

52. Several informants wrote their names in this way as graffiti on fences, tables, and pillars in their hangouts, and also on the questionnaire I gave them.

53. See *BBA,* 201–2.

54. Chaps. 4 and 5.

55. Thompson, *Hell's Angels,* 89–90.

56. Roy Wagner, *The Invention of Culture* (Chicago: University of Chicago Press, 1981), 76.

57. Goffman, *Frame Analysis,* chap. 8.

58. See Frank Tannenbaum, *Crime and Community* (New York: McGraw-Hill, 1938); Kanji Mori, "Becoming *Bosozoku,*" *Shonen Hodo* September (1979): 9–17, and idem, "*Bosozoku* Boy," in *Juvenile Delinquency in Japan,* ed. Katei Saibansho Gendai Hiko Kenkyukai (Tokyo: Taisei Shuppan, 1979).

CHAPTER THREE

1. Kaneto, "*Bosozoku,*" 207–10.

2. Kikuchi, "A Treatise on *Bosozoku,*" 15, 16.

3. See, for example, *BA '80,* 187.

4. See chap. 7.

5. Joseph Gusfield, *The Culture of Public Problems* (Chicago: University of Chicago Press, 1981). For more general discussions about various types of "dramaturgical" and "dramatistic" analyses of society, see Brissette and Edgley, *Life as Theater;* Paul Hare and Herbert Blumberg, *Dramaturgical Analysis of Social Interaction* (New York: Praeger, 1988); and Clifford Geertz, "Blurred Genres," *The American Scholar* 49 (1980): 165–79. For anthropological applications of theatrical metaphor, see Victor Turner, *From Ritual to Theatre* (New York: Performing Arts Publications, 1982); and John MacAloon, ed., *Rite, Drama, Festival, Spectacle* (Philadelphia: ISHI, 1984).

6. Stanley Cohen, *Folk Devils and Moral Panics* (New York: St. Martin's, 1980); Orrin Klapp, *Heroes, Villains, and Fools* (San Diego: Aegis, 1972); Gusfield, *Culture of Public Problems.*

7. Boorstin, *Image.*

8. See MacAloon, *Rite, Drama, Festival, Spectacle,* Introduction.

9. See chap. 7.

10. Hebdige, *Subculture,* 92–93.

11. *AS,* 23 June 1975; *MS,* 28 May 1983.

12. Shuppan Nyususha, *Publication Yearbook 1982* (Tokyo: Shuppan Nyususha, 1982).

13. An informant even asked me, "Which *shokan* [publishing firm] are you working for?" Although the use of *shokan* (書館) to designate a publishing company is rather unusual, it was synonymous with "publisher" for him.

14. See Appendix A.

15. Shuppan Nyususha, *Publication Yearbook 1982.*

16. Shuppan Nyususha, *Publishing Yearbook 1980* (Tokyo: Shuppan Nyususha, 1980), 65.

17. Klapp, *Heroes, Villains, and Fools,* 147.

18. Cohen, *Folk Devils and Moral Panics,* 11–12.

19. He even suggests a "government subsidy for the publicity of high types of char-

acter, either in real life or in fiction and drama" (Klapp, *Heroes, Villains, and Fools,* 155–56).

20. Barbara Babcock, "Liberty's a Whore," in *The Reversible World,* ed. Barbara Babcock (Ithaca, N.Y.: Cornell University Press, 1978), 100.

21. Ibid., 101.

22. Arnold van Gennep, *The Rites of Passage,* trans. Monika Vizedon and Gabrielle Caffee (Chicago: University of Chicago Press, 1960); Victor Turner, *Dramas, Fields, and Metaphors* (Ithaca: Cornell University Press, 1974).

23. Babcock, "Liberty's a Whore," 118; See also Mikhail Bakhtin, *On Dostoevsky,* Japanese trans. Keizaburo Araya (Tokyo: Tikisha, 1974), 155–70; idem, *Spatiotemporal Structure of the Novel,* Japanese trans. Seiji Kitaoka (Tokyo: Shinjidaisha, 1987), 230; and Masao Yamaguchi, *Culture and Ambiguity* (Tokyo: Iwanami Shoten, 1975), passim.

24. van Gennep, *Rites of Passage;* Turner, *Dramas, Fields, and Metaphors.*

25. Turner, *Dramas, Fields, and Metaphors,* 232.

26. Babcock, "Liberty's a Whore," 101–2.

27. *B100,* 120.

28. *BD II,* 200.

29. *BD I,* from the editor's commentary.

30. Yoshiharu Urita, *Only Saturday Is Left for Us* (Tokyo: Futami Shobo, 1975), 20.

31. *BD III,* 238.

32. *BB,* 136.

33. Turner, *Dramas, Fields, and Metaphors,* 232.

34. Babcock, "Liberty's a Whore," 102–3.

35. Ibid., 105.

36. *B100,* 129.

37. Dojo, Bosozoku *Documentary,* 26.

38. *BB,* 249.

39. Kiichiro Nakamura, *The* Bosozoku *Boy* (Tokyo: Tairiku Shobo, 1981), 74, from a statement inserted by the editor.

40. Urita, *Only Saturday Is Left for Us,* 28–29.

41. Antonio Gramsci, *Prison Notebooks,* trans. Quintin Hoare and Geoffrey Smith (New York: International Publishers, 1971); Georg Lukács, *History and Class Consciousness,* trans. R. Livingstone (Cambridge: MIT Press, 1983); Peter Berger and Thomas Luckman, *The Social Construction of Reality* (New York: Doubleday, 1967).

42. Dojo, Bosozoku *Documentary,* 48.

43. *BB,* 188.

44. *BA '81,* 90.

45. Bakhtin, *On Dostoevsky,* 230, comments that there is a fundamental affinity between the picaresque genre and the tradition of carnival.

46. *BA '81,* 99.

47. *B100,* 128.

48. Jugatsu Toi, ed., *Nobody Can Stop Us* (Tokyo: Daisan Shokan, 1979), introduction.

49. Turner, *Dramas, Fields, and Metaphors,* 232.

50. Babcock, "Liberty's a Whore," 111.

51. *B100,* passim; *BA '80,* 74–89.

52. Toru Mita, *The Frontline of Boso Driving* (Tokyo: Rippu Shobo, 1981), 95.

53. *BB,* 344.

54. *BA '81,* 22.

55. *BD II,* 2.

56. Urita, *Only Saturday Is Left for Us*, 195–96.
57. *BB*, 338.
58. Jun Takemura, ed., *Explosion! Ladies* (Tokyo: Tairiku Shobo, 1980), 217.
59. *BA '81*, 398.
60. *BB*, 139.
61. *BB*, 344.
62. Minoru Umegaki, *Slang Dictionary* (Tokyo: Tokyodo Shuppan, 1961), 166, 316.
63. See Erving Goffman, "Where the Action Is," in *Interaction Ritual* (New York: Doubleday, 1967), 149–270.
64. Mita, *Frontline of Boso Driving*, 92.
65. *BA '81*, 53.
66. *BA '80*, 178.
67. *BA '81*, 049.
68. *BA '81*, 086.
69. *B100*, 207.
70. *BD I*, 24.
71. *B100*, 100.
72. Amitai Etzioni, *Comparative Analysis of Complex Organization* (New York: The Free Press, 1961).
73. The fictive character of the *koha* image is also apparent in criticisms of other groups. As a few statements already mentioned have shown, self-assertion as *koha* is often accompanied by the criticism of other groups. "Other groups" are viewed as *"nanpa" bosozoku* who lack self-control and engage in despicable deviant acts such as theft, gang rape, and paint-thinner-inhaling. See, for example, *BD I*, 133; *BB*, 19–22; and Mori, "Becoming *Bosozoku*," 11.
The image of morally degraded "other groups" is very close to public stereotypes of the *bosozoku* to be discussed in chapter 7. The stereotypic distinction between the praiseworthy "our group" and detestable "other groups" suggests that the contrast is an exaggerated one and that *nanpa* acts exist also among "our group."
74. Cf. Goffman, "Where the Action Is"; Katz, *Seductions of Crime*.
75. Babcock, "Liberty's a Whore," 108; Cf. Bakhtin, *Spatiotemporal Structure of the Novel*, 156–70.
76. *BA '80*, 187.
77. Edwin Lemert, *Social Pathology* (New York: McGraw-Hill, 1951), 65–68; Cohen, *Folk Devils and Moral Panics*, 139–40.
78. Thompson, *Hell's Angels*, 90.
79. *BA '80*, 308.
80. *BA '80*, 230.
81. *B100*, 192.
82. Boorstin, *Image*.
83. Ibid., 74.
84. Ibid., 61.
85. Klapp, *Heroes, Villains, and Fools*, 155.
86. Urita, *Only Saturday Is Left for Us*, 13.
87. *AS*, 23 June 1975; *MS*, 20 September 1980; *MS*, 5 December 1981; *MS*, 28 May 1983; *YS*, 19 November 1981.
88. Cohen, *Folk Devils and Moral Panics*.
89. John Clarke, "Style," in *Resistance through Ritual*, ed. Hall and Jefferson, 188–89; John Irwin, *Scenes* (Beverly Hills: Sage, 1977), chap. 4; Hedbige, *Subculture*, 92–99; Cohen, *Folk Devils and Moral Panics*, 139–41, 201–2.

90. *BA '80,* 344.

91. The title of the book *Nammennayo* literally means "Don't lick me!" which in Japanese figuratively means "Don't mess around with me!" Thus the title includes a wordplay about a docile, licking cat and the defiant words of rebellious youths.

92. Asahi Shimbunsha, *Contemporary Schools* (Tokyo: Asahi Shimbunsha, 1983).

93. M. Granovetter, "Threshold Models of Collective Behavior," *AJS* 83 (1978): 1420–43.

94. *AS,* 4 November 1977; *AS,* 3 December 1981; Asahi Shimbunsha, *Minors* (Tokyo: Asahi Shimbunsha, 1978), 67–68.

95. Among the *bosozoku* groups I studied, the history of Yakyo (Midnight Crazies) typically illustrates these developments. This group started as an anonymous gang consisting of schoolboys from several junior high schools. They imitated *bosozoku* poses when they took their own pictures. (Such photographs then were put in their albums.) They soon formed a bicycle *bosozoku* group called the "Pink Panther" and wore *tokkofuku* with the name "Nagare" (Flow), from a *bosozoku* group in their neighborhood. Some became passengers when this group went on *boso* drives. After graduating from their junior high schools, they formed a group called "Ann Lewis," using motorcycles of small displacement. They also participated frequently in the *boso* driving of other groups in their neighborhood. After groups in their community formed an association, the Ukyo Rengo, "Ann Lewis" operated under the name "Yakyo," using motorcycles with large displacement or automobiles. Eikichi Yazawa was among their favorite singers. They played his songs aloud on car stereos during their *boso* driving, bought or shoplifted copies of his autobiography, and attended one of his concerts in Osaka.

96. Walter Benjamin, *Art in the Age of Reproduction,* Japanese trans. Hisao Takagi and Hirohira Takahara (Tokyo: Shobunsha, 1970); Boorstin, *Image;* Orrin Klapp, *Overload and Boredom* (Westport, Conn.: Greenwood Press, 1986).

97. Irwin, *Scenes,* chap. 4.

98. See Yasuko Kasaki, *Harajuku Bamboo Shoot Tribe* (Tokyo: Daisan Shokan, 1981); Yuji Namae, *We Beat Up Teachers* (Tokyo: Kadokawa Shoten, 1983).

99. Cf. Claude Lévi-Strauss, *The Savage Mind* (Chicago: University of Chicago Press, 1966), 232.

100. *Bosozoku* subculture includes various "actable ideas" or schemes of action ranging from "those that are relatively simple and vague to those that are complex and provide detailed descriptions of the roles to be played" (Hare and Blumberg, *Dramaturgical Analysis,* 58).

101. Bateson, "Theory of Play and Fantasy," 182; MacAloon, *Rite, Drama, Festival, Spectacle,* 13.

102. Turner, *From Ritual to Theater.*

103. Irwin, *Scenes,* 211.

CHAPTER FOUR

1. While in American usage the accent in the word "Yankee" falls on the first syllable, in spoken Japanese of the Kansai region *yankii* is stressed on the second syllable.

2. Jiyu Kokuminsha, *The Basic Knowledge of Contemporary Words* (Tokyo: Jiyu Kokuminsha, 1984), 1010.

3. Shimpei Takuma, Yasunori Chiba, and Sakuichi Nakagawa, "*Bosozoku* and Juvenile Problems, Part I," *IATSS Review* 1 (1975), 22; Kaneto, "*Bosozoku,*" 182–84; Nagayama et al., *Report on* Bosozoku *Problem.*

4. Gans, *Urban Villagers,* passim.

5. Robert Park and Ernest Burgess, *Introduction to the Science of Sociology* (Chicago: University of Chicago Press, 1921), 16–24; Thrasher, *Gang*, part I, p. 70.

6. S. Eisenstadt, *From Generation to Generation* (Glencoe, Ill.: The Free Press, 1956), 162.

7. *WPP 1981*, 31; Masayuki Tamura, "A Multivariate Analysis of *Bosozoku* Members," *Kagaku Keisatsu Kenkyujo Hokoku* 22 (1981): 42–48; Mori, "Becoming *Bosozoku*."

8. See chap. 2.

9. Cf. Thomas Scheff, *Catharsis on Healing, Ritual, and Drama* (Berkeley: University of California Press, 1979).

10. Duncan, *Communication and Social Order*, chap. 28.

11. Umegaki, *Slang Dictionary*, 447–48.

12. See Makoto Akimoto, *Who Is to Blame!? School Violence* (Tokyo: Dainamikku Serazu, 1983); Asahi Shimbunsha, *Contemporary Schools*.

13. Kyoto Shimbunsha, *The Junior High School Student* (Kyoto: Kyoto Shimbunsha, 1980).

14. In the 1984 *White Paper on the Police, tamariba* (hangout) is defined as a "place where adolescents gather and misbehave, as in smoking, drinking, and impure sexual acts." The white paper mentions 16,473 hangouts investigated by the police in July 1983 during the campaign to "prevent adolescents from delinquency." Of these, snack bars or tearooms made up 22.4 percent, apartments 15.1 percent, and video arcades 14.8 percent. See *WPP 1984*, 140–41.

15. In 1980, there were some 4.6 million vending machines in Japan, while the United States had 5.1 million. A large portion of these machines dispense cigarettes and alcoholic beverages. In Japan minors are rarely asked their age when they buy cigarettes or alcohol, even in stores. See Yoshihiro Ishikawa, ed., *American Culture in Japan, '70s* (Tokyo: Sanseido, 1981), 187.

16. For similar observations, see Suttles, *Social Order of the Slum*, chap. 10; Paul Willis, *Learning to Labor* (New York: Columbia University Press, 1977), chap. 2; Paul Corrigan, *Schooling the Smash Street Kids* (London: Macmillan, 1979), passim.

17. Katz, *Seductions of Crime*, 110–12.

18. Cf. Gerald Suttles, "Friendship as a Social Institution," in *Social Relationships*, ed. G. McCall (Chicago: Aldine, 1970).

19. In some cases, *yakuza* members intervene in a dispute between Yankees at the request of the Yankees or in expectation of exploiting their differences. Extorting a certain sum of money from young hoodlums by intervening in their dispute is a "hustle" (*shinogi*) for low-level *yakuza* members. Such *yakuza* intervention also precludes a report to the police.

20. See Irwin, *Scenes*.

21. Matza, *Delinquency and Drift*, chap. 6; Csikszentmihalyi and Larson, *Being Adolescent*, passim.

22. Hannerz, *Soulside*, chap. 5; Leary, "White Guys' Stories." See also chap. 5 of this volume.

23. Cf. Lyn Lofland, *A World of Strangers* (New York: Basic Books, 1973).

CHAPTER FIVE

1. Garvey, *Play*, 86–96.

2. Sutton-Smith and Kelly-Byrne, "Masks of Play," 195; see also idem, "The Idealization of Play," in *Play*, ed. Peter Smith (Oxford: Basil Blackwell, 1984), 305–21.

3. Garvey, *Play*, 88.

4. Gary Fine, *Shared Fantasy* (Chicago: University of Chicago Press, 1983).

5. Garvey, *Play,* 91–92.

6. Fine, *Shared Fantasy,* chap. 7.

7. *KS,* 21 September 1982.

8. The others are: three technical school students (4.5 percent), two technical school graduates (3.0 percent), three part-time high school dropouts (4.5 percent), and seven full-time high school dropouts (10.6 percent).

9. Ministry of Education, *Summary Statistics on Education, 1983* (Tokyo: Monbusho), 142–47; *WPYA 1980,* 108.

10. As was shown in chap. 3, the "Group Full Throttle," free-lance journalists, emphasized resentment on the part of *bosozoku* and depicted the *bosozoku* as a hero revolting against the meritocratic society. A member of the group recently published a book on postwar development of youthful stylistic deviations, or various *zoku* (Kosuke Umabuchi, *The Postwar History of* Zoku [Tokyo: Sanseido, 1989]; see also chap. 7 of this volume). He repeatedly argues that the chief reason of gang participation is not resentment but enjoyment of sociability and high-speed racing.

11. My informants' skepticism regarding the financial rewards of post-compulsory education corresponds with the declining economic utility of higher education in the last decade. The income differential for an academic pedigree is relatively low in Japan, because of the improvement in salaries across the board and because of the rapid increase in college enrollment. The "diploma disease" in Japan has produced too many college graduates for available white-collar jobs; many don't even make it to the level of "mere salary man." See Morikazu Ushiogi, *Transformation of Academic-Pedigree-Oriented Society* (Tokyo: Tokyo Daigaku Shuppankai, 1978); Ronald Dore, *The Diploma Disease* (Berkeley, Calif.: University of California Press, 1976); and Ryoichi Iwanai, *Is There No Academic Pedigreeism?* (Tokyo: Nihon Keizai Shuppannsha, 1980). For the changes of "internal rates of return" (a rate of discount equating the present value of return on education with the present value of cost), see Motohisa Kaneko, "Educational Expansion in Postwar Japan," (Ph. diss., University of Chicago, 1984). See also Hiroshi Ishida, "Educational Credentials and Socio-Economic Status Attainment," *Shakaigaku Hyoron* 40 (1989): 252–66.

12. Kaneto, *"Bosozoku,"* 202.

13. Takuma et al., "Psychological Study of *Bosozoku,"* 91.

14. For my informants, then, achievement of higher academic pedigree is not a "culturally-induced deep motivation" inculcated by society to such a degree that, when unsatisfied, it leads to rebellious behavior resulting from Mertonian "anomy."

15. For possible parental influences on my informants' evaluation of academic advancement, see chap. 6, n. 17.

16. Garvey, *Play,* 92.

17. Ibid., 92.

18. See Paul Hare and Herbert Blumberg, *Dramaturgical Analysis,* chap. 6.

19. *BB,* 239.

20. Leary, "White Guys' Stories," 61; Lee Rainwater, *Behind Ghetto Walls* (Chicago: Aldine, 1970), chap. 13.

21. See Howard Becker, "Becoming a Marihuana User," in *Outsiders* (New York: The Free Press, 1963), 41–58.

22. Cf. Hannerz, *Soulside,* chap. 5.

23. See Leary, "White Guys' Stories," 66.

24. Matza, *Delinquency and Drift;* Leary, "White Guys' Stories"; William Labov, *Language in the Inner City* (Philadelphia: University of Pennsylvania Press, 1972); Thomas Kochman, *Black and White Styles in Conflict* (Chicago: University of Chicago Press, 1981).

25. Erving Goffman, *The Presentation of Self in Everyday Life* (Woodstock, N.Y.: Overlook Press, 1959), chap. 3.

26. Hannerz, *Soulside,* 112; Cf. Leary, "White Guys' Stories," 66.

27. Garvey, *Play,* 95.

28. Thirty-one percent of all shops and 42 percent of all shop employees do business in the Nakagyo and Shimogyo wards; within this area 57 percent of all consumer sales in Kyoto are transacted (Kyoto City Office, *Commerce in Kyoto 1983,* 143). Kawaramachi Avenue between Sanjo and Shijo Streets, and Shijo Street between Higashioji and Karasuma Avenues constitute two major shopping districts, which include large department stores as well as smaller enterprises offering traditional goods. The wide assortment of merchandise, from electric appliances to kimonos to fashionable imported clothes, will give foreign visitors the impression of an enormous urban toy bin.

29. *KS,* 1979–81; Kyoto Prefecture Police, *The Present State of Bosozoku 1982.*

30. Etzioni, *A Comparative Analysis of Complex Organization;* see also D. Ellis, "The Hobbesian Problem of Order," *ASR* 36 (1971): 692–703.

31. Kyoto Prefecture Police, *Present State of Bosozoku,* 1.

32. They were Ken'ichi (June 1976–July 1980), Susumu (July 1980–September 1981), Shintaro (September 1981–February 1982), Masahiko (February 1982–June 1982), Saburo (June 1982–March 1983), Kenji (March 1983–September 1983), Taro (September 1983–December 1983), Tokio (December 1983–).

33. *KS,* 28 January 1980.

34. *KS,* 30 November 1979.

35. Cf. Mori, "Becoming *Bosozoku,*" 9–17.

36. *KS,* 2 September 1983; *YS,* 29 September 1983; *AS,* 29 September 1983.

37. See Thrasher, *Gang;* Suttles, *Social Order of the Slum,* chap. 10; Lewis Yablonsky, *The Violent Gang* (Maryland: Penguin, 1970).

38. See Kyoto Prefecture Police, *Present State of Bosozoku.*

CHAPTER SIX

1. Tamura, "The Present State of *Bosozoku,*" *Hanzai to Hiko* 38 (1978): 67–84; Mori, "Becoming *Bosozoku*"; idem, "*Bosozoku* Boy," in *Juvenile Delinquency in Japan,* ed. Katei Saibansho Gendai Hiko Mondai Kenkyukai (Tokyo: Taisei Shuppan, 1979).

2. B. Wooton, *Social Science and Social Pathology* (London: Allen & Unwin, 1959), chap. 5.

3. See, for example, S. Glueck and E. Glueck, *Juvenile Delinquency Grown up* (New York: Commonwealth, 1940); M. Sullivan and J. Grant, "The Development of Interpersonal Maturity," *Psychiatry* 20 (1957): 373–85; C. Jesness, "Comparativeness of Behavior Modification and Transactional Analysis Programs for Delinquents," *Journal of Consulting and Clinical Psychology* 43 (1975): 758–79.

4. Wooton, *Social Science and Social Pathology,* 163–64.

5. Daniel Glaser and K. Rice, "Crime, Age and Employment," *AJS* 24 (1959): 679–86; L. Karacki and Jackson Toby, "The Uncommitted Adolescent," *Sociological Inquiry* 32 (1962): 203–15; Daniel Glaser, *Crime in Our Changing Society* (New York: Holt, Rinehart & Winston, 1978); H. Cline, "Criminal Behavior over the Life Span," in *Constancy and Change in Human Development,* ed. O. Brim and J. Kagan (Cambridge: Harvard University Press, 1980). For a critical commentary on these studies, see Travis Hirschi and Michael Bottfredson, "Age and the Explanation of Crime," *AJS* 89 (1982): 552–84.

6. The three categories of factors roughly correspond to the three categories of "compliance" relationship mentioned in chap. 5.

7. For an outline of the juvenile justice system in Japan, see M. Shikata and S.

Tsuchiya, "The Juvenile System in Japan," in *Juvenile Justice,* United Nations Social Defense Research Institute, Publication No. 12 (1976): 55–81.

8. Some informants erroneously believe that, even if they are sent to training schools, their delinquency records will be automatically burned when they become twenty.

9. See chap. 4.

10. For a more detailed discussion of this belief, see Ikuya Sato, *Yankee,* Bosozoku, *Man of Society* (Tokyo: Shin'yosha, 1985), chap. 8.

11. For criticism of the subcultural theory of delinquency, see Suttles, *Social Order of the Slum,* chap. 10; Hirschi, *Causes of Delinquency;* Kornhauser, *Social Sources of Delinquency.*

12. Stanford Lyman and Marvin Scott, *Sociology of the Absurd,* (New York: Appleton-Century-Crofts, 1970), 116.

13. See, for example, Bernice Neugarten, J. Moore, and J. Lowe, "Age Norms, Age Constraints and Adult Socialization," *AJS* 70 (1965): 710–17; D. Plath and K. Ikeda, "After Coming of Age," in *Socialization and Communication in Primary Groups,* ed. T. Williams (The Hague: Mouston, 1975); G. Elder, "Age Differentiation and the Life Course," *Annual Review of Sociology* 1 (1975): 165–90.

14. It should be noted that the age norms regarding juvenile misconduct and subcultural styles have changed over time. Older informants all agreed that one could participate in *boso* driving in one's twenties before 1980. They also said there had been no strict age norm about the use of motorcycles at that time. Many members began their *bosozoku* career in their late teens and participated in *boso* driving in their twenties. Official reports on *bosozoku* in Kyoto correspond with their observations about the change in the age structure of the *bosozoku* population. While 82.2 percent of those *bosozoku* youths on the Kyoto Prefecture police lists were minors in 1978, 90.6 percent were minors in 1983 (Kyoto Prefecture Police, *The Present State of* Bosozoku *1979; KS,* 28 March 1984). Although the police documents do not specify ages of *bosozoku* youths, the documents published in 1980 and 1982 record the increasing number of minors in the *bosozoku* population (Kyoto Prefecture Police, *The Present State of* Bosozoku *1980, 1982*). During my field research, informants who were active gang members regarded nineteen as the approximate graduation age. Most of them began participating in *boso* driving at the age of fifteen, following graduation from junior high school. It seems to me that "juvenescence" of the *bosozoku* symbolism and increased risk of gang activity are two major causes of this change in the age structure and age norms. The changes in age structure of the gang population and in age norms would attest to the hypothesis that "maturational reform" of my informants is a social rather than a biological process.

15. Hoichoi Production, *Official Mie Handbook* (Tokyo: Shogakukan, 1983), 166–68.

16. Robert Stebbins, "On Misunderstanding the Concept of Commitment," *Social Forces* 48 (1970), 527; idem, *Amateur* (Beverly Hills: Sage, 1979), 39. For the original formulation of the sociological concept of commitment, see Howard Becker, "Note on the Concept of Commitment," *AJS* 66 (1960): 32–40.

17. In many cases, the attitudes and expectations that my informants have about occupation seem to reflect those of their parents. At least twenty out of some seventy informants had parents who were self-employed. Most of the self-employed parents were not poor and some were well-to-do. It seems that these parents who could lead a decent life without any significant "academic pedigree" provided an important role model for my informants and led to their low commitment to academic work. Senior members or ex-members who could spend a relatively affluent consumer life without a high school diploma provided another role model.

Kaneto reports that sons of self-employed parents are overrepresented in 100 *bosozoku* boys investigated by the Tokyo Family Court: Forty-three boys had self-employed parents. See Shimpei Takuma, Yasunori Chiba, and Yoshiichi Kaneto, "*Bosozoku* and Juvenile Problems, Part I," *IATSS Review* 1 (1975), 29, 39.

18. Cf. A. Hollingshead, *Elmtown's Youth* (New York: John Wiley, 1949), 369–71.

19. See Tamara Hareven, *Transitions* (New York: Academic Press, 1978).

20. I did not include the item of "adolescence" in the tentative version of the questionnaire administered to the girls. Their responses to the item of "regular jobs" were excluded from figure 6.3 because most of them expected not to work after marriage.

21. See Dennis Hogan, "The Transition to Adulthood as a Career Contingency," *ASR* 45 (1980): 261–76: and idem, *Transitions and Social Change* (Chicago: University of Chicago Press, 1981).

22. See Helen Ebaugh, *Becoming an Ex* (Chicago: University of Chicago Press, 1988).

CHAPTER SEVEN

1. *WPP, 1981,* 49–50.

2. *WPP, 1983.*

3. *AS,* 14 July 1981.

4. Stylistic deviations, especially those including the element of make-believe, are "mirrors" in still another sense. Make-believe offers one an opportunity for detachment both from one's part in everyday life and from a role in the make-believe world. The performance in the make-believe world includes two seemingly contradictory messages, "I am what I pretend to be," and "I am *not* what I pretend to be" and provides commentary on both roles and on outside elements such as other people's roles, or the make-believe setting. In other words, make-believe, as a self-reflexive communication, does not simply "reflect" its social backgrounds as antecedents but "reflects upon" them. See Schwartzman, *Transformations,* 232–36; Geertz, "Deep Play"; Garvey, *Play;* and MacAloon, *Rite, Drama, Festival, Spectacle.*

In this volume, then, I have examined *bosozoku* as a "mirror" in three senses: 1) as a manifestation of affluent society—chap. 7; 2) as a projective test for public anxiety—chap. 7; and 3) as a "metasocial commentary" by *bosozoku* youths on Japanese society—chaps. 3–6.

5. I. Destler and H. Sato, *Coping with the U.S.-Japanese Conflicts* (Lexington, Mass.: Lexington Books, 1982).

6. Ministry of Labor, *White Paper on Labor, 1983* (Tokyo: Okurasho Insatsukyoku, 1983), p. 156; ILO, *Yearbook of Labor Statistics* (Geneva: ILO Publications, 1984), table 9; Takafusa Nakamura, *The Postwar Japanese Economy,* trans. Jacqueline Kaminsky (Tokyo: University of Tokyo Press, 1981), pp. 254–56.

7. Nakamura, *Postwar Japanese Economy,* 115–21.

8. Economic Planning Agency, *White Paper on National Life, 1983* (Tokyo: Okurasho Insatsukyoku, 1983), table I-2-3.

9. *JSY, 1957,* table 223; *JSY, 1984,* table 15–19.

10. *SA, 1966,* table 97; *SA, 1985,* table 122.

11. NHK Hoso Seron Chosabu, *National Time Budget Study, 1980* (Tokyo: NHK Shuppan, 1981), p. 6.

12. Yoka Kaihatsu Senta, *Recreation Handbook, 1982* (Tokyo: Nikkan Kogyo Shimbunsha, 1982), 14–21.

13. Some 50 percent of junior high school graduates entered senior high school and only about 10 percent went on to college in 1955. See Ministry of Education, *Summary Statistics on Education, 1980* (Tokyo: Monbusho, 1980), 142; *WPYA, 1984,* 146.

14. According to a survey, the average monthly allowance was ¥2,045 ($9.30) for twelve- to fourteen-year-olds, and ¥15,682 ($71.10) for those fifteen to twenty years old (Yoka Kaihatsu Sentaa, *1982 Recreation Handbook*, 1240, 1943).

15. Japanese students spend about 59 hours a week in school or studying, and have only 28 hours for leisure (Sorifu, *WPYA 1980*, 10–91). And the Japanese school year is 243 days. A study of teenagers in a Chicago suburb shows that on a weekly basis they spend about 38 hours on schoolwork and 42 hours at leisure. In the United States, the school year is generally 174 days (Csikszentmihalyi and Larson, *Being Adolescent*, 63–67).

16. Tutoring comprises 43.5 percent and jobs in service industries 20.8 percent of part-time jobs taken on a regular basis. From the part-time jobs, 46.7 percent of the students earn more than $200 per month (Gakusei Engokai, *White Paper on Part-Time Jobs of Students* [Tokyo: Gakusei Engokai, 1981], pp. 109, 117, 120, 161). Most Japanese students use income from part-time jobs as spending money.

17. Jiyu Kokuminsha, *The Basic Knowledge of Contemporary Words, 1983* (Tokyo: Jiyu Kokuminsha, 1983).

18. Ministry of Labor, *White Paper on Labor, 1984* (Tokyo: Okurasho Insatsukyoku, 1984), Appendix 43, Document 121.

19. *SA, 1981*, table 114.

20. Shuppan Nyususha, *Publication Yearbook, 1982*, 1275.

21. Over 5 million copies of *Jump* were sold in 1988 (*AS* 14 December 1988).

22. *Nikkei Anthropos* 3 (1990), 34.

23. Cf. John Brooks, *Showing-off in America* (Boston: Little Brown, 1979).

24. Herbert Gans, *Popular Culture and High Culture* (New York: Basic Books, 1974); Cf. Pierre Bourdieu, *Distinction*, trans. Richard Nice (Cambridge: Harvard University Press, 1984).

25. For a similar bipolarization of styles of American high school boys, between "soshes" (or "elites") and "hoods," see Irwin, *Scenes*, 64–66. For a more detailed analysis of the interrelationship between the two taste cultures and their subtypes, see Sato, *An Ethnography of Bosozoku*, chap. 6.

The overrepresentation of high school dropouts and junior high school graduates in the *bosozoku* population seems, then, a matter of taste and stake in conformity, rather than psychological strains such as "inferiority complex" and "frustration" arising from poor academic pedigrees. In essence, the pathetic characterization of *bosozoku* rests upon an assumption of Mertonian anomy which is supposed to arise from the discrepancy between "culturally-induced deep motivation" for higher academic pedigree and legitimate means of attaining it. In almost all cases, the generality of the aspiration for academic pedigree is merely assumed and never empirically examined.

26. Urita, *Only Saturday Is Left for Us*, 45.

27. Hoichoi Production, *Official Mie Handbook*, 168.

28. Eisenstadt, *From Generation to Generation*; James Coleman, *The Adolescent Society* (New York: The Free Press, 1961); idem, *Youth* (Chicago: University of Chicago Press, 1974); Elder, "Age Differentiation and the Life Course."

29. M. Riley, M. Johnson, and B. Forster, *Aging and Society* (New York: Russell Sage, 1972).

30. S. Strong, "Social Types in the Negro Community of Chicago " (Ph.D. diss., University of Chicago, 1940); R. Angell, "A Critical Review of the Development of the Personal Document Method in Sociology 1920–1940," in *The Use of Personal Documents in History, Anthropology and Sociology*, ed. L. Gottschalk, C. Kluckhohn, and R. Angell (New York: Social Science Research Council, 1945), 177–232; Klapp, *Heroes, Villains, and Fools*.

254 Notes to Pages 189-94

31. Talcott Persons, "Age and Sex in the Social Structure of the United States," *ASR* 7 (1942): 604–16.

32. Theodore Sarbin, "On the Distinction between Social Roles and Social Types, with Special Reference to the Hippie," *American Journal of Psychiatry* 125 (1969), 1028–29.

33. In 1960 there were fewer than 16,000 licensed passenger cars, and only 1.2 percent of all households owned automobiles. The number of cars rose to about 6.8 million in 1970, and reached 23.4 million in 1982. Some 65 percent of all households owned passenger cars in 1984 (*JSY, 1962*, table 127; *JSY, 1984*, table 8–5; *SA, 1966*, table 97; *SA, 1985*, table 122). Among them, about 22 percent owned more than two automobiles. Increased use of motor vehicles has been associated with the improvement of roads. The "pavement ratio," which was as low as 2.1 percent in 1956, increased to 50.7 percent in 1982. The total real length of national expressways was about 3,000 km (1,875 miles) in 1982 while it had been some 200 km (125 miles) in 1965 (*JSY, 1985*, table 8–2). Around the mid-1970s, then, the "objects and settings" are provided for the massive participation in youthful, stylistic deviation with motor vehicles, something that had been almost unimaginable for older generations.

34. See for example, *AS*, 15 September 1959.

34. Burke, "Dramatism"; Duncan, *Communication and Social Order*; Cohen, *Folk Devils and Moral Panics*.

36. Since the word *bosozoku* first appeared in an official document (a police memorandum, "On Strengthening the Regulation of *Bosozoku*," dated May 25) in 1974, the mass media invariably came to use the word as the preferred label for such gangs, first with square brackets or quotation marks, and soon without them. *Yomiuri Shimbun* has used the word *bosozoku* consistently since June 1974, *Asahi Shimbun* since August 1974, and *Mainichi Shimbun* since July 1974. Previously the three papers applied various labels to motorcycle gangs.

37. Kobe-shi Seishonen Mondai Kyogikai, Bosozoku: *A Contemporary Youth Problem* (Kobe: Kobe-shi).

38. There was a temporary resurgence of public concern with *bosozoku* in the summer of 1989. A *"bosozoku* murder case" in April, in which a drunken newspaper editor assaulted two youths but was killed by his intended victims, triggered the resurgence. The editor assaulted two youngsters with an iron pipe in his hand, while the two had no weapons. There was wide news coverage about the incident and the *bosozoku* problem in general. As was the case with similar incidents in the heyday of motorcycle gang activities, the news industry treated the case as one of *"bosozoku* murder" before the two perpetrators were identified and arrested in June. Although it eventually turned out that the two were ex-*bosozoku* members, they were actually youths who "looked like *bosozoku* from their appearance and kind of automobile" in April.

Several times I was interviewed by journalists about this incident and I myself appeared on TV twice. While all the journalists I met personally acknowledged that the victim himself was largely responsible for precipitating the incident, the news industry almost unanimously treated him as a sort of martyr in the public campaign against *bosozoku*. Two of the journalists who interviewed me tried to make contact with active *bosozoku* members but could not do so largely because *bosozoku* activity had dwindled considerably. Yet the mass media reported the incident as if *bosozoku* were still a serious youth problem. See *Asahi Shimbun* 19 April, 23 April, 24 April, 9 June, 1989; *Shukan Shincho* 22 June, 26 October, 1989; and *Asahi Journal*, 19 May, 1989.

39. *WPP, 1981*, 9.

40. *AS*, 14 July 1981.

41. *YS*, 14 July 1981.

42. Tamura, "Present State of *Bosozoku*," 78; *B100*, 242; Kaneto, "*Bosozoku*," 211.

43. *AS*, 27 October 1982.

44. *AS*, 24, 25 January 1978.

45. *YS*, 26 January 1978.

46. For case studies of false reports in which ordinary youths were treated as gang members, see Asahi Shimbunsha, *Minors*, 47–54; and *BA '80*, 32–53.

47. *B100*, 204–25.

48. Cohen, *Folk Devils and Moral Panics*, 41–42.

49. Becker, *Outsiders*, 32–33.

50. See, for example, *AS*, 14 July 1981; Tamura and Mugishima, "Present State of *Bosozoku*"; Yasuo Goto, "Contemporary Youths," *Hanzai to Hiko* 38 (1978): 85–105; Kaneto, "*Bosozoku*"; Yoshihiro Ikeda, "*Bosozoku*," in *Contemporary Juvenile Delinquency*, ed. Toshio Utena and Takao Yaku (Tokyo: Kyoiku Shuppan, 1983).

51. Ikeda, "*Bosozoku*," 141.

52. Quoted in Kaneto, "*Bosozoku*," 165.

53. Hideo Ogawa et al., "Frontline of the Police Control over *Bosozoku*," *Shonen Hodo* September (1976), 20.

54. Police statistics show that the *bosozoku* population jumped from some 25,000 to 40,000 in 1980 and since has been over 37,000, though it declined to some 35,500 in 1987 (*WPC, 1983, WPC, 1988*). It seems to me that these figures reflect increased vigilance of the police against non-gang members, and do not necessarily reflect actual fluctuations in the *bosozoku* population.

55. *AS*, 16 May 1976, on the Kobe Festival Incident.

56. *AS*, 19 September 1977.

57. See chap. 3.

58. Cohen, *Folk Devils and Moral Panics*.

59. Lemert, *Social Pathology*; Rotenberg, "Self-Labeling Theory."

60. Duncan, *Communication and Social Order*, 137; Lyman and Scott, *Sociology of the Absurd*, 138; William Goode, *The Celebration of Heroes* (Berkeley: University of California Press, 1978), 280–82; Anthony Harris and Gary Hill, "The Social Psychology of Deviance," *Annual Review of Sociology*, 8 (1982): 164–65.

61. See Takuma et al., "Psychological Study on *Bosozoku*," 5–11.

62. *YS*, 20 June 1977.

63. Takuma et al., "Psychological Study on *Bosozoku*," 91.

64. See Gusfield, *The Culture of Public Problems*, 84.

65. See for example, Kaneto, "*Bosozoku*"; Kobe-shi Seishonen Mondai Kyogikai, *Bosozoku*, 19–22.

66. See for example, Kikuchi, "Treatise on *Bosozoku*"; Takuma, Chiba, and Nakagawa, "*Bosozoku* and Juvenile Problem, Part I"; Takuma et al., "Psychological Study on *Bosozoku*."

67. See for example, Kazunori Kikuchi, "*Bosozoku*," *Hanzai to Hiko* 38 (1978): 106–25; Kaneto, "*Bosozoku*"; Yasunori Chiba, "Social and Psychological Background of *Bosozoku*," in *Integration and Diffusion*, ed. Keigo Okonogi (Tokyo: Shiseido, 1980); idem, *How to Prevent* Bosozoku; Tamura, "Social Psychology of *Bosozoku*," *Seishin Igaku* 25 (1983): 1035–40. Tamura and Mugishima, "Present State of *Bosozoku*," and Takuma et al., "Psychological Study on *Bosozoku*" attempt to corroborate their hypothesis about psychological stress by employing a questionnaire and psychological tests. The studies include serious methodological defects and do not present any convincing evidence. For a criticism of the studies, see Sato, *An Ethnography of* Bosozoku, 169–72.

256 Notes to Pages 200–206

68. See for example, Chiba, *Bosozoku;* idem, *How to Prevent* Bosozoku; Tamura and Mugishima, "Present State of *Bosozoku"*; and Kaneto, *"Bosozoku."*

69. *WPC, 1976,* p. 253.

70. Junkichi Abe, *Social Psychology of Crime* (Tokyo: Shin'yosha, 1957); O. Takuwa and Y. Ono, *Juvenile Delinquency and Scientific Diagnosis of Delinquents* (Tokyo: Kyosei Fukushikai, 1973); Y. Okukawa and K. Osanai, *The History of Juvenile Delinquency and Correctional Treatment in Postwar Japan* (Tokyo: Sorifu).

71. *WPC, 1984,* 266. The number of juveniles arrested on charges of "heinous offenses" (homicide, rape, burglary, and arson) has steadily decreased since the early 1960s. In 1983, less than 0.3 per 1,000 juveniles committed such crimes. See National Police Agency, *Criminal Statistics in 1984* (Tokyo: Okurasho Insatsukyoku, 1984), 364–65.

72. Kikuchi and Horiuchi, *Playlike Delinquency,* 38–88.

73. *WPC, 1980,* p. 278; National Police Agency, *Criminal Statistics in 1984,* 364–65.

74. *WPP, 1983,* 18–19; see also Marshall Clinard, *Cities with Little Crime* (Cambridge: Cambridge University Press, 1978).

75. D. Bayley, *Forces of Order* (Berkeley: University of California Press, 1976); W. Clifford, *Crime Control in Japan* (Lexington, Mass.: Lexington Books, 1976).

76. Unlike in the United States, "violence in the family" in modern Japan usually refers to children's violent attacks on other family members (especially parents) rather than child abuse or wife-beating.

77. Since 1977 the *White Paper on Youth and Adolescence* has treated the problem of violence in the schools and the *bosozoku* in specific subsections of its chapter about delinquency; and violence in the family received a separate subsection in 1981. The *White Paper on the Police* treated *bosozoku* in its feature article in 1981, and in that year the *White Paper on Youth and Adolescents* dealt with problems of violence in the schools and the family in an independent section (not subsection) of twenty pages.

78. Masaaki Takane, "A Comparative Study on School Violence in Japan and the United States," *Shokun* October (1981): 175–87.

79. *MS,* 16 July 1982; emphasis added.

80. Eisho Omura, "'The Worst Record of Delinquency' and 'The Best Record of Homicide'," *Shonen Hodo* September (1981), p. 39; Kazunori Kikuchi, "Is Juvenile Delinquency Getting More Violent and Malicious?" *Shonen Hodo* October (1981): 13–21.

81. *WPC, 1983,* 301.

82. Cf. Scheff, *Catharsis in Healing, Ritual, and Drama.*

83. See, for example, Ezra Vogel, *Japan as Number One* (New York: Harper & Row, 1979); William Ouchi, *Theory Z* (Reading, Mass.: Addison-Wesley, 1981); Richard Pascal and Anthony Athos, *The Art of Japanese Management* (New York: Simon and Schuster, 1981).

84. The first chapter of the book bears the title "A Mirror for America." It seems to me that the book serves as a vanity mirror for Japanese readers than as a "lesson" for American readers.

85. Nakamura, *Postwar Japanese Economy,* 122; see also Michiko Ishimure, *Minamata* (Tokyo: Kodansha, 1962); Jun Ui *General Treatise on Environmental Pollution* (Tokyo: Aki Shobo, 1973–74).

86. Although unemployment increased almost steadily during the period between 1983 and 1987, reaching over 2.8 percent in 1986 and 1987, it dropped to 1.9 percent in 1988 (*AS,* 24 March 1989).

87. The number of bankruptcies in 1984 exceeded that of 1983, but it has decreased since that year (*AS,* 14 April 1989).

88. Ministry of Health and Welfare, *Estimate of Future Population in Japan* (Tokyo: Okurasho Insatsukyoku, 1983).

89. *AS*, 13 March 1983; Kikuchi and Horiuchi, *Playlike Delinquency*, 38–39.

90. Kikuchi and Horiuchi, *Playlike Delinquency*.

91. *WPP, 1982*.

92. *AS*, 19 May 1976; emphasis added.

93. Shigemori Kyutoku, *Mother-related Syndrome* (Tokyo: San Maku Shuppan, 1979).

94. Kunio Miyauchi, "Home Violence," in *Violence of Adolescents*, ed. Yoshiichi Kaneto (Tokyo: Tachibana Shobo, 1981), 78–85.

CONCLUSION

1. *Time*, August 31, 1987; *Time*, September 28, 1987.

2. Katz, *Seductions of Crime*, chap. 4.

3. See for example, Hall and Jefferson, *Resistance through Ritual*; Hebdige, *Subculture*; Willis, *Learning to Labor*; Corrigan *Schooling the Smash Street Kids*; and Simon Frith, *Sound Effects* (New York: Pantheon, 1981).

4. David Bordua, "Delinquent Subcultures," *Annals of the American Academy of Political and Social Sciences* 338 (1961): 119–36; Downes, *Delinquent Solution*, 81.

5. For a more extensive review of this genre of literature, see Katz, *Seductions of Crime*.

6. Bordua, "Delinquent Subcultures," 120–21.

7. See for example, Clifford Shaw, *The Jack-Roller* (Chicago: University of Chicago Press, 1930), 50; Clifford Shaw, Henry McKay, and James McDonald, *Brothers in Crime* (Chicago: University of Chicago Press, 1938), 354.

8. Thrasher, *Gang*, 82.

9. William Thomas, *The Unadjusted Girl*; Paul Cressey, *The Taxi-Dance Hall* (Chicago: University of Chicago Press, 1932).

10. Gerald Suttles, "Urban Ethnography," 8.

11. Gans, *Urban Villagers*; Muzafer Sherif and Caroline Sherif, *Reference Groups* (New York: Harper and row, 1964); Downes, *Delinquent Solution*; Suttles, *Social Order of the Slum*; Hannerz, *Soulside*.

12. Harold Finestone, "Cats, Kicks, and Color"; Walter Miller, "Lower-Class Culture as a Generating Milieu of Gang Delinquency," *Journal of Social Issues* 15 (1958): 5–19; Yablonsky, *Violent Gang*; James Short and Fred Strodbeck, *Group Process and Gang Delinquency* (Chicago: University of Chicago Press, 1965); Rainwater, *Behind Ghetto Walls*.

13. Elijah Anderson, *A Place on the Corner* (Chicago: University of Chicago Press, 1976); Leary, "White Guys' Stories"; Ruth Horowitz, *Honor and the American Dream* (New Brunswick, N.J.: Rutgers University Press, 1983).

14. For criticism of works by the Birmingham school, see Cohen, *Folk Devils and Moral Panics*, i–xxxiv.

15. Cohen, *Folk Devils and Moral Panics*, 182.

16. Marsh, Rosser, and Harré, *Rules of Disorder*, 97.

17. Goffman, "Where the Action Is," 185.

18. Gans, *Urban Villagers*, 64–73.

19. Thomas, *Unadjusted Girl*, 109, 120.

20. E. Liebow, *Tally's Corner* (Boston: Little, Brown, 1967); Hannerz, *Soulside*; Rainwater, *Behind Ghetto Walls*; Anderson, *A Place on the Corner*.

21. Cressey, *Taxi-Dance Hall*, chap. 5.

22. Shaw, McKay, and McDonald, *Brothers in Crime*, 355; Tannenbaum, *Crime and Community*, 13–17, 52–62.

23. Johan Huizinga, *Homo Ludens* (Boston: Beacon, 1950), 28.

24. Roger Caillois, *Man, Play and Games*, trans. M. Barash (New York: Schocken, 1961), chap. 1.

25. Bateson, "A Theory on Play and Fantasy"; Goffman, *Frame Analysis*.

26. Caillois, *Man, Play and Games*, chap. 4.

27. Martin Gold and Richard Peteronio "Delinquent Behavior in Adolescence," in *Handbook of Adolescent Psychology*, ed. J. Adelson (New York: John Wiley, 1980), p. 525; see also Scott and Vaz, "A Perspective on Middle-Class Delinquency," 329; and Gary Fine, *With the Boys* (Chicago: University of Chicago Press, 1987), p. 120.

28. Suttles, *Social Order of the Slum*, 183, 198–201; Short and Strodbeck, *Group Process and Gang Delinquency*, chaps. 8 and 9.

29. See Smith, "Aestheticism and Social Structure"; and Hebdige, *Subculture*.

30. Thomas, *Unadjusted Girl*, 119; Cressey, *Taxi-Dance Hall*, 85; Granovetter, "Threshold Models of Collective Behavior."

31. Irwin, *Scenes*, 27.

32. Thrasher, *Gang*; Short and Strodbeck, *Group Process and Gang Delinquency*; Horowitz, *Honor and the American Dream*.

33. Thrasher, *Gang*, 138.

34. Ibid., 391.

35. Hugh Duncan, *Symbols in Society* (New York: Oxford University Press, 1968); see also Burke, "Dramatism," 450.

36. Roger Caillois, *Man and the Sacred*, trans. Meyer Barash (New York: The Free Press, 1959); see also Francis Hearn, "Toward a Critical Theory of Play," *Telos* 30 (1976–77), 145–60; and Shun Inoue, *Sociology of Play* (Tokyo: Sekai Shisosha, 1977).

37. Goffman, "Where the Action Is," 193.

38. It is mainly serious action which Goffman treats in his seminal paper "Where the Action Is." He declares that he uses the term "action" in a non-Parsonian sense (149) and criticizes the traditional or functionalist view of man that emphasises socialization to socially delineated goals and conformity to normative regulations (258–59) as a basis of social order. Goffman, however, offers his own version of a functional theory of action by pointing out "latent functions" of action and the image of "character."

39. Goffman, "Where the Action Is," 238.

40. Ibid., 259.

41. Katz, *Seductions of Crime*, passim.

42. Goffman, "Where the Action Is," 192.

43. See Emile Durkheim, *The Division of Labor in Society*, trans. George Simpson (New York: The Free Press, 1933); Peter Berger, Brigitte Berger, and Hansfield Kellner, *The Homeless Mind*, (New York: Random House, 1973); Orrin Klapp, *Collective Search for Identity* (New York: Holt, Rinehart & Winston, 1969); and Irwin, *Scenes*.

44. Berger, Berger, and Kellner, *The Homeless Mind*.

45. Erich Fromm, *Escape from Freedom* (New York: Holt, Rinehart & Winston, 1941).

46. Abner Cohen, *Two-Dimensional Man* (Berkeley: University of California Press, 1974).

47. Stanley Cohen and Laurie Taylor. *Escape Attempts* (London: Allen Lane, 1976).

48. Irwin, *Scenes*: Lofland, *World of Strangers*.

49. Matza, *Delinquency and Drift*.

50. Huizinga, *Homo Ludens;* idem, *In The Shadow of Tomorrow*, trans. J. H. Huizinga (New York: Norton, 1936); see Caillois, *Man and the Sacred*, 161.

51. Cohen, *Two-Dimensional Man*.

52. According to a police report (*WPP, 1984,* 197), there were somewhat more than half the number of *yakuza* members in 1983 as in 1963. During the same period the number of "young hoodlums" fell to one-fourth of the number there were in 1963.

References

Abe, Junkichi. *Hanzai no Shakaishinrigaku* (Social psychology of crime). Tokyo: Shin'yosha, 1957.

Akimoto, Makoto. *Warui nowa Dareda!? Gakunai Boryoku* (Who is to blame!? School violence). Tokyo: Dainamikku Serazu, 1983.

Anderson, Elijah. *A Place on the Corner.* Chicago: University of Chicago Press, 1976.

Angell, R. "A Critical Review of the Development of the Personal Document Method in Sociology, 1920–1940." In *The Use of Personal Documents in History, Anthropology, and Sociology,* edited by L. Gottschalk, C. Kluckhohn, and R. Angell. New York: Social Science Research Council, 1945.

Asahi Shimbunsha. *Miseinen* (Minors). Tokyo: Asahi Shimbunsha, 1978.

———. *Ima Gakkode* (Contemporary schools). Tokyo: Asahi Shimbunsha, 1983.

Babcock, Barbara. "Liberty's a Whore." In *The Reversible World,* edited by Barbara Babcock. Ithaca, N.Y.: Cornell University Press, 1978.

Bakhtin, Mikhail. *Rabelais and His World.* Translated by Helen Iswolsky. Cambridge, Mass.: MIT Press, 1968.

———. *Dostoevsky Ron* (On Dostoevsky). Translated into Japanese by Keizaburo Araya. Tokyo: Tokisha, 1974.

———. *Shosetsu no Jikukan* (Spatiotemporal structure of the novel). Translated into Japanese by Seiji Kitaoka. Tokyo: Shinjidaisha, 1987.

Balint, M. *Thrills and Regressions.* London: Hogarth, 1959.

Ball, Donald. "The Definition of the Situation." *Journal of Social Behavior* 2 (1972): 61–82.

Balsley, Gene. "The Hot-Rod Culture." *American Quarterly* 2 (1950): 353–58.

Bateson, Gregory. "A Theory of Play and Fantasy." In *Steps to an Ecology of Mind.* San Francisco: Chandler, 1972.

Bauman, R. "Verbal Act as Performance." *American Anthropologist* 77 (1974): 290–312.

Bayley, D. *Forces of Order.* Berkeley: University of California Press, 1976.

Becker, Howard. "Note on the Concept of Commitment." *American Journal of Sociology* 66 (1960): 32–40.

———. "Becoming a Marihuana User." In *Outsiders.* New York: The Free Press, 1963.

Benjamin, Walter. *Fukuseigijutsu Jidai no Geijutsu* (Art in the age of reproduction). Translated into Japanese by Hisao Takagi and Hirohira Takahara. Tokyo: Shobunsha, 1970.

Berger, Peter, and Thomas Luckman. *The Social Construction of Reality.* New York: Doubleday, 1967.

Berger, Peter, Brigitte Berger, and Hansfield Kellner. *The Homeless Mind.* New York: Random House, 1973.

Blumer, Herbert. *International Encyclopedia of the Social Sciences.* S.v. "Fashion."

———. "Fashion." *Sociological Quarterly* 10 (1969): 275–91.

Boorstin, Daniel. *The Image*. New York: Harper & Row, 1961.

Bordua, David. "Delinquent Subcultures." *Annals of the American Academy of Political and Social Sciences* 338 (1961): 119–36.

Bourdieu, Pierre. *Distinction*. Translated by Richard Nice. Cambridge: Harvard University Press, 1984.

Brissette, Dennis, and Charles Edgley. *Life as Theater*. Chicago: Aldine, 1975.

Brooks, John. *Showing-off in America*. Boston: Little, Brown, 1979.

Brown, Richard. *A Poetic for Sociology*. Chicago: University of Chicago Press, 1989.

Burke, Kenneth. *International Encyclopedia of the Social Sciences*. S.v. "Dramatism."

Caillois, Roger. *Man and the Sacred*. Translated by Meyer Barash. New York: The Free Press, 1959.

———. *Man, Play and Games*. Translated by Meyer Barash. New York: Schocken, 1961.

Chiba, Yasunori. *Bosozoku (Bosozoku)*. Tokyo: Nihon Keizai Shimbunsha, 1975.

———. "Bosozoku no Kodo no Kiso" (Social and psychological background of *bosozoku*). In *Togo to Kakusan* (Integration and diffusion), edited by Keigo Okonogi. Tokyo: Shiseido, 1980.

———. *Mizen ni Fusego Bosozoku* (How to prevent youths from becoming *bosozoku*). Tokyo: Kumon Sugaku Kenkyu Senta, 1981.

Clarke, J. "Style." In *Resistance through Ritual*, edited by Edward Hall and Tony Jefferson. London: Hutchinson, 1976.

Clifford, W. *Crime Control in Japan*. Lexington, Mass.: Lexington Books, 1976.

Clinard, Marshall. *Cities with Little Crime*. Cambridge: Cambridge University Press, 1978.

Cline, H. "Criminal Behavior over the Life Span," In *Constancy and Change in Human Development*, edited by O. Brim and J. Kagan. Cambridge: Harvard University Press, 1980.

Cloward, R., and L. Ohlin. *Delinquency and Opportunity*. New York: The Free Press, 1960.

Cohen, Abner. *Two-Dimensional Man*. Berkeley: University of California Press, 1974.

Cohen, Albert. *Delinquent Boys*. New York: The Free Press, 1955.

Cohen, Stanley, and Laurie Taylor. *Escape Attempts*. London: Allen Lane, 1976.

Cohen, Stanley. *Folk Devils and Moral Panics*. New York: St. Martin's, 1980.

Coleman, James. *The Adolescent Society*. New York: The Free Press, 1961.

———, ed. *Youth*. Chicago: University of Chicago Press, 1974.

Corrigan, Paul. *Schooling the Smash Street Kids*. London: Macmillan, 1979.

Cressey, Paul. *The Taxi-Dance Hall*. Chicago: University of Chicago Press, 1932.

Csikszentmihalyi, Mihaly, et al. *Flow: Studies of Enjoyment*. PHS Grant Report, 1974.

Csikszentmihalyi, Mihaly. *Beyond Boredom and Anxiety*. San Francisco: Jossey-Bass, 1975.

Csikszentmihalyi, Mihaly, and Reed Larson. *Being Adolescent*. New York: Basic Books, 1984.

Csikszentmihalyi, Mihaly, and Isabella Csikszentmihalyi, eds. *Optimal Experience*. New York: Cambridge University Press.

Denzin, Norman. *The Research Act*. New York: McGraw-Hill, 1978.

Destler, I., and H. Sato, *Coping with the U.S.-Japanese Conflicts*. Lexington, Mass.: Lexington Book, 1982.

Dojo, Takeshi. *Dokyumento Bosozoku (Bosozoku* documentary). Kobe: Kobe Simbun Shuppan Senta, 1982.

Dore, Ronald. *The Diploma Disease*. Berkeley, Calif.: University of California Press, 1976.

Douglas, Mary. *Purity and Danger*. London: Routledge & Kegan Paul, 1966.

Downes, D. *The Delinquent Solution*. New York: The Free Press, 1966.

Duncan, Hugh. *Communication and Social Order*. London: Oxford University Press, 1962.

————. *Symbols in Society.* New York: Oxford University Press, 1968.

Durkheim, Emile. *The Elementary Forms of the Religious Life.* Translated by J. W. Swain. New York: The Free Press, 1912.

————. *The Division of Labor in Society.* Translated by George Simpson. New York: The Free Press, 1933.

Ebaugh, Helen. *Becoming an Ex.* Chicago: University of Chicago Press, 1988.

Economic Planning Agency. *Showa 58 Nendo Seikatsu Hokusho* (White paper on national life 1983). Tokyo: Okurasho Insatsukyoku, 1983.

————. *Kurashi no Tokei* (Statistical abstracts). Tokyo: Okurasho Insatsukyoku, 1966–83.

Eisenstadt, S. *From Generation to Generation.* Glencoe, Ill.: The Free Press, 1956.

Elder, G. "Age Differentiation and the Life Course." *Annual Review of Sociology* 1 (1975): 165–90.

Ellis, D. "The Hobbesian Problem of Order." *American Sociological Review* 36 (1971): 692–703.

Etzioni, Amitai. *Comparative Analysis of Complex Organization.* New York: The Free Press, 1961.

Fine, Gary, and S. Kleinman. "Rethinking Subculture." *American Journal of Sociology* 85 (1979): 1–20.

Fine, Gary, "Small Groups and Culture Creation." *American Sociological Review* 44 (1979): 733–45.

————. *Shared Fantasy.* Chicago: University of Chicago Press, 1983.

————. *With the Boys.* Chicago: University of Chicago Press, 1987.

Finestone, Harold. "Cats, Kicks, and Color." *Social Problems* 5 (1957): 3–13.

Frith, Simon. *Sound Effects.* New York: Pantheon, 1981.

Fromm, Erich. *Escape from Freedom.* New York: Holt, Rinehart & Winston, 1941.

Gakusei Engokai. *Arubaito Hakusho* (White paper on part-time jobs of students). Tokyo: Gakusei Engokai, 1981.

Gans, Herbert. *Popular Culture and High Culture.* New York: Basic Books, 1974.

————. *The Urban Villagers.* New York: The Free Press, 1962.

Garvey, Catharine. *Play.* Cambridge: Harvard University Press, 1977.

Geertz, Clifford. "Deep Play." In *The Interpretation of Cultures.* New York: Basic Books, 1973.

————. "Blurred Genres." *The American Scholar* 49 (1980): 165–79.

Glaser, Daniel. *Crime in Our Changing Society.* New York: Holt, Rinehart and Winston, 1978.

Glaser, Daniel, and K. Rice. "Crime, Age, and Employment." *American Journal of Sociology* 24 (1959): 679–86.

Glueck, S., and E. Glueck. *Juvenile Delinquency Grown Up.* New York: Commonwealth, 1940.

Goffman, Erving. *The Presentation of Self in Everyday Life.* Woodstock, N.Y.: Overlook Press, 1959.

————. "Where the Action Is." In *Interaction Ritual.* New York: Doubleday, 1967.

————. *The Frame Analysis.* New York: Harper, 1974.

————. "Reply to Denzin and Keller." *Contemporary Sociology* 10 (1981): 60–68.

Gold, Martin, and Richard Peteronio. "Delinquent Behavior in Adolescence." In *Handbook of Adolescent Psychology,* edited by J. Adelson. New York: John Wiley, 1980.

Gold, Raymond. "Role in Sociological Field Observations." *Social Forces* 36 (1958): 217–23.

Goode, William. *The Celebration of Heroes.* Berkeley: University of California Press, 1978.

Goto, Yasuo. "Seishun Gunzo" (Contemporary youths). *Hanzai to Hiko* 38 (1978): 85–105.

Gramsci, Antonio. *Prison Notebooks*. Translated by Quintin Hoare and Geoffrey Smith. New York: International, 1971.

Granovetter, M. "Threshold Models of Collective Behavior." *American Journal of Sociology* 83 (1978): 1420–43.

Group Full Throttle, eds. *Boso Retto* (*Bosozoku* Archipelago). Tokyo, Daisan Shokan, 1979–82.

———. *Za Bosozoku* (The *bosozoku*). Tokyo: Daisan Shokan, 1980.

———. *Boa Appu! Bosozoku* (Bore up! *Bosozoku*). Tokyo: Daisan Shokan, 1980.

———. *Rediisu* (Ladies). Tokyo: Daisan Shokan, 1981.

Gusfield, Joseph. *The Culture of Public Problems*. Chicago: University of Chicago Press, 1981.

Hall, Edward, and Tony Jefferson, eds. *Resistance through Ritual*. London: Hutchinson, 1976.

Handel, Warren. "Normative Expectations and the Emergence of Meaning as Solutions to Problems." *American Journal of Sociology* 84 (1979): 855–81.

Hannerz, Ulf. *Soulside*. New York: Columbia University Press, 1969.

Hare, Paul, and Herbert Blumberg. *Dramaturgical Analysis of Social Interaction*. New York: Praeger, 1988.

Hareven, Tamara. *Transitions*. New York: Academic Press, 1978.

Harris, Anthony, and Gary Hill. "The Social Psychology of Deviance." *Annual Review of Sociology* 8 (1982): 161–86.

Hearn, Francis. "Toward a Critical Theory of Play." *Telos* 30 (1976–77): 145–60.

Hebdige, Dick. *Subculture*. London: Methuen, 1979.

Hirschi, Travis. *Causes of Delinquency*. California: University of California Press, 1969.

Hirschi, Travis, and Michael Bottfredson. "Age and the Explanation of Crime." *American Journal of Sociology* 89 (1982): 552–84.

Hiyama, Shiro, and Mori Yamazaki. *Shonen Boryoku no Haikei to Yobo* (The background of youthful violence and its prevention). Tokyo: Gyosei, 1981.

Hogan, Dennis. "The Transition to Adulthood as a Career Contingency," *American Sociological Review* 45 (1980): 261–76.

———. *Transitions and Social Change*. Chicago: University of Chicago Press, 1981.

Hoichoi Production. *Mie Koza* (Official *mie* handbook). Tokyo: Shogakukan, 1983.

Hollingshead, A. *Elmtown's Youth*. New York: John Wiley, 1949.

Horowitz, Ruth. *Honor and the American Dream*. New Brunswick, N.J.: Rutgers University Press, 1983.

Huizinga, Johan. *In the Shadow of Tomorrow*. Translated by J. H. Huizinga. New York: Norton, 1936.

———. *Homo Ludens*. Boston: Beacon, 1950.

Ikeda, Yoshihiro. "Bosozoku" (*Bosozoku*). In *Gendai no Hiko* (Contemporary juvenile delinquency), edited by Toshio Utena and Takao Yaku. Tokyo: Kyoiku Shuppan, 1983.

ILO. *Yearbook of Labor Statistics*. Geneva: ILO Publications, 1984.

Inoue, Shun. *Asobi no Shakaigaku* (Sociology of play). Tokyo: Sekai Shisosha, 1977.

Inukai, Nagatoshi, ed. *Boso Kaido no Seishun* (Adolescence in *boso* driving). Tokyo: Daisan Shokan, 1980.

———. *Shashinshu: Boso Saizensen* (Picture book: The frontline of *boso* driving). Tokyo: Daisan Shokan, 1981.

Irwin, John. *Scenes*. Beverly Hills: Sage, 1977.

Ishida, Hiroshi. "Gakureki to Shakai-Keizaiteki Chii no Tassei" (Educational credentials and socio-economic status attainment). *Shakaigaku Hyoron* 40 (1989): 252–66.

Ishikawa, Yoshihiro, ed. *Amerikan Karucha 1970s* (American culture in Japan, 1970s). Tokyo: Sanseido, 1981.

Ishimure, Michiko. *Kukai Jodo* (Minamata). Tokyo: Kodansha, 1962.

Iwanai, Ryoichi. *Gakureki Shugi was Hokaishitaka?* (Is there no academic pedigreeism?). Tokyo: Nihon Keizai Shuppannsha, 1980.

Janowitz, Morris. *The Last Half Century.* Chicago: University of Chicago Press, 1978.

Jesness, C. "Comparativeness of Behavior Modification and Transactional Analysis Programs for Delinquents." *Journal of Consulting and Clinical Psychology* 43 (1975): 758–79.

Jiyu Kokuminsha. *Showa 58 Nenban Gendai Yogo no Kisochishiki* (The basic knowledge of contemporary words, 1983). Tokyo: Jiyu Kokuminsha, 1983.

———. *Showa 59 Nenban Gendai Yogo no Kisochishiki* (The basic knowledge of contemporary words, 1984). Tokyo: Jiyu Kokuminsha, 1984.

Kaneko, Motohisa. "Educational Expansion in Postwar Japan." Ph.D. diss., University of Chicago, 1984.

Kaneto, Yoshiichi. "Bosozoku" (*Bosozoku*). In *Shonen no Boryoku* (Violence of adolescents), edited by Yoshiichi Kaneko. Tokyo: Tachibana Shobo, 1981.

Karacki, L., and Jackson Toby. "The Uncommitted Adolescent." *Sociological Inquiry* 32 (1962): 203–15.

Kasaki, Yasuko. *Harajuku Takenoko-zoku* (Harajuku bamboo shoot tribe). Tokyo: Daisan Shokan, 1981.

Katz, Jack. *Seductions of Crime.* New York: Basic Books, 1988.

Kikuchi, Kazunori. "Soboka, Kyoakuka no Jitsujo" (Is juvenile delinquency getting more violent and malicious?). *Shonen Hodo* October (1981): 13–21.

———. "Bosozoku ni tsiteno Ichikosatsu" (A treatise on *bosozoku*). *Katei Saibansho Geppo.* July (1981): 10–25.

Klapp, Orrin. *Collective Search for Identity.* New York: Holt, Rinehart & Winston, 1969.

———. *Heroes, Villains, and Fools.* San Diego: Aegis, 1972.

———. *Overload and Boredom.* Westport, Conn.: Greenwood Press, 1986.

Kobe-shi Seishonen Mondai Kyogikai. *Bosozoku: Konnichi no Seishonen Mondai* (*Bosozoku:* A contemporary youth problem). Kobe: Kobe-shi.

Kochman, Thomas. *Black and White Styles in Conflict.* Chicago: University of Chicago Press, 1981.

Kornhauser, Ruth. *Social Sources of Delinquency.* Chicago: University of Chicago Press, 1978.

Kyoto City Office. *Showa 58 nen Kyoto no Shogyo* (Commerce in Kyoto, 1983).

Kyoto Prefecture Police. *Bosozoku no Jittai to Taisaku* (The present state of *bosozoku*). 1979–82.

Kyoto Shimbunsha. *Chugakusei* (The junior high school student). Kyoto: Kyoto Shimbunsha, 1980.

Kyutoku, Shigemori. *Bogenbyo* (Mother-related syndrome). Tokyo: San Maku Shuppan, 1979.

Labov, William. *Language in the Inner City.* Philadelphia: University of Pennsylvania Press, 1972.

Lakoff, George, and Mark Johnson. *Metaphors We Live by.* Chicago: University of Chicago Press, 1980.

Lakoff, George. *Women, Fire, and Dangerous Things.* Chicago: University of Chicago Press, 1987.

Leary, James. "White Guys' Stories of the Night Street." *Journal of the Folklore Institute* 14 (1977): 59–71.

Lemert, Edwin. *Social Pathology.* New York: McGraw-Hill, 1951.

Lévi-Strauss, Claude. *The Savage Mind.* Chicago: University of Chicago Press, 1966.

Liebow, E. *Tally's Corner.* Boston: Little, Brown, 1967.

Lofland, Lyn. *A World of Strangers.* New York: Basic Books, 1973.

Lukács, Georg. *History and Class Consciousness.* Translated by R. Livingstone. Cambridge: MIT Press, 1983.

Lyman, Stanford, and Marvin Scott. *Sociology of the Absurd.* New York: Appleton-Century-Crofts, 1970.

MacAloon, John, ed. *Rite, Drama, Festival, Spectacle.* Philadelphia: ISHI, 1984.

Marsh, Peter, Elizabeth Rosser, and Rom Harré. *The Rules of Disorder.* London: Routledge & Kegan Paul, 1978.

Matza, David. *Delinquency and Drift.* New York: John Wiley, 1964.

Mead, George. *Mind, Self, and Society.* Chicago: University of Chicago Press, 1934.

Miller, Walter. "Lower-Class Culture as a Generating Milieu of Gang Delinquency." *Journal of Social Issues* 15 (1958): 5–19.

Ministry of Education. *Mombu Tokei Yoran* (Summary statistics on education), 1980, 1983. Tokyo: Mombusho.

Ministry of Health and Welfare. *Nihon no Shorai Suikei Jinko* (Estimate of future population in Japan). Tokyo: Okurasho Insatsukyoku, 1983.

Ministry of Justice. *Hanzai Hakusho* (White paper or crime). Tokyo: Okurasho Insatsukyoku, 1976–84.

Ministry of Labor. *Rodo Hakusho* (White paper on labor). Tokyo: Okurasho Insatsukyoku, 1983–84.

Mita, Toru. *Boso Saizensen* (The frontline of *boso* driving). Tokyo: Rippu Shobo, 1981.

Mitchell, Richard. *Mountain Experience.* Chicago: University of Chicago Press, 1983.

Miyauchi, Kunio. "Kateinai Boryoku" (Home violence). In *Shonen no Boryoku* (Violence of adolescents), edited by Yoshiichi Kaneto. Tokyo: Tachibana Shobo, 1981.

Mori, Kanji. "Bosozoku ni Nariyuku Wakamonotachi" (Becoming *bosozoku*). *Shonen Hodo,* September (1979): 9–17.

———. "Bosozoku Shonen" (*Bosozoku* boy). In *Nihon no Shonen Hiko* (Juvenile delinquency in Japan), edited by Katei Saibansho Gendai Hiko Mondai Kenkyukai. Tokyo: Taisei Shuppan, 1979.

Nagayama et al., *Bosozoku Mondai ni Kansuru Chosa Hokokusho* (Report on *bosozoku* problem). Osaka: Osaka Bosozoku Modai Kenkyukai, 1981.

Nakabe, Hiroshi, ed. *Bosozoku 100 Nin no Shisso* (The *boso* driving of 100 *bosozoku* guys). Tokyo: Daisan Shokan, 1979.

Nakamura, Kiichiro. *Bosozoku Shonen* (The *bosozoku* boy). Tokyo: Tairiku Shobo, 1981.

Nakamura, Takafusa. *The Postwar Japanese Economy.* Translated into English by Jacqueline Kaminsky. Tokyo: University of Tokyo Press, 1981.

Namae, Yuji. *Oretachi wa Sensei o Nagutta* (We beat up teachers). Tokyo: Kadokawa Shoten, 1983.

National Police Agency, *Showa 59 Nen no Hanzai* (Criminal statistics in 1984). Tokyo: Okurasho Insatsukyoku, 1984.

National Police Agency. *Keisatsu Hakusho* (White paper on the police). Tokyo: Okurasho Insatsukyoku, 1976–84.

Neugarten, Bernice, J. Moore, and J. Lowe. "Age Norms, Age Constraints and Adult Socialization." *American Journal of Sociology* 70 (1965): 710–17.

NHK Hoso Seron Chosabu. *Showa 55 Nendo Kokumin Seikatsu Jikan Chosa* (National time budget study, 1980). Tokyo: NHK Shuppan, 1981.

Office of the Prime Minister. *Seishonen Hakusho* (White paper on youth and adolescence). Tokyo: Okurasho Insatsukyoku, 1976–84.

Office of the Prime Minister. *Nihon Tokei Nenkan* (Japan statistical yearbook). 1962–84.

Ogawa, Hideo et al. "Kochira 'Bosozoku' Torishimari Saizensen" (Frontline of the police control over *bosozoku*). *Shonen Hodo,* September (1976): 18–31.

Okukawa, Y., and K. Osanai. *Sengo ni Okeru Shonen Hiko no Yotai to Shogu Taisaku no Hensen* (The history of juvenile delinquency and correctional treatment in postwar Japan). Tokyo: Sorifu.

Omura, Eisho. "'Hiko Sengo Saiaku' to 'Satsujin Sengo Sairyo'" ('The worst record of delinquency' and 'The best record of homicide'). *Shonen Hodo,* September (1981): 36–41.

Ouchi, William. *Theory Z.* Reading, Mass.: Addison-Wesley, 1981.

Park, Robert, and Ernest Burgess. *Introduction to the Science of Sociology.* Chicago: University of Chicago Press, 1921.

Parsons, Talcott. "Age and Sex in the Social Structure of the United States." *American Sociological Review* 7 (1942): 604–16.

Pascal, Richard, and Anthony Athos. *The Art of Japanese Management.* New York: Simon and Schuster, 1981.

Perinbanayagam, R. "Definition of the Situation." *Sociological Quarterly* 15 (1974): 521–41.

Plath, D., and K. Ikeda. "After Coming of Age." In *Socialization and Communication in Primary Groups,* edited by T. Williams. The Hague: Mouton, 1975.

Project Liberty Bell. *Sakebi: Urakaido no Seishun* (Cry: Adolescence on the byroad). Tokyo: Taiyo Shobo.

Rainwater, Lee. *Behind Ghetto Walls.* Chicago: Aldine, 1970.

Ricoeur, Paul. *The Rules of Metaphor.* Toronto: University of Toronto Press, 1977.

Riley, M., M. Johnson, and B. Forster, eds. *Aging and Society.* New York: Russell Sage, 1972.

Rotenberg, M. "Self-labeling Theory." *British Journal of Criminology* 15 (1975): 360–75.

Sahlins, Marshall. *Culture and Practical Reason.* Chicago: University of Chicago Press, 1976.

Sarbin, Theodore. "On the Distinction between Social Roles and Social Types, with Special Reference to the Hippie." *American Journal of Psychiatry* 125 (1969): 1024–31.

Sato, Ikuya. *Bosozoku no Esunogurafi* (An ethnography of *bosozoku*). Tokyo: Shin'yosha, 1984.

———. *Yanki, Bosozoku, Shakaijin* (Yankee, *bosozoku,* man of society). Tokyo: Shin'yosha, 1985.

Scott, J., and E. Vaz. "A Perspective on Middle-Class Delinquency." *Canadian Journal of Economics and Political Science* 29 (1963): 324–35.

Schwartzman, Helen. *Transformations.* New York: Plenum, 1978.

Shaw, Clifford, Henry McKay, and James McDonald. *Brothers in Crime.* Chicago: University of Chicago Press, 1938.

Shaw, Clifford. *The Jack-Roller.* Chicago: University of Chicago Press, 1930.

Scheff, Thomas. *Catharsis in Healing, Ritual, and Drama.* Berkeley: University of California Press, 1979.

Sherif, Muzafer, and Caroline Sherif. *Reference Groups.* New York: Harper and Row, 1964.

Shikata, M., and S. Tsuchiya. "The Juvenile System in Japan." In *Juvenile Justice,* United Nations Social Defense Research Institute, Publication No. 12 (1976), 55–81.

Short, James, and Fred Strodbeck, *Group Process and Gang Delinquency.* Chicago: University of Chicago Press, 1965.

Shuppan Nyususha. *Shuppan Nenkan '80* (Publication yearbook, 1980). Tokyo: Shuppan Nyususha, 1980.

Shuppan Nyususha. *Shuppan Nenkan '82* (Publication yearbook, 1982). Tokyo: Shuppan Nyususha, 1982.

Simmel, Georg. *The Sociology of Georg Simmel.* Translated and edited by Kurt Wolff. New York: The Free Press, 1950.

————. "Fashion." *American Journal of Sociology* 62 (1957): 541–58.

Smith, Thomas. "Aestheticism and Social Structure." *American Sociological Review* 39 (1974): 725–43.

Stebbins, Robert. "On Misunderstanding the Concept of Commitment." *Social Forces* 48 (1970): 526–29.

————. *Amateur.* Beverly Hills: Sage, 1979.

————. "The Definition of the Situation." In *Social Behavior in Context,* edited by Adrian Furnham. Boston: Allyn and Bacon, 1986.

Strong, S. "Social Types in the Negro Community of Chicago." Ph.D. diss., University of Chicago, 1940.

Sullivan, M., and J. Grant. "The Development of Interpersonal Maturity." *Psychiatry* 20 (1957): 373–85.

Suttles, Gerald. *The Social Order of the Slum.* Chicago: University of Chicago Press, 1968.

————. "Friendship as a Social Institution." In *Social Relationships,* edited by G. McCall. Chicago: Aldine, 1970.

————. "Urban Ethnography." *Annual Review of Sociology* 2 (1976): 1–18.

Sutton-Smith, Brian, and Diana Kelly-Byrne. "The Masks of Play." In *The Masks of Play,* edited by Brian Sutton-Smith and Diana Kelly-Byrne. New York: Leisure Press, 1984.

————. "The Idealization of Play." In *Play,* edited by Peter Smith. Oxford: Basil Blackwell, 1984.

Sykes, Gresham, and David Matza. "Juvenile Delinquency and Subterranean Values." *American Sociological Review* 26 (1961): 712–19.

Takane, Masaaki. "Nichibei Konai Boryoku Hikakuron" (A comparative study on school violence in Japan and the United States). *Shokun* October (1981): 175–87.

Takemura, Jun, ed. *Bakuso! Rediisu* (Explosion! Ladies). Tokyo: Tairiku Shobo, 1980.

Takuma, Shimpei, Yasunori Chiba, and Sakuichi Nakagawa. "Bosozoku to Seishonen Modai I" (*Bosozoku* and juvenile problems, Part I). *IATSS Review* 1 (1975): 12–43.

Takuma, Shimpei, Yasunori Chiba, and Yoshiichi Kaneto, "Bosozoku to Seishonen Modai II" (*Bosozoku* and juvenile problems, Part II). *IATSS Review* 1 (1975): 84–102.

Takuma, Shimpei, et al. "Bosozoku no Shinrigakuteki Kenkyu" (A psychological study of *bosozoku*). *IATSS Review* 3 (1977): 76–93.

Takuwa, O., and Y. Ono, *Shonen Hiko to Kanbetsu Kagaku* (Juvenile delinquency and scientific diagnosis of delinquents). Tokyo: Kyosei Fukushikai, 1973.

Tamura, Masayuki, and Fumio Mugishima. "Bosozoku no Jittai Bunseki" (The present state of *bosozoku*). *Kagaku Keisatsu Kenkyujo Hokoku* 16 (1975): 38–72.

Tamura, Masayuki. "Kanyusha Tokusei no Patan Bunseki" (A multivariate analysis of *bosozoku* members). *Kagaku Keisatsu Kenkyujo Hokoku* 22 1981): 42–48.

————. "Bosozoku no Shakaishinri" (Social psychology of *bosozoku*). *Seishin Igaku* 25 (1983): 1035–40.

Taniguchi, Masayasu. "Bosozoku" (*Bosozoku*). In *Asobigata Hiko* (Playlike delinquency), edited by Kazunori Kikuchi and Mamoru Horiuchi. Tokyo: Gakuji Shuppan, 1982.

Tannenbaum, Frank. *Crime and Community.* New York: McGraw-Hill, 1938.

Tazaki, Yoshinobu. "Bosozoku wa Kuruma Shakai no Onikko" (*Bosozoku* are a manifestation of motorized society). In *Bosozoku no Jittai to Taisaku* (The present state of *bosozoku* and countermeasures to be taken), edited by Hyogo Kenkei. Kobe: Hyogo Kenkei, 1981.

Thomas, William. *The Unadjusted Girl.* New York: Little, Brown, 1923.

Thomas, William, and Florian Znaniecki. *The Polish Peasant in Europe and America.* New York: Alfred A. Knopf, 1927.

Thomas, William, and Dorothy Thomas. *The Child in America.* New York: Alfred A. Knopf, 1928.

Thomposon, Hunter. *Hell's Angels.* New York: Ballantine, 1966.

Thrasher, Frederick. *The Gang.* Chicago: University of Chicago Press, 1927.

Toi, Jugatsu, ed. *Tomerareruka Oretachio* (Nobody can stop us). Tokyo: Daisan Shokan, 1979.

Tsuda, Takeshi. *Namennayo!* (Don't mess around with me!). Tokyo: Shjnko Gakufu Shuppan, 1981.

Tsukamoto, Kunio. *Kotoba Asobi Etsuranki* (The pleasure of wordplay). Tokyo: Kadokawa Shobo Shinsha, 1980.

Tsuruoka, Ken'ichi. "Asobi to Hiko" (Play and delinquency). *Choken Kiyo* 30 (1981): 71–89.

Turner, Victor. *The Ritual Process.* New York: Aldine, 1969.

———. *Dramas, Fields, and Metaphors.* Ithaca: Cornell University Press, 1974.

———. *From Ritual to Theatre.* New York: Performing Arts Publications, 1982.

Tyler, Stephen. *The Said and the Unsaid.* New York: Academic Press, 1978.

Ueno, Jiro. *Dokyumento Bosozoku* (*Bosozoku* documentary), 3 vols. Tokyo: Futami Shobo, 1980.

Ui, Jun. *Kogai Genron* (General treatise on environmental pollution). Tokyo: Aki Shobo, 1973–74.

Umabuchi, Kosuke. *Zokutachi no Sengoshi* (The postwar history of *zoku*). Tokyo: Sanseido, 1989.

Umegaki, Minoru. *Ingo Jiten* (Slang dictionary). Tokyo: Tokyodo Shuppan, 1961.

Urita, Yoshiharu. *Oretachi niwa Doyo shikanai* (Only saturday is left for us). Tokyo: Futami Shobo, 1975.

Ushiogi, Morikazu. *Gakureki Shakai no Tenkan* (Transformation of academic-pedigree-oriented society), Tokyo: Tokyo Daigaku Shuppankai, 1978.

van Gennep, Arnold. *The Rites of Passage.* Translated by Monika Vizedon and Gabrielle Caffee. Chicago: University of Chicago Press, 1960.

Vogel, Ezra. *Japan as Number One.* New York: Harper and Row, 1979.

Wagner, Roy. *The Invention of Culture.* Chicago: University of Chicago Press, 1981.

Willis, Paul. *Learning to Labor.* New York: Columbia University Press, 1977.

———. *Profane Culture.* London: Routledge & Kegan Paul, 1978.

Wooton, B. *Social Science and Social Pathology.* London: Allen & Unwin, 1959.

Yablonsky, Lewis. *The Violent Gang.* Maryland: Penguin, 1970.

Yamaguchi, Masao. *Bunka to Ryogisei* (Culture and ambiguity). Tokyo: Iwanami Shoten, 1975.

Yinger, Milton. *Countercultures.* New York: The Free Press, 1982.

Yoka Kaihatsu Senta. *Yoka Handobukku 1982* (Recreation handbook, 1982). Tokyo: Nikkan Kogyo Shimbunsha, 1982.

Znaniecki, Florian. *Cultural Sciences.* Urbana, Ill.: University of Illinois Press, 1952.

Name Index

Tsuruoka, Ken'ichi, 241
Turner, Victor, 32, 78, 241, 242, 244,
    245, 247
Tyler, Stephen, 243

Ueno, Jiro, 94, 104, 239
Ui, Jun, 256
Umabuchi, Kosuke, 249
Umegaki, Minoru, 246
Urita, Yoshiharu, 72, 93, 103, 157, 188,
    245, 246, 253
Ushiogi, Morikazu, 249
Utena, Toshio, 255

van Gennep, Arnold, 78, 244
Vaz, E., 242, 258

Vizeden, Monika, 245
Vogel, Ezra, 256

Wagner, Roy, 244
Williams, T., 251
Willis, Paul, 242, 248, 257
Wolff, Kurt, 242
Wooton, B., 250

Yablonsky, Lewis, 250, 257
Yaku, Takao, 255
Yamaguchi, Masao, 245
Yamazaki, Mori, 242
Yazawa, Eikichi, 98, 247
Yinger, Milton, 243

Znaniecki, Florian, 224, 240

Subject Index

Academic pedigree (*gakureki*): of *bosozoku* population, 109, 200, 253; and inferiority complex, 108–9, 135–36, 138; of informants, 134–35, 249; reliance on, in Japan, 3, 79, 182, 185, 199, 205, 208. *See also* Dropouts

Action: *boso* driving as, 131–32; *bosozoku* and, 7, 50, 133, 143; defined, 213; in ethnographic studies, 8, 212–13; and the routine-seeker, 213; and the sacred, 218–19; seeker of, 213, 221; serious and playlike, 213–14, 220, 221; territorial scope of, and vehicle, 142; Yankee and, 31, 48, 109, 118, 120–30, 140, 143, 175. *See also* Iwazu; Thrills

Addiction: and corruption of play, 212, 217; paint thinner, 163–64. *See also* Drugs

Adolescence. *See* Age; *Seishun;* Youth

Affluence: and changing life-style in Japan, 7, 183–85; and youths, 185–90; delinquency in an affluent society, 7, 185, 200, 207–8

Age: and definition of play, 161–62; and fights, 123–24, 128; hierarchy, 87, 112–13, 151, 155, 162–64; and mobilization, 151; norm, 159, 161–65; and paraphernalia, 52, 164–65, 242; and reference groups, 162–64; segregation by, 7, 189, 209

AJK (All-Japan Kyoto Racing Club), 148–56

America (the United States): influence of on action scenes in Japan, 119, 189, 204, 219–20; as a mirror for Japan, 205–9

Amphetamine. *See* Drugs

Anomy, 208, 219, 221; Merton's concept of, 240, 249, 253

Asobi (play), 36, 39, 161, 173; *-gata hiko* (playlike delinquency), 2, 207

Attraction theory of delinquency, 3–5, 8, 109

Automobiles: and flow, 35; modification of, 38, 43–45; motorization in Japan, 184, 254; youths and, 184, 186–87

Birmingham school, 211, 213, 257

Brand name, significance of, 42–44, 50, 69, 187

Calligraphy, and group names, 56–57

Campaign: against *bosozoku,* 181–82; against delinquency, 201

Carnival: *boso* driving as, 19, 32, 47, 49, 83; and the picaresque, 245. *See also* Festival

Cats, comical representation of *bosozoku* as, 98–99, 101, 247

Catharsis, by *boso* driving, 27, 204

Celebrity, *bosozoku* as, 69, 94–97, 102

Class: *bosozoku* as leisure, 109, 156, 176, 187; *bosozoku* as middle-, 2, 137–38; *bosozoku* as working-, 137–38; theory of delinquency, xiii–xiv, 211, 213

Collective effervescence, 25, 32, 36. *See also* Communitas

Commercialism: and *bosozoku* artifacts, 97–101; and exploitation of *bosozoku,* 73, 93, 97

Communitas, 31–33

Conflict: adult-youth, 188–90; between *bosozoku* and the police, 140, 192; between two definitions of the

273